Westmoreland County, Virginia

Deed and Will Abstracts

1742–1745

Ruth and Sam Sparacio

HERITAGE BOOKS
2018

HERITAGE BOOKS
AN IMPRINT OF HERITAGE BOOKS, INC.

Books, CDs, and more—Worldwide

For our listing of thousands of titles see our website
at
www.HeritageBooks.com

Published 2018 by
HERITAGE BOOKS, INC.
Publishing Division
5810 Ruatan Street
Berwyn Heights, Md. 20740

International Standard Book Number
Paperbound: 978-16-8034-989-4

pp. 235- 240

THIS INDENTURE made the Sixteenth day of August in the Sixteenth year of the Reign of our Sovereign Lord George the Second by the grace of God of Great Brittain France and Ireland, King, Defender of the faith, Anno Domini one thousand seven hundred and forty two; Between SAMUEL ATTWELL of Parish of Cople in County of Westmoreland, Planter, of one part and THOMAS REDDALL, Joyner, of the afsd. Parish and County of other part; Witnesseth that SAMUEL ATTWELL in consideration of the sum of Five shillings current money of Virginia to him in hand paid by THOMAS REDDALL, the receipt whereof SAMUEL ATTWELL doth hereby acknowledge, hath and by these presents doth bargain and sell unto THOMAS REDDALL, his heirs all that parcel of land containing Ninety five acres fifty three perches scituate in LOWER MACHOTIQUE NECK in Parish and County afsd., bounded, Begining at a marked Gum standing at the No. East side of the said ATTWELLs Spring Branch and corner to Colo. HENRY LEE, thence No. forty degrees East twenty two poles, thence down the North side of the Branch still binding on the land of said LEE, No. sixty five degrees East twenty poles to South side of said Branch the several courses thereof reduced to a right line is No. fifty six degrees East thirty poles to the said LEE's corner in YEWEL's Line out the side of said Branch and opposite to the land of THOMAS REDDALL, thence with said REDDALL's line South fifty six and a half degrees East one hundred and nine poles to a small Cedar upon the head of a Creek corner between the aforesaid ATTWELL and REDDALL, thence up a Branch of said Creek South thirty five and a quarter degrees West sixty eight poles to a dead white Oak corner to ATTWELL & ALLERTON and side line to KENNER, thence along KENNER's line South sixty nine degrees West one hundred and eighteen poles to within half a Chain East of a marked live Oak corner to aforesaid LEE, thence along a line of the said LEE's North six degrees East one hundred thirty one poles to the begining; containing ninety five acres, fifty three perches, Together with all houses orchards & appurtenances to the same belonging; To have and to hold the parcel of land and premises unto THOMAS REDDALL his heirs during the term of one whole year paying therefore unto SAMUEL ATTWELL the rent of one year of Indian Corn at the expiration of the said term if lawfully demanded to the intent that by virtue of these presents and of the Statute for transferring uses into possession the said REDDALL may be in actual possession of the premises and hereby be the better enabled to accept a release of the inheritance thereof to him and his heirs; In Witness whereof the parties first above named to these present Indentures have interchangeably set their hands and seals the day and year first above written
Signed Sealed & Delivered in presence of
JOHN ATTWELL, FRANCIS ATTWELL,   SAMUEL ATTWELL
THOMAS SORRELL

Westmoreland sct. At a Court held for the said County the 31st day of August 1742 SAMUEL ATTWELL personally acknowledged this Deed of Lease for Land by him passed to THOMAS REDDALL to be his proper act and deed which at the instance of the said REDDALL is admitted to Record

Recorded the Ninth day of September 1742
Test GEO: LEE, C.W.C.

THIS INDENTURE made the Seventeenth day of August in the Sixteenth year of the Reign of our Sovereign Lord George the Second by the grace of God of Great Brittain

France and Ireland, King, Defender of the faith &c., Anno Domini one thousand seven hundred and forty two; Between SAMUEL ATTWELL of Parish of Cople in County of Westmoreland, Planter, of one part and THOMAS REDDALL, Joyner, of aforesaid Parish and County of other part; Witnesseth that SAMUEL ATTWELL in consideration of the sum of One hundred and two pounds, Ten shillings and one penny current money of Virginia to him in hand paid by THOMAS REDDALL, the receipt whereof SAMUEL ATTWELL doth hereby acknowledge, hath and by these presents doth bargain sell and release unto THOMAS REDDALL in his actual possession now being by virtue of a bargain and sale to him made and by force and virtue of the Statute for transferring uses into possession, his heirs all that parcel of Land containing Ninety five acres and Fifty three perches scituate in LOWER MACHOTIQUE NECK and bounded; Begining (the bounds of the land repeated as in the Lease); To have and to hold the parcel of land and other the premises unto THOMAS REDDALL his heirs, and SAMUEL ATTWELL his heirs the parcel of land and premises against every person shall warrant and forever defend by these presents; In Witness whereof the parties first above named to these present Indentures have interchangeably set their hands and seals the day and year first above written; Signed Sealed & Delivered in presence of

JOHN ATTWELL, FRANS: ATTWELL,   SAMUEL ATTWELL
THOMAS SORRELL

Westmoreland sct. At a Court held for the said County the 31st day of August 1742 SAMUEL ATTWELL personally acknowledged this Deed of Release for land by him passed to THOMAS REDDALL to be his proper act and deed, and MARTHA, Wife of the said SAMUEL (being first privily examined according to Law) relinquished her right of Dower and Thirds in and to the Land by the said Deed conveyed which at the instance of the said REDDALL are admitted to Record

Recorded the Ninth day of September 1742
Test GEO: LEE, C.W.C.

KNOW ALL MEN by these presents that I SAMUEL ATTWELL of the Parish of Cople in County of Westmoreland, Planter, and held & firmly bound unto THOMAS REDDALL of aforesaid Parish and County, Joyner, in the um of Two hundred & six pounds current money of Virginia to the which payment well and truly to be made I bind myself my heirs firmly by these presents; In Witness whereof I have hereunto set my hand and fixt my seal this Seventeenth day of August Anno Domin one thousand seven hundred and forty two and in the Sixteenth year of the Reign of our Sovereign Lord George the Second by the grace of God of Great Brittain France and Ireland, King, Defender of the faith &c.,

THE CONDITION of the above obligation is such that if the above bound SAMUEL ATTWELL his heirs shall perform and keep all the Covenants which on his and their parts ought to be performed and kept comprized in a certain Indenture of Bargain and Sale made between SAMUEL ATTWELL and THOMAS REDDALL (the bounds of the land as in the Lease and Release are repeated in this Bond) according to the true intent of the said Indentures, Then the above obligation to be void and of none effect otherwise to be and remain in full force power & virtue

Signed Sealed and Delivered in presence of

JOHN ATTWELL, FRANS: ATTWELL,   SAMUEL ATTWELL
THOMAS SORRELL

Westmoreland sct. At a Court held for the said County the 31st day of August 1742 SAMUEL ATTWELL personally acknowledged this Bond for performance of Covenants by him passed to THOMAS REDDALL to be his proper act and deed, which at the instance of

the said REDDALL, is admitted to Record
        Recorded the ninth day of September 1742
                Teste GEORGE LEE, C. W. C.

pp.   THIS INDENTURE made the fourteenth day of July in the year of our Lord God
240-   one thousand seven hundred and forty two and in the Sixteenth year of the
242   Reign of our Sovereign Lord George the Second by the grace of God of Great
        Brittain France and Ireland, King, Defender of the faith &c., Between JEREMIAH
MURDOCK and JANE his Wife of KING GEORGE County of one part and SAMUEL KENDALL,
JUNR. of the County of Westmoreland of other part; Witnesseth that JEREMIAH MUR-
COCK and JANE his Wife in consideration of Fifty pounds current money of Virginia in
hand paid by SAMUEL KENDALL, JUNR. the receipt whereof JEREMIAH MURDOCK and
JANE his Wife doth own and acknowledge, hath and by these presents doth bargain and
sell unto SAMUEL KENDALL JUNR. his heirs during the natural life of SAMUEL KEN-
DALL SIGNR. and SARAH his Wife during her Widowhood and after marriage two years
at Five hundred and thirty pounds of lawfull tobacco pr. annum all that parcel of land
that SAMUEL KENDALL now liveth on, the said SAMUEL KENDALL to make no use or
waste of the wood or Timber any farther than for the necessary use of the Plantation,
the tract of land containing Seventy acres and bounded; Begining at a red Oak, corner
tree to a tract of land belonging to JEREMIAH MURDOCK, extending South 72 poles to a
red Oak standing in a line that divides this land from the land of JEREMIAH MURDOCK
greater tract bought of THOMAS MUSE and now marked by JEREMIAH MURDOCK for a
corner to SAMUEL KENDALL seventy acres, extending thence East crossing a Branch
155 poles to a red Oak standing in the back line of MURDOCKs whole tract and now
marked as a course for the said KENDALL, thence North 72 poles to a white Oak, corner
tree to this Land and the Land of AARON HARDIGE, thence West 155 poles to the begining; Together with all houses orchards advantages and appurtenances to the land
and premises belonging; To have and to hold the land and premises unto SAMUEL
KENDALL, SIGNR, during the natural life of SAMUEL KENDALL and SARAH his Wife and
her Widowhood and after her marriage two years at five hundred and thirty pounds of
tobacco per annum; and JEREMIAH MURDOCK for himself his heirs shall warrant and
defend the premises and the appurtenances from the claims of all manner of persons;
In Witness whereof JEREMIAH MURDOCK to this present Indenture hath set his hand
and seal the day and year above written
Signed Sealed & Delivered in presence of us
        ORIGINAL BROWN,   JEREMIAH MURDOCK
        CHARLS WRIGHT, THOMAS ROBINS
    Westmoreland sct. At a Court held for the said County the 31st day of August 1742
This Deed of Dale for lives from JEREMIAH MURDOCK, Gent., to SAMUEL KENDALL, was
this day proved in open Court by the Oaths of the witnesses thereto subscribed, which is
ordered to be recorded
        Recorded the Ninth day of September 1742
                Teste GEORGE LEE, C. W. C.

(On margin: MURDOCK's Bond to KENDALL)
KNOW ALL MEN by these presents that I JEREMIAH MURDOCK of KING GEORGE County
am held and firmly bound unto SAMUEL KENDALL, SIGNR. of Westmoreland County his
heirs &c. in the sum of One hundred pounds current money to which payment well and
truly to be made I bind myself my heirs firmly by these presents; Sealed with my Seal
& dated this 14th day of July 1742

THE CONDITION of this obligation is such that if the above bound JEREMIAH MURDOCK his heirs shall perform and keep all the Covenants which on his or their parts ought to be performed and kept comprized in a certain Deed of Sale of Land for the natural lives of SAMUEL KENDALL and SARAH his Wife made between JEREMIAH MURDOCK and SAMUEL KENDALL according to the true intent of the same Deed without any fraud or deceit, Then this obligation to be void otherwise to remain in full force and virtue Signed Sealed and delivered in the presence of us

> ORIGINAL BROWN,   JEREMIAH MURDOCK
> CHARLES WRIGHT,   THOMAS ROBINS

Westmoreland Sct. At a Court held for the said County the 31st day of August 1742 This Bond for performance of Covenants for Lives from JEREMIAH MURDOCK, Gent. to SAMUEL KENDLL was this day proved in open Court by the Oaths of the witnesses thereto which is ordered to be recorded

> Recorded the Ninth day of September 1742, pr. G. L. C. C. W.
> Test GEORGE LEE, C. C. W.

pp.   (On margin: FOX's Lease to SHROPSHIRE)
242-   THIS INDENTURE made the twentyeth day of November in the Fifteenth year of
244   the Reign of our Sovereign Lord George the Second by the grace of God of Great Brittain France and Ireland, King, Defender of the faith &c., and in the year of our Lord God one thousand seven hundred forty and one; Between JOHN FOX of Parish of Hannover in KING GEORGE County within the Dominion of Virginia, Blacksmith, of one part and WINKFIELD SHROPSHIRE of aforesaid Parish and County within the Dominion of Virginia, Planter, of other part; Witnesseth that JOHN FOX in consideration of Five shillings current money of Virginia to him in hand paid by WINKFIELD SHROPHSIRE, the receipt whereof JOHN FOX doth hereby acknowledge, hath and by these presents doth bargain and sell unto WINKFIELD SHROPSHIRE a certain parcel of land containing Fifty acres scituate some part in County of Westmoreland and some part in KING GEORGE County and bounded; Begining in the line of the land of Mr. JOHN WASHINGTON in Westmoreland County opposite to the corner of JOHN DRAGENs Cornfield Fence, then with WASHINGTONs line crossing the Main Ridge Road to the head of a Swamp to the line of the land of JOHN PLUNKETT in KING GEORGE County, thence along a Hedge Row to the Ridge Road, thence along the Ridge Road to DRAGENs Fence, thence with the Fence to the place where it begun; Together with all houses orchards and commodities to the same belonging; To have and to hold the premises unto WINKFIELD SHROPSHIRE and his heirs during the term of one whole year paying therefore the rent of one Pepper Corn on the first day of Saint Michael the Archangel if lawfully demanded to the intent that by virtue of these presents and of the Statute for transferring uses into possession WINKFIELD SHROPSHIRE may be in the actual possession of the premises and may be thereby the better enabled to take a release of the inheritance thereof to him and his heirs; In Witness whereof JOHN FOX hath to these presents set his hand and fixt his seal the day month and year first

Sealed and Delivered in the presence of
Test   ST. JOHN SHROPSHIRE,   JOHN FOX
        JOHN JETT, WILLIAM PEIRCE

Westmoreland sct. At a Court held for the said County the thirty first day of August 1742   JOHN FOX personally acknowledged this Deed of Lease for Land by him passed to WINKFIELD SHROPSHIRE to be his proper act and deed which at the instance of the said SHROPSHIRE is ordered to be recorded

> Recorded the tenth day of September 1742
> Test GEORGE LEE, C. C. W.

(On margin: FOX's Release to SHROPSHIRE)

THIS INDENTURE made the one and twentyeth day of November in the fifteenth year of the Reign of our Sovereign Lord George the Second by the grace of God of Great Brittain France and Ireland, King, Defender of the faith &c., And in the year of our Lord God one thousand seven hundred forty and one, Between JOHN FOX of Parish of Hannover in KING GEORGE County within the Dominion of Virignia, Blacksmith, of one part and WINKFIELD SHROPSHIRE of aforesaid Parish and County within the Dominion of Virginia, Planter of other part; Witnesseth that JOHN FOX in consideration of the sum of Twenty and five pounds current money of Virginia to him in hand paid by WINKFIELD SHROPSHIRE, the reciept whereof JOHN FOX doth hereby confess and acknowledge, and for several other good causes and considerations him thereunto moving, hath and by these presents doth bargain and sell unto WINKFIELD SHROPSHIRE and his heirs being in his actual possession by virtue of a Lease to him made and of the Statute for transferring uses into possession, a certain parcel of land containing Fifty acres scituate some part in the County of Westmoreland and some in KING GEORGE County and bounded Begining (the bounds of the land repeated as in the Lease) To have and to hold the land and premises free and clear to WINKFIELD SHROPSHIRE and his heirs; In Witness whereof JOHN FOX hath to these presents set his hand and fixt his seal the day month and year first above written

Sealed and Delivered in presence of

    ST. JOHN SHROPSHIRE,   JOHN FOX
    JOHN JETT,   WILLIAM PEIRCE

Westmoreland sct. At a Court held for the said County the thirty first day of August 1742   JOHN FOX personally acknowledged this Deed of Release for Lands by him passed to WINKFIELD SHROPSHIRE to be his proper act and deed, which at the instance of the said SHROPSHIRE is admitted to Record

        Recorded the tenth day of September 1742, pr. G. L., C. C. W.
            Test GEORGE LEE, C. C. W.

pp.   (On margin: LAZARUS SMITH's Will)
244   IN THE NAME OF GOD, Amen this Sixteenth day of July 1742, I LAZARUS SMITH of
245   Cople Parish in the County of Westmoreland being sick and weak but of perfect
        mind and memory, thanks be given unto God therefore, calling to mind the mortality of my body and knowing that it is appointed for all men once to die, doe make this my Last Will and Testament in manner and form following, (that is to say) first and principally I give my Soul to God who gave it me hoping at the general ressurection to receive it again by the mighty power of God and my body to be buryed at the discretion of my Executor hereafter named; And as for what worldly Estate it hath pleased Almigty God to bestow upon me, I give and bequeath as folloeth;

Imprs. I give and bequeath to my Brother, JAMES SMITH, my wearing Cloaths which is now at his house and all my pewter and working tools which is at his house, and a sett of Turners tools which I have at JOHN McCAVEs and two casque which is at the said McCAVEs and I also give him what is due from him to me for the hire of my Negro boy provided he will pay what I am indebted to JOHN CULLY.

Item. I give and bequeath unto my Godson, SPENCER SMITH, Son of THOMAS SMITH, deced., Twenty pounds current money of Virginia to be paid to him the said SPENCER, when he shall arive to the age of Twenty one years which said sum of Twenty pounds is to be paid by my Executor hereafter named.

Item. I give and bequeath to my Cozen, RICHARD NUTT, Son of RICHARD NUTT and ELIZABETH his Wife, my Riding Horse, bridle saddle and saddle cloth and housing;

Item. I give and bequeath unto my God Daughter, JUDITH SMITH, Daughter of WILLIAM SMITH, all my Cattle which is at the said WILLIAM SMITH's

Item. I give also to the above named JAMES SMITH my Cloaths which is at the Cullies and all other my wearing cloaths and some Bottles which I have at WILLIAM WELCH's, provided he pays what I am indebted to Mr. JACKSON, And what I am indebted to JOHN RHODS.

Item. I give and bequeath to my Brother, JOHN SMITH, my Negro Boy, Harry, and what money Mr. WILLOUGHBY NEWTON is indebted to me and all other debts together with all monies goods chattels and movables to me belonging (except before bequeathed). I also appoint him the said JOHN SMITH, my whole and sole Executor of this my Last Will and Testament revoaking and disannulling all other and former Will by me made and ratifying and confirming this and not other to be my Last Will and Testament. In Witness I have hereunto sett my hand and seal this day and year above written

Signed Seal'd published and declared by him the said
LAZARUS SMITH to be his Last Will and Testament in
the presence of us   WILLIAM HARTLEY,   LAZARUS SMITH
        GEORGE his mark Ⓒ FEAGINS,
        ELINOR her mark ℰ YEATTS

Westmoreland sct. At a Court held for the said County the 31st day of August 1742 This Last Will and Testament of LAZARUS SMITH, deced., was presented into Court by JOHN SMITH, his Brother and Executor, who made Oath thereto, and being proved by the Oaths of GEORGE FEAGINS and ELEANOR YATES, two of the witnesses thereto, is admitted to Record; And upon the motion of the said Executors and his performing what is usual in such cases, Certificate is granted him for obtaining a Proabe thereof in due form
        Recorded the 10th day of September 1742   pr. G. L. C. C. W.
            Test GEORGE LEE, C. C. W.

pp.   (On margin: ELLIOTT & Ux. their Feofment to VAULX)
246-   THIS INDENTURE made the 26th day of October in the Sixteenth year of the
248   Reign of our Sovereign Lord George the Second by the grace of God, King of
       Great Brittain France and Ireland, Defender of the faith &c., Anno Domini one
thousand seven hundred and forty two; Between JOHN ELLIOTT of Parish of Washington in County of Westmoreland, Gent. and ISABELLA, his Wife of one part and ROBERT VAULX of the aforesaid Parish and County, Gent., of other part; Witnesseth that JOHN ELLIOTT and ISABELLA his Wife in consideration of the sum of Seventy five pounds of current money of Virginia to them in hand paid by ROBERT VAULX, the receipt whereof they do hereby acknowledge, hath and by these presents doth bargain and sell unto ROBERT VAULX, (in his actual possession now being) and to his heirs one Water Grist Mill scituate erected and built in the County of Westmoreland on a Run that falls into RAPPAHANNOCK CREEK, and three acres of land next adjoining the Mill, that is to say, one acre that was part of lands late Coll. WILLIAM FITZHUGH's, and two acres that was part of the lands of Mr. THOS: STURMAN, deced., which two acres of land was sold to THOMAS NEWTON, Gent., as by a Deed of Feoffment bearing date the 26th day of September one thousand seven hundred and five, wch: Mill with the lands formerly belonged to THOMAS NEWTON and by him sold to AUGUSTINE HIGGINS, and conveyed after the decease of the said AUGUSTINE to PENELOPE HIGGINS, Daughter and sole heir of said AUGUSTINE HIGGINS as by a Deed bearing date the 27th day of July one thousand seven hundred and twenty will more fully appear; wch: Mill with the land and appurtenances thereunto belonging fell after the decease of said PENELOPE (among other lands and

Negroes) to ISABELLA ELLIOTT party to these presents and PENELOPE OSBORN as coheirs
of PENELOPE HIGGINS, and after an equal division made of the Lands and Negroes between ISABELLA and PENELOPE, the Mill together with three acres of land fell to and
was allotted JOHN ELLIOTT and ISABELLA his Wife, parties to these presents as part of
said ISABELLA's Estate, with all its rights members and appurtenances thereunto belonging; To have and to hold the Water Grist Mill and Three acres of land unto ROBERT
VAULX his heirs and JOHN ELLIOTT and ISABELLA his Wife and their heirs the Mill and
three acres of land unto ROBERT VAULX his heirs shall warrant and forever defend by
these presents against the claim of any person; In Witness whereof the parties first
above named to these presents have interchangable set their hands and seals the day
and year first above written
Sign'd Seal'd and delivered in presence of
    JOHN, MARTIN,   JAMES BERRYMAN,   JNO: ELLIOTT
    B. WEEKS   ZEABELLA her mark ╱ ELLIOTT
    Received the day and year first written in the within Indenture of ROBERT VAUX the
sum of Seventy five pounds current money of Virginia being the full consideration
within mentioned, L. 75.
                                    JNO: ELLIOTT
    Westmoreland sct. At a Court held for the said County the 26th day of September 1742
JOHN ELLIOTT, Gent., and ZEABELLA his Wife (she being first privily examined according to Law relinquished her right of Inheritance) personally acknowledged this Deed
of Feoffment for lands and premises by them passed to ROBERT VAULX, Gent. (And the
said ELLIOTT also acknowledged his receipt for the consideration endorsed) to be their
proper act and deed which at the instance of the said VAULX are admitted to Record
        Recorded the 29th day of October 1742, pr. G. L., C. C. W.
                 Test GEORGE LEE, C. C. W.

(On margin: ELLIOTT's Bond to VAULX)
    KNOW ALL MEN by these presents that I JOHN ELLIOTT of Washington Parish in Coun-
ty of Westmoreland, Gent., am held and firmly bound unto ROBERT VAULX of the aforesaid Parish and County in the sum of Six hundred pounds current money of Virgina
which payment well and truly to be made I bind myself my heirs firmly by these presents; Sealed with my seal and dated this 26th day of October Anno Domini 1742
    THE CONDITION of the above obligation is such that if the above bound JOHN ELLIOTT
his heirs shall perform and keep all the Covenants which on his or their parts ought to
be performed and kept mentioned in a certain Indenture of Feoffment of the sale of one
Water Grist Mill and three acres of Land made between JOHN ELLIOTT and ROBERT
VAULX according to the intent of the Indenture, then the above obligation to be void
and of none effect else to remain in full force power and virtue
Signed Seal'd and delivered in presence of
    JOHN MARTIN,   JAMES BERRYMAN   JNO: ELLIOTT
    B. WEEKS
    Westmoreland sct. At a Court held for the said County the 26th day of October 1742
JOHN ELLIOTT, Gent., personally acknowledged this Bond for performance of Covenants
by him passed to ROBERT VAULX, Gent., at whose motion the same is admitted to Record
        Recorded the 29th day of October 1742 pr. G. L., C. C. W.
               Test GEORGE LEE, C. C. W.

pp.   (On margin: JOHN MURPHY's Will)
248-   IN THE NAME OF GOD, Amen. I JOHN MURPHY of Parish of Copley and County of
249   Westmoreland being in perfect sence and memory do make this my Last Will
           and Testament. I commit my Soul into the hands of God who gave it me and my
body to the Earth to be decently buried, As for such worldly Estate which it hath pleased
God to bless me with, I dispose of it as followeth;
    Itum. I give to my Son, JOHN MURPHY, all my Land whereon I now live to him my
said Son, JOHN, and the male heirs of his body lawfully begotten and for want of such to
the female heirs of the body of my Son, JOHN, and for the want of such to the male heirs
of the body of my Son, SAMUEL, and to his or their heirs forever;
    Itum. I give to my Son, SAMUEL, Ten pounds current money to be paid him out of my
Estate and that he be of age and for himself at the age of Sixteen; But to dwell with and
be under the care and jurisdiction of his Mother til he shall arive at that age;
    Itum. The rest of my Estate to be equally divided between my Son, JOHN, and Daughter
ELIZABETH MURPHEY, and that my Daughter, ELIZABETH, shall have ondly her reason-
able part when she shall arive at the age of Sixteen or day of Marriage not to debar or
hinder her Mother from her part as may be understood;
    Itum. I give to my Loving Wife, MARY MURPHEY, the whole use of this my Estate till
my Son, JOHN, shall be of the age of twenty one, or till my Daughter, ELIZABETH, arive
to her above mentioned age or day of marriage which shall first happen, provided she
use the same well and to waste or be extravagant in any thing for then by this Will I
give my Executors in Trust full power to take the same out of her hand and that she
have ondly what the Law will allow;
    Lastly, I nominate and ordain my Trusty Friends, JOHN ATTWELL, THOMAS REDDALL
and WILLIAM RICE, Executors in Trust of this my Will. In Witness hereof set my hand
this 19th day of July 1742
           JAMES # JOHNSTON   JOHN MURPHY
           JOHN ATTWELL   his John w mark
Westmoreland sct. At a Court held for the said County the 26th day of October 1742
This Last Will and Testament of JOHN MURPHEY, deceased, was presented into Court by
JOHN ATTWELL and WILLIAM RICE, two of the Executors in Trust in the said Will named
who made Oath thereto, and being proved by the Oath of JAMES JOHNSTON, one of the
witnesses thereto, is admitted to Record; And upon the motion of the said Executors and
their performing what is usual in such cases, Certificate is granted them for obtaining
a Probate thereof in due form
           Recorded the 29th day of October 1742, pr. G. L., C. C. W.
              Test   GEORGE LEE, C. C. W.

pp.   (On margin: MINOR JUNIOR's Lease for Lives to NEWMARCH)
249-   THIS INDENTURE made the first day of September in the year of our Lord one
251   thousand seven hundred and forty two, Between NICHOLAS MINOR, JUNIOR of
           County of Westmoreland, Gent., of one part and JONATHAN NEWMARCH of said
County, Planter, of other part; Witnesseth that NICHOLAS MINOR, JUNIOR in consideration of the Rents and Covenants herein after reserved on part of JONATHAN NEWMARCH
to be paid and kept hath granted and to farm let one parcel of land containing One hundred and fifty acres of land scituate in County of Westmoreland and bounded; Begining
at a stooping red Oak on East side of the Main Road and runing thence North 59 degrees East 104 poles to a small red Oak, thence runing into the Land North 40 degrees
West 294 poles to the land called MOXLEYs, thence South 10 degrees West 59 poles, thence
South West 58 poles, thence South East 210 poles along THOMAS SANFORDs line to the

first begining; including 150 acres of land with all houses orchards profits and appurtenances to the same belonging; To have and to hold the parcel of land and premises
with the appurtenances unto JONATHAN NEWMARCH his heirs during the natural life of
JONATHAN NEWMARCH, ANN NEWMARCH his Wife and THOMAS NEWMARCH his Son or
the life of the longest liver of them, paying therefore unto NICHOLAS MINOR, JUNIOR
his heirs every year on the Feast of St. Luke, being the Eighteenth of October, the neat
sum and quantity of Six hundred pounds of tobacco and cask, the tobacco to be made
upon the said Land and from thence rolled to such convenient Rolling Houses or Warehouses on the water as the Laws from time to time shall appoint as also at the time
aforesaid four hens, Capins or Pullets; And JONATHAN NEWMARCH within three years
from the date of these presents plant fifty Apple trees and the same take care of and
keep the houses and buildings in needful reparations as often as need shall require;
And every year pay the quitrents of the land to the Chief Lord of the Fee and save
NICHOLAS MINOR his heirs harmless and indemnified from the same; In Witness
whereof the parties above named have hereunto interchangeably set their hands and
seals the day and year first above written
Sealed & Delivered in presence of us
    P. NEALE, GABRIEL JOHNSTON   NICH: MINOR, JUNR.
    Westmoreland Sct. At a Court held for the said County the 26th day of October 1742
NICHOLAS MINOR, JUNIOR personally acknowledged this Deed of Lease for Lands for
Lives by him passed to JONATHAN NEWMARCH at whose mostion the same is admitted to
Record   Recorded the 29th day of October 1742, pr. G. L., C. C. W.
        Test GEORGE LEE, C. C. W.

pp.   (On margin: OMOHUNDRO's Lease to CHILTON)
251-   THIS INDENTURE made the 25th day of October in the Sixteenth year of the
256   Reign of our Sovereign Lord George the Second by the grace of God of Great
        Brittain France and Ireland, King, Defender of the faith &c., And in the year of
our Lord one thousand seven hundred and forty two; Between RICHARD OMOHUNDRO of
Parish of Cople in County of Westmoreland, Planter, of one part and THOMAS CHILTON of
the same Parish and County, Gent., of other part; Witnesseth that RICHARD OMOHUNDRO
in consideration of Five shillings current money to him in hand paid by THOMAS CHIL-
TON the receipt whereof is hereby acknowledged, hath and by these presents doth bargain and sell unto THOMAS CHILTON all that parcel of land including the Land whereon
RICHARD OMOHUNDRO now liveth scituate in County aforesaid and bounded Easterly
upon the Land of JOHN SANFORD being divided by a small Branch and Swamp, Northerly
upon a small parcel of Land formerly by WILLIAM MOXLEY given and made over unto
WILLIAM MOXLEY, JUNIOR, runing up the Old Field, the Old Riding Way that was formerly used to goe from MRS. SANFORDs up the County so to extend along the said Road as far
as WASHINGTONs PATH, thence Westerly upon the Land of LAWRENCE WASHINGTON,
Southerly upon a a Great Swamp called the QUARTER SWAMP, finally down the Swamp to
the Branch first mentioned dividing this from the Land of JOHN SANFORD, which parcel
of land including the Plantation were given and conveyed to RICHARD OMOHUNDRO by
his Grand Father, WILLIAM MOXLEY, as appears by a Deed thereof by WILLIAM MOXLEY
acknowledged in legal form in the Court of the County aforesaid bearing date the
Eighth day of May one thousand seven hundred and thirteen being recorded in the said
County Records may more fully appear; And all the houses orchards profits and appurtenances belonging; To have and to hold the land and premises with appurtenances
unto THOMAS CHILTON his heirs during the term of one whole year paying therefore
the rent of one Pepper Corn upon the Feast of Saint Michael the Archangel if lawfully

demanded, to the intent that by virtue of these presents and by force of the Statute for transferring of uses into possession, THOMAS CHILTON may be in the actual possession of the premises and thereby be enabled to accept a release of the inheritance thereof to him and his heirs; In Witness whereof RICHARD OMOHUNDRO hath hereunto set his hand and seal the day month and year first above written
Sealed and delivered in the presence of
    B. WEEKS,   PETER RUST   RICHARD his mark ℞ OMOHUNDRO
    B. HARNETT
   Westmoreland Sct. At a Court held for the said County the 26th day of October 1742 RICHARD OMOHUNDRO personally acknowledged this Deed of Lease for Land by him passed to THOMAS CHILTON, Gent., to be his proper act and deed which is ordered to be recorded   Recorded the first of November 1742, pr. G. L., C. C. W.
          Test. GEORGE LEE, C. C. W.

   (On margin: OMOHUNDRO's Release to CHILTON)
   THIS INDENTURE made the 26th day of October in the Sixteenth year of the Reign of our Sovereign Lord George the Second by the grace of God of Great Brittain France and Ireland, King, Defender of the faith &c., And in the year of our Lord one thousand seven hundred and forty two; Between RICHARD OMOHUNDRO of Parish of Cople in County of Westmoreland, Planter, of one part and THOMAS CHILTON of the same Parish and County, Gentleman, of other part; Witnesseth that RICHARD OMOHUNDRO in consideration of the sum of Twelve thousand pounds of transfer tobo: to him in hand paid, the receipt whereof RICHARD OMOHUNDRO doth hereby acknowledge, hath and by these presents doth bargain sell and release unto THOMAS CHILTON (in his actual possession now being by virtue of a bargain and sale to him thereof made for one year and by force of the Statute for transferring of uses into possession), all that parcel of land including the Plantation whereon RICHARD OMOHUNDRO now liveth scituate in Parish and County aforesaid and bounded (the bounds of the land and the passing of the land repeated as in the Lease) To have and to hold the land and premises with appurtenances unto THOMAS CHILTON his heirs; without the interruption of RICHARD OMOHUNDRO his heirs freed and discharged from and sufficient saved and kept harmless and indemnified from all incumbrances, the Rents and Services due for the premises to the Lord or Lords of the Fee or Fees only excepted; In Witness whereof RICHARD OMOHUNDRO hath hereunto set his hand and seal the day month and year first above written
Sealed and delivered in the presence of
    B. WEEKS,   PETER RUST,   RICHARD his mark ℞ OMOHUNDRO
    B. HARNETT
   Received of THOMAS CHILTON the sum of Twelve thousand pounds of transfer tobacco being the consideration mentioned in the within Deed to be paid by him to me on the perfection thereof; Witness my hand this 26th day of 8br: Anno Domini 1742
Witness B. WEEKS, PETER RUST   RICHD. his mark ℞ OMOHUNDRO
    B. HARNETT
   Westmoreland Sct. At a Court held for the said County the 26th day of October 1742 RICHARD OMOHUNDRO personally acknowledged this Deed of Release for Lands by him passed to THOMAS CHILTON, Gent., together with the receipt for the consideration thereon endorsed to be his proper act and deed, And ANN, Wife of the said RICHARD OMOHUNDRO (she being first privily examined according to Law), relinquished her right of Dower of in and to the lands by the said Deed conveyed, all which ordered to be recorded
    Recorded the first day of November 1742, pr. G. L, C. C. W.
      Test GEORGE LEE, C. C. W.

(On margin: OMOHUNDRO's Bond to CHILTON)

KNOW ALL MEN by these presents that I RICHARD OMOHUNDRO of the Parish of Cople in County of Westmoreland, Planter, and held and firmly bound unto THOMAS CHILTON, of said Parish and County, Gentleman, in the sum of Twenty four thousand pounds of transfer tobacco, to which payment well and truly to be made I bind myself my heirs firmly by these presents; Sealed with my Seal the 26th day of 8br: in the Sixteenth year of the Reign of our Sovereign Lord George the Second and in the year of our Lord 1742

THE CONDITION of the above written obligation is such that if the above bound RICHARD OMOHUNDRO his heirs shall perform and keep all the Covenants which on his or their part ought to be performed and kept mentioned in certain Deeds of Lease and Release made between RICHARD OMOHUNDRO and THOMAS CHILTON according to the true intent of the Deeds, That then the above written obligation to be void and of none effect otherwise to be and remain in full force power and virtue

Sealed and Delivered in the presence of

B. WEEKS,   PETER RUST   RICHARD his mark ℛ OMOHUNDRO
B. HARNETT

Westmoreland Sct. At a Court held for the said County the 26th day of October 1742 RICHARD OMOHUNDRO personally acknowledged this Bond for performance of Covenants by him passed to THOMAS CHILTON, Gent., which is ordered to be recorded

Recorded the first day of November 1742, pr. G. L, C. C. W.

Test GEORGE LEE, C. C. W.

pp.   (On margin: BUSH alias RIDLY Lease to SHAW)
256-   THIS INDENTURE made the twenty fifth day of October in the Sixteenth year of
260   the Reign of our Sovereign Lord George the Second by the grace of God of Great
         Brittain France and Ireland, King, Defender of the faith &c., And in the year of
our Lord one thousand seven hundred and forty two; Between EDWARD BUSH alias RIDLY, Carpenter, born on the body of MARGARET RIDLY, of the County of ORANGE in Parish of Saint Marks of one part and THOMAS SHAW of County of Westmoreland in Parish of Washington, Planter, of other part; Witnesseth that EDWARD BUSH Carpenter alias RIDLY in consideration of the sum of Five shillings of lawfull money to him in hand paid by THOMAS SHAW, the receipt whereof is hereby acknowledged, hath and by these presents doth bargain and sell unto THOMAS SHAW all that Plantation or parcel of Land containing by estimation Eighty acres be the same more or less scitaute in Parish of Washington in County of Westmoreland nigh the head of POPES CREEK a little above the Mill of NATHANIEL POPE, and begining at a marked Spanish Oak standing near the Plantation of LAWRENCE POPE and runing along the line of marked trees to the head of a Branch runing into the head of POPES CREEK and from thence along the said head of the Creek to the Branch that divides CHARLES GOODARDs Land from the Land of WILLIAM LORD and so up the Branch to GODDARDs Line and so along the line to the first begining; Together with all houses orchards profits and appurtenances to the Plantation or parcel of land belonging; To have and to hold the land and premises with appurtenances unto THOMAS SHAW during the term of one whole year paying therefore the rent of one Ear of Indian Corn upon the last day of the term if lawfully demanded, to the intent that by virtue of these presents and of the Statute for transferring of uses into possesion, THOMAS SHAW may be in the actual possession of the premises and thereby be the better enabled to take a release of the inheritance thereof to him and his heirs; In Witness whereof the parties to these presents have interchangeably set their hands and seals the day and year first above written

Sealed and delivered in the presence of us
      LAWR: BUTLER,   EDWAD: BUSH alias RIDLY
      HUMPHRY POPE, P. NEALE
    Westmoreland Sct. At a Court held for the said County the 26th day of October 1742
EDWARD BUSH alias RIDLY personally acknowledged this Deed of Lease for Lands by
him passed to THOMAS SHAW to be his proper act and deed, at whose motion the same is
admitted to Record
      Recorded the first day of November 1742, pr. G. L., C. C. W.
        Test GEORGE LEE, C. C. W.

    (On margin: BUSH alias RIDLY's Release to SHAW)
    THIS INDENTURE made the 26th day of October in the Sixteenth year of the Reign of
our Sovereign Lord George the Second by the grace of God of Great Brittain France and
Ireland, King, Defender of the faith &c., And in the year of our Lord one thousand
seven hundred and forty two; Between EDWARD BUSH alias RIDLY, Carpenter, born on
the body of MARGARET RIDLY, of the County of ORANGE in the Parish of Saint Marks of
one part and THOMAS SHAW of County of Westmoreland in Parish of Washington, Planter, of other part; Witnesseth that EDWARD BUSH alias RIDLY in consideration of the
sum of Forty pounds current money to him in hand paid by THOMAS SHAW, the receipt
whereof EDWARD BUSH alias RIDLY doth hereby acknowledge, hath and by these presents doth bargain sell and release unto THOMAS SHAW (in his actual possession now
being by virtue of a bargain and sale to him thereof made for one whole year and by
force of the Statute for transferring of uses into possession) and to his heirs all that
Plantation or parcel of Land containing by estimation Eighty acres scituate in Parish of
Washington in County of Westmoreland nigh the head of POPES CREEK (this Release continues as in the Lease including the description of the bounds of the land); To have and to hold
the parcel of land with appurtenances unto THOMAS SHAW his heirs; And EDWARD
BUSH alias RIDLY his heirs the Plantation and parcel of land unto THOMAS SHAW his
heirs against the claims of all persons shall warrant and forever defend by these presents; In Witness whereof the parties to these presents have interchangeably sett their
hands and seals the day and year first above written
Sealed and delivered in the presence of us
      LAWR: BUTLER,   EDWD. BUSH alias RIDLY
      HUMPHRY POPE, P. NEALE
    Received the twenty sixth day of October one thousand seven hundred and forty two
of THOMAS SHAW the sum of Forty pounds current money being the consideration
money in the within Deed to be paid by him to me on the perfection thereof; Witness
my hand
Test P. NEALE, HUMPHRY POPE   EDWD. BUSH alias RIDLY
    Westmoreland Sct. At a Court held for the said County the 26th day of October 1742
EDWARD BUSH alias RIDLY personally acknowledged this Deed of Release for Lands by
him passed to THOMAS SHAW, together with the Receipt for the consideration endorsed
to be his proper act and deed, all which at the instance of the said SHAW are admitted to
Record   Recorded the 1st day of November 1742, pr. G. L., C. C. W.
        Test GEORGE LEE, C. C. W.

    (On margin: BUSH alias RIDLY Bond to SHAW)
    KNOW ALL MEN by these presents that I EDWARD BUSH, Carpenter, alias RIDLY of the
County of ORANGE in the Parish of Saint Marks am held and firmly bound unto THOMAS
SHAW of County of Westmoreland in Parish of Washington, Planter, in the sum of One

hundred pounds current money, to the which payment well and truly to be made I bind myself my heirs firmly by these presents; Sealed with my seal and dated the twenty sixth day of October in the Sixteenth year of the Reign of our Sovereign Lord George the Second by the grace of God of Great Brittain France and Ireland, King, Defender of the faith &c., Anno Domini 1742

THE CONDITION of this obligation is such that if the above bound EDWARD BUSH alias RIDLY his heirs shall perform and keep all the Covenants which on his or their part ought to be performed and kept particularly mentioned in one Indenture of Release made between EDWARD BUSH, Carpenter, alias RIDLY and THOMAS SHAW according to the true intent of the said Indenture, Then the above obligation to be void otherwise to be and remain in full force and virtue

Sealed and delivered in the presence of us

  LAWR: BUTLER, HUMPHRY POPE, EDWD. BUSH alias RIDLY
  P. NEALE

  Westmoreland Sct. At a Court held for the said County the 26th day of October 1742 EDWARD BUSH alias RIDLY personally acknowledged this Bond for the performance of Covenants by him passed to THOMAS SHAW, at whose motion the same is admitted to Record Recorded the 1st day of November 1742, pr. G. L., C. C. W.

    Test GEORGE LEE, C. C. W.

pp. (On margin: WASHINGTON's Lease to MacCARTY)
260- THIS INDENTURE made the Seventh day of August in the Sixteenth year of the
262 Reign of our Sovereign Lord George the Second by the grace of God of Great
    Brittain France and Ireland, King, Defender of the faith &c., Anno Domini 1742;
Between AUGUSTINE WASHINGTON of the Parish of Brunswick in County of KING GEORGE Gent., of one part and DANIEL McCARTY of the Parish of Washington in County of Westmoreland, also Gent., of other part; Witnesseth that AUGUSTINE WASHINGTON in consideration of the sum of five shillings to him in hand paid (the receipt whereof is hereby acknowledged) hath and by these presents doth bargain and sell unto DANIEL McCARTY all the parcel of land containing Two hundred acres be the same more or less scituate in Parish of Cople in County of Westmoreland upon the falling Branches of NOMINI RIVER bounded by the Lands of WILLIAM STURMAN, THOMAS STONE, THOMAS & RICHARD SANFORD, MICHAEL ROBINSON, WILLIAM STURMAN ASHTON and McCARTY party to these presents; the same being conveyed unto AUGUSTINE WASHINGTON by Deeds of Lease and Release bearing date the first and second days of June Anno Domini 1724, Together with all houses orchards profits and appurtenances to the same belonging; To have and to hold the land and premises with appurtenances unto DANIEL McCARTY his heirs during the term of one whole year paying therefore the Rent of one Ear of Indian Corn if lawfully demanded To the intent that by virtue of these presents and by virtue of the Statute for transferring uses into possession DANIEL McCARTY may be the better enabled to take a grant of the inheritance thereof to him and his heirs; In Witness whereof, the parties to these presents have interchangeably set their hands and affixed their seals the day and year above written

Sign'd Sealed and delivered in the presence of

  R. VAULX, JOS: MORTON,   AUGUST: WASHINGTON
  HENRY WASHINGTON, JUNR.

  Westmoreland Sct. At a Court held for the said County the 30th day of November 1742 AUGUSTINE WASHINGTON, Gent., personally acknowledged this Deed of Lease for Lands by him passed to DANIEL McCARTY, Gent., to be his proper act and deed, which at the

instance of the said McCARTY is admitted to Record
Recorded the Seventh day of December 1742, pr. G. L., C. C. W.
Test GEORGE LEE, C. C. W.

(On margin: WASHINGTON's Release to MacCARTY)
THIS INDENTURE made the twenty eighth day of August in the Sixteenth year of the
Reign of our Sovereign Lord George the Second by the grace of God of Great Brittain
France and Ireland, King, Defender of the faith &c., And in the year of our Lord 1742,
Between AUGUSTINE WASHINGTON of Parish of Brunswick in County of KING GEORGE,
Gent., of one part and DANIEL McCARTY of Parish of Washington in County of West-
moreland, also Gent., of other part; Witnesseth that AUGUSTINE WASHINGTON in consideration of the sum of Seventy pounds Sterling to him in hand paid, the receipt whereof is hereby acknowledged, hath (the same being now in possession of DANIEL McCAR-
TY by virtue of a Lease for one whole year) and by these presents doth bargain sell and
release unto DANIEL McCARTY all that parcel of land containing by estimation Two
hundred acres scituate in Parish of Cople in County of Westmoreland (this Release continues as in the Lease naming the lands of those on which this land is bounded) To have and to
hold the land and premises with appurtenances unto DANIEL McCARTY his heirs free
and clear from all incumbrances and AUGUSTINE WASHINGTON his heirs doth for himself his heirs the demised premises unto DANIEL McCARTY his heirs shall warrant and
forever defend by these presents; In Witness whereof the parties to these presents
have interchangeably set their hands and affixed their seals the day and year above
written.
Signed Sealed and Delivered in presence of
        R. VAULX,   JOS: MORTON,   AUGUST: WASHINGTON
        HENRY WASHINGTON, JUNR.
Then received of DANIEL McCARTY the within mentioned consideration money
Seventy pounds Sterling money
        (no witnesses recorded)   (no signature recorded)
Westmoreland Sct. At a Court held for the said County the 30th day of November 1742
AUGUSTINE WASHINGTON, Gent., personally acknowledged this Deed of Release for Land
by him passed to DANIEL McCARTY, Gent., together with the Receipt for the considera-
tion endorsed to be his proper act and deed, which on the motion of said McCARTY are
admitted to Record
Recorded the Seventh day of December 1742, pr. G. L., C. C. W.
Test   GEORGE LEE, C. C. W.

(On margin: WASHINGTON's Bond to MacCARTY)
KNOW ALL MEN by these presents that I AUGUSTINE WASHINGTON of Parish of Bruns-
wick in County of KING GEORGE, Gent., am held and firmly bound unto DANIEL McCARTY
of Parish of Washington in County of Westmoreland, also Gent., in the full and just sum
of One hundred and forty pounds Sterling, to which payment well and truly to be made
I bind myself my heirs firmly by these presents; Sealed with my Seal and dated the
Twenty sixth day of September Anno Domini 1742
THE CONDITION of the above obligation is such that if the above bound AUGUSTINE
WASHINGTON his heirs shall perform and keep all the Covenants which on his or their
part ought to be performed and kept mentioned in certain Deeds of Lease and Release
made between AUGUSTINE WASHINGTON and DANIEL McCARTY according to the true intent thereof; Then the above obligation to be void, otherwise to remain in full force and
virtue

Signed Sealed and Delivered in the presence of
    R. VAULX,   JOS: MORTON,   AUGUST: WASHINGTON
    HENRY WASHINGTON, JUNR.
    Westmoreland Sct. At a Court held for the said County the 30th day of November 1742 AUGUSTINE WASHINGTON, Gent., personally acknowledged this Bond for performance of covenants by him passed to DANIEL McCARTY, also Gent., at whose motion the same is admitted to Record
        Recorded the Seventh day of December 1742, pr. G. L., C. C. W.
            Test GEORGE LEE, C. C. W.

pp.   (On margin: VEALE's Bond to JERVASE. Lease and Release recorded in this Book
263-   page 152)
264   KNOW ALL MEN by these presents that I MAURICE VEALE of County of PRINCE
        WILLIAM am held and firmly bound unto JOHN JERVASE of Parish of Washington and County of Westmoreland in the sum of Fifty pounds Sterling money of Great Brittain, to which payment well and truly to be made I bind myself my heirs firmly by these presents; Sealed with my Seal dated the thirty first day of March 1742
    THE CONDITION of the above obligation is such that if the above bound MAURICE VEALE his heirs shall perform and keep all the Covenants which on his or their part ought to be performed and kept particularly mentioned in certain Indentures of Lease and Release bearing date the thirtieth day of October one thousand seven hundred and forty made between MAURICE VEALE and JOHN JERVASE according to the true intent and MAURICE VEALE shall also when thereunto required execute such further Deed or Deeds for the indefeasable right of inheritance in the premises with their appurtenances as JOHN JERVASE or his Council learned in the Law shall require, In Witness whereof I have hereunto sett and seal the date above within
Sealed and Delivered in presence of us
    NATHL: BUTLER,   MORRIS his mark)W VEALE
    CHARLES CARTER,   LAWR: BUTLER
    Westmoreland Sct. At a Court held for the said County the 30th day of November 1742 This Bond for performance of Covenants from MAURICE VEALE to JOHN JERVASE was proved in open Court by the Oaths of NATHANIEL BUTLER and LAWRENCE BUTLER, two of the witnesses thereto, which on motion of the said JERVASE is admitted to Record
        Recorded the Eighth day of December 1742, pr. G. L, C. C. W.
            Test GEORGE LEE, C. C. W.

p.   (On margin: ELIZABETH STONEHOUSE her Will)
264   IN THE NAME OF GOD, Amen, so be it I ELIZABETH STONEHOUSE of Parish of
        Washington and County of Westmorland, Widow, being sound of mind and memory though very weak of body do make this my Last Will and Testament.
    Imprimis. I being confident that my body shall be raised incorruptible and glorious am desirous that it may be decently interr'd in or near the Grave of my first Husband, SAINT JOHN SHROPSHIRE,
    Item. I desire that my whole Estate and whatsoever may be due to me at the time of my death may be equally divided between my two Sons, SAINT JOHN SHROPSHIRE and WINKFIELD SHROPSHIRE;
    Item. I appoint and constitute my Son, SAINT JOHN SHROPSHIRE, the only Executor of this my Last Will and Testament. In Witness whereof I have hereunto set my hand and seal this fourteenth day of April MDCCXXXVIII

Signed and Sealed in presence of
    RODERICK MACCULLOCK,   ELIZABETH her mark $\mathcal{E}$ STONEHOUSE
    ROBERT SANFORD

    Westmorland Sct. At a Court continued and held for the said County the first day of December 1742   This Last Will and Testament of ELIZABETH STONEHOUSE, deceased, was presented into Court by SAINT JOHN SHROPSHIRE her Executor who made Oath thereto, And being proved by the Oath of the Reverend RODERICK MACCULLOCK, one of the witnesses thereto, is admitted to Record; And upon the motion of the said Executor and his performing what is usual in such cases, Certificate is granted him for obtaining a Probate thereof in due form
        Recorded the Eighth day of December 1742 pr. G. L., C. C. W.
          Test GEORGE LEE, C. C. W.

pp.   (On margin: RICHARD SANFORD's Deed of Feofment to RICHD: MOXLEY)
264-   THIS INDENTURE made this Twenty second day of February in the Sixteenth
268   year of the Reign of our Sovereign Lord George the Second by the grace of God
        of Great Brittain France and Ireland, King, Defender of the faith &c., And in the year of our Lord Christ one thousand seven hundred and forty two; Between RICHARD SANFORD of County of Westmorland in Collony of Virginia of one part and RICHARD MOXLEY of County of Westmorland in the Collony of Virginia, Planter, of other part; Witnesseth that RICHARD SANFORD for divers good causes and considerations him thereunto moving but more especially in consideration of the sum of Forty pounds current money of Virginia to him in hand paid by RICHARD MOXLEY, the receipt whereof RICHARD SANFORD doth hereby acknowledge, hath and by these presents doth bargain and sell unto RICHARD MOXLEY his heirs all that parcel of land with its rights members and appurtenances together with all houses orchards and hereditaments belonging; scituate within the Parish of Cople in County of Westmorland and being one moiety of Three hundred acres of land which ROBERT SANFORD, deceased, Father to the aforesaid RICHARD SANFORD, devised to his two Sons, JOHN SANFORD and THOMAS SANFORD, which the said JOHN SANFORD dying without issue, RICHARD SANFORD being in full possession by virtue of his Father's Last Will and Testament, bounded on the South side by JOHN PARRY, deceased, line thence up the Branch East to a marked black Oak and Maple, thence by a line of marked trees South to a corner Chesnutt bounded on the South side by RICHARD SANFORDs land, thence runing Easterly bound by THOMAS SANFORD Land to a corner Locust standing near the Race Pathes, thence runing North bounded by THOMAS SANFORD line to JOSEPH SANFORDs, deced., line, thence runing West by JOSEPH SANFORDs line to a marked Gumm standing in the Spring Branch, thence down the Branch to the Main Run, bounded by JOSEPH SANFORD, deceased, line, thence down the Run to the begining, bounded by Capt. THOMAS CHILTON land; And the rents and yearly profits thereof; To have and to hold the said hundred and fifty acres of land and other the appurtenances unto RICHARD MOXLEY his heirs; freely and clearly discharged from all incumbrances (Annual Rent from henceforth to grow due to the Proprietor or Chief Lord or Lords of the Fee or Fees of the premises only excepted and foreprized); In Witness whereof the party first above mentioned have hereunto interchangeably set my hand and affixed my seal the day and year first above written
Signed & Sealed in presence of us
    RICHD: SANFORD, JUNR.   RICHARD SANFORD
    JOHN SANFORD, THOMAS COCKERILL
    Memorandum; That this day full and peaceable possession of Livery of Seizin by the delivery of Turff and Twigg on part of the within mentioned Land in the name of the

whole by RICHARD SANFORD unto RICHARD MOXLEY according to the tenure and true meaning of the within Indenture

In the presence of us

    RICHD: SANFORD,   RICHARD SANFORD

    JOHN SANFORD, THOMAS COCKERILL

Westmorland Sct. At a Court held for the said County the 22nd day of February 1742 RICHARD SANFORD personally acknowledged this Deed of Feofment for Land by him passed to RICHARD MOXLEY together with the Livery of Seizin to be his proper act and deed, And SUSANNAH, Wife of RICHARD SANFORD (she being first privily examined) relinquished her right of Dower and Thirds in and to the Lands by the said Deed conveyed all which on the motion of the said MOXLEY are admitted to Record

        Recorded the 28th day of February 1742, pr. G. L., C. C. W.

            Test   GEORGE LEE, C. C. W.

    (On margin: RICHARD SANFORD's Bond to RICHARD MOXLEY)

KNOW ALL MEN by these presents that I RICHARD SANFORD of County of Westmorland in Parish of Cople, Planter, am held and firmly bound unto RICHARD MOXLEY of the Parish of Washington in County of Westmorland, Planter, in the sum of Eighty pounds current money of Virginia, to which payment well and truly to be made I bind myself my heirs firmly by these presents; Sealed with my Seal and dated this 22nd day of February in the year of our Lord 1742

THE CONDITION of the above obligation is such that if the above bound RICHARD SANFORD his heirs shall perform and keep all the Covenants which on his or their part ought to be performed and kept particularly expressed in one Indenture of Livery and Seizin made between RICHARD SANFORD and RICHARD MOXLEY according to the true intent of the Indenture, Then the above obligation to be void, otherwise to be and remain in full force power and virtue

Sealed and delivered in the presence of us

    RICHD: SANFORD, JUNR.   RICHARD SANFORD

    JOHN SANFORD, THOMAS COCKERILL

Westmorland Sct. At a Court held for the said County the 22nd day of February 1742 RICHARD SANFORD personally acknowledged this Bond for performance of Covenants by him passed to RICHARD MOXLEY to be his proper act and deed, which at the instance of the said MOXLEY is admitted to Record

        Recorded the 28th day of February 1742, pr. G. L., C. C. W.

            Test GEORGE LEE, C. C. W.

pp.   (On margin: JAMES McDANIEL's Deed of Feofment to W. MOOR)

268-   THIS INDENTURE made the Twenty first day of February in the Sixteenth year

271   of the Reign of our Sovereign Lord George the Second by the grace of God of

        Great Brittain France and Ireland, King, Defender of the faith &c., And in the year of our Lord one thousand seven hundred and forty two, Between JAMES McDANIEL and JANE his Wife of County of Westmorland of one part and WILLIAM MOOR of the same County of other part; Witnesseth that in consideration of the sum of Fourteen pounds current money to JAMES McDANIEL in hand paid by WILLIAM MOOR, the receipt whereof JAMES McDANIEL doth hereby acknowledge, have and by these presents do bargain and sell unto WILLIAM MOOR his heirs all that parcel of land containing Sixty six acres by estimation scituate in County aforesd. being the Land which JAMES McDANIEL purchased of JOHN MARMADUKE and WINIFRED his Wife by Indenture of Feofment bearing date the last day of July one thousand seven hundred and forty one, with all its rights

members and appurtenances to the parcel of land belonging; To have and to hold the
Sixty six acres of land be the same more or less and all other the premises and appurtenances to said land belonging; and that freely and clearly discharged from and suffi-
ciently saved harmless by JAMES McDANIEL his heirs from all manner of incumbrances; In Witness whereof the parties to these presents have interchangeably set
their hands and seals the day and year first above written
Signed Sealed and delivered in presence of
    JAS: BALEY,   JAMES his mark ⨏ McDANIEL
    PETER his mark ⅄ SMITH   JANE her mark ℘ McDANIEL
    JOHN his mark ⨎ SELF
    WILLIAM GROVE
   Received the 21st day of February 1742 of WILLIAM MOOR fourteen pounds, it being
the consideration money to be by him paid to me
Test   JAS: BALEY, WILLIAM GROVE   JAMES his mark ⨏ McDANIEL
   Memorandum; That full and peaceable possession and seizin of and in the premises
within written with the appurtenances was delivered by JAMES McDANIEL and JANE his
Wife to WILLIAM MOOR to the use and behoof within limitted according to the effect of
this present writing and moreover that the said JAMES and JANE have delivered to said
WILLIAM Turff and Twigg on the land; To have and to hold according to the form and
effect of the Deed in the presence of us whose names are hereunto subscribed this 21st
day of February 1742
    JAS: BALEY, JOHN his mark ⨎ SELF,
    PETER his mark ⅄ SMITH, WILLIAM GROVE
   Westmorland Sct. At a Court held for the said County the 22nd day of February 1742
JAMES McDANIEL personally acknowledged this Deed of Bargain and Sale for Land by
him and his Wife, JANE, passed to WILLIAM MOOR, together with livery of seiin and receipt for the consideration thereon endorsed to be his proper act and deed, Also JAMES
BAILEY by virtue of a Power of Attorney for that purpose made by the said JANE, relinquished her the said JANE's right of Dower and Thirds at the Common Law of in and to
the Land by the said Deed conveyed, all which at the instance of the said MOOR are admitted to Record
    Recorded the Twenty eighth day of February 1742 pr. G. L. C. C. W.
      Test GEORGE LEE, C. C. W.

  (On margin: JAMES McDANIEL's Bond to WILLIAM MOOR)
   KNOW ALL MEN by these presents that I JAMES McDANIEL of County of Westmorland
do owe and justly stand indebted and by these presents firmly bound and obliged unto
WILLIAM MOOR of the same County in the penal sum of Twenty eight pounds current
money to the which payment well and truly to be made I bind myself my heirs firmly
by these presents; Sealed with my Seal and dated this 21st day of February in the Sixteenth year of the Reign of our Sovereign Lord George the Second by the grace of God
of Great Brittain France and Ireland, King, Defender of the faith and in the year of our
Lord 1742
   THE CONDITION of the above obligation is such that if the above bound JAMES
McDANIEL his heirs shall perform and keep all the Covenants which on his or their
part ought to be performed and kept mentioned in one Indenture of Bargain and Sale
made between JAMES McDANIEL and JANE his Wife and WILLIAM MOOR according to the
true meaning of the said Indenture, that then the above obligation to be void and of
none effect, otherwise to stand remain and be in full force power strength and virtue
Signed Sealed and delivered in the presence of us

JAS: BALEY, PETER his mark ⊂ SMITH   JAMES his mark Ɪ McDANIEL
JOHN his mark Ɪ SELF, WILLIAM GROVE

Westmorland Sct. At a Court held for the said County the 22nd day of February 1742
JAMES McDANIEL personally acknowledged this Bond for performance of Covenants by
him passed to WILLIAM MOOR to be his proper act and deed at whose motion the same is
admitted to Record

Recorded the 28th day of Febry, 1742, pr. G. L., C. C. W.,
Test GEORGE LEE, C. C. W.

(On margin: McDANIEL's Power of Attorney to JAS: BAILEY)

KNOW ALL MEN by these presents that I JANE McDANIEL of the County of Westmorland do hereby make appoint and ordain my trusty Friend, JAMES BAILEY, my lawfull
Attorney for me and in my name to acknowledge one certain Indenture of Bargain and
Sale made between JAMES McDANIEL and JANE his Wife of one part and WILLIAM MOOR
of other part for certain lands lying in County aforesaid bearing date the 21st day of
February 1742 in as full and ample manner as if I was there present my self; As Witness my hand and seal this 21st day of February 1742

Signed & Sealed in presence of
PETER his mark ⊥ SMITH   JANE her mark Ɪ McDANIEL
JOHN his mark Ɪ SELF
WILLIAM GROVE

Westmorland Sct. At a Court held for the said County the 22nd day of February 1742
JAMES BAILEY personally acknowledged this Power of Attorney from JANE McDANIEL,
Wife of JAMES McDANIEL, to him the said BAILEY made, and by virtue of the said Power
relinquished the said JANE's right of Dower to certain Lands by the said JAMES
McDANIEL sold and conveyed to WILLIAM MOOR, which on motion of the said MOOR is
admitted to Record

Recorded the 28th day of February 1742, pr. G. L., C. C. W.
Test GEORGE LEE, C. C. W.

pp.   (On margin: JOHN EDWARDS's Lease to THOMAS PRATT)
271-   THIS INDENTURE made the Eighteenth day of October in the Sixteenth year of
274   the Reign of our Sovereign Lord George the Second by the grace of God of Great
         Brittain France and Ireland, King, Defender of the faith &c., And in the year of
our Lord God one thousand seven hundred and forty two; Between JOHN EDWARDS of
Parish of Washington in County of Westmorland, Carpenter, of one part and THOMAS
PRATT of Parish of Sittinburn in County of KING GEORGE, Planter, of other part; Witnesseth that JOHN EDWARDS in consideration of the sum of five shillings of Virginia current to him in hand paid by THOMAS PRATT, the receipt whereof he doth hereby acknowledge, hath and by these presents doth bargain and sell unto THOMAS PRATT all that
Plantation or parcel of land that THOMAS PRATT has in his possession containing Forty
acres of land or thereeabouts to the same belonging scituate in Parish of Washington in
County of Westmorland and bounded; Begining at a white Oak standing near a small
Run called and known by the name of THE BLACK SWAMP, runing thence along a line
of marked trees made by and with the consent of DANIEL WHITE and JOHN EDWARDS
dividing this land from the land of DANIEL WHITE to ROGER's DAM, thence down the
Dam to the mouth of the BLACK SWAMP, thence up the Swamp to the place where it first
began being part of a Pattent granted by the Proprietors of the Northern Neck of Virginia for Two hundred ninety and two acres of land unto DANIEL WHTIE, SENR., late of
said County, deced., and the same parcel or quantity sold by WILLIAM BOALTROP unto

DANIEL WHITE, as by the Records of said County may more fully appear; with all houses orchards rents issues and profits thereof; To have and to hold the premises unto THOMAS PRATT and his heirs during the term of one year paying the rent of an Ear of Indian Corn on the first day of the Lords Birth next ensuing if lawfully demanded to the intent that by virtue of these presents and of the Statute for transfering uses into possession THOS: PRATT may be in the actual possession of the premises and be thereby the better enabled to take a release of the inheritance thereof; In Witness whereof the parties aforesaid have to these presents set his hand and seal the day month and year first above wrightten

Signed Sealed and delivered in the presence of
    BENJA: TYLER,   WM: TYLER,   JOHN his mark *E* EDWARDS
    JOHN DEGGE,   EDWD: his mark *ET* TANCIL

Westmorland Sct. At a Court held for the said County the 22nd day of February 1742 This Deed of Lease for Lands from JOHN EDWADS to THOMAS PRATT was proved in open Court by the Oaths of WILLIAM TYLER, Gent., JOHN DEGGE and EDWARD TANCILL, three of the witnesses thereto, and on the motion of the said PRATT the same is admitted to Record   Recorded the Second day of March 1742, pr. G. L., C. C. W.
         Test GEORGE LEE, C. C. W.

(On margin: JOHN EDWARDS's Release to THOMAS PRATT)
    THIS INDENTURE made the Nineteenth day of October in the Sixteenth year of the Reign of our Sovereign Lord George the Second by the grace of God of Great Brittain France and Ireland, King, Defender of the faith &c., And in the year of our Lord God one thousand seven hundred and forty two; Between JOHN EDWARDS of the Parish of Washington in County of Westmorland, Carpenter, of one part and THOMAS PRATT of Parish of Sittinburn in County of King George, Planter, of other part; Witnesseth that JOHN EDWARDS in consideration of the sum of Fore pounds of Virginia currence to him in hand paid by THOMAS PRATT, the receipt whereof JOHN EDWARDS doth hereby acknowledge, hath and by these presents doth bargain sell and release unto THOMAS PRATT his heirs, the said THOMAS PRATT being in actuall possession of the premises by virtue of a Lease thereof and of the Statute for transfering uses into possession; all that Plantation or parcel of land containing Forty acres of land or thereabouts being in Parish of Washington and County of Westmorland being part of a Pattent (the Pattent and passing of the land and the bounds repeated as in the Lease); To have and to hold the premises unto THOMAS PRATT his heirs and JOHN EDWARDS his heirs their whole right and title in the premises wholly to belong unto THOMAS PRATT his heirs; In Witness whereof the parties aforesaid to these presents sett his hands and seals the day month and year first above written

Signed Sealed and delivered in the presence of
    BENJA: TYLER,   WM: TYLER,   JOHN his mark *E* EDWARDS
    JOHN DEGGE,   EDWD. his mark *ET* TANCIL

Westmorland Sct. At a Court held for the said County the 22nd day of February 1742 This Deed of Release for Land from JOHN EDWARDS to THOMAS PRATT was this day proved in open Court by the Oaths of WILLIAM TYLER, Gent., JOHN DEGGE and EDWARD TANCIL, three of the witnesses thereto, And on motion of the said PRATT the same is admitted to Record
        Recorded the Second day of March 1742, pr. G. L., C. C. W.
         Test GEORGE LEE, C. C. W.

(On margin: JOHN EDWARDS's Bond to THOMAS PRATT)
KNOW ALL MEN by these presents that I JOHN EDWARDS of Parish of Washington in
County of Westmorland, Carpenter, am held and firmly bound unto THOMAS PRATT of
the Parish of Sittinburn in County of KING GEORGE, Planter, in the sum of Fifty pounds
of Sterling money of Great Brittain to the which payment well and truly to be made I
bind myself my heirs firmly by these presents; Sealed with my Seal and dated this
Eighteen day of October in the Sixteen year of the Reign of our Sovereign Lord George
the Second of Great Brittain France and Ireland, King, Defender of the faith Annoque
Domini
THE CONDITION of the above obligation is such that if the above bounded JOHN
EDWARDS his heirs shall perform and keep all the Covenants which on his or their part
ought to be performed and kept mentioned in certain Indenture of Bargain and Sale
made between JOHN EDWARDS and THOMAS PRATT according to the true intent of the
said Indenture; Then this obligation to be void and of none effect otherwise to be and
remain in full power and virtue
Sealed and Delivered in presence of
    BENJ: TYLER, WM. TYLER,   JOHN his mark   EDWARDS
    JOHN DEGGE, EDWD. his mark TANCIL
Westmorland Sct. At a Court held for the said County the 22nd day of February 1742
This Bond for performance of Covenants from JOHN EDWARDS to THOMAS PRATT was
this day proved in open Court by the Oaths of WILLIAM TYLER, Gent., JOHN DEGGE and
EDWARD TANCIL, three of the witnesses thereto, And on motion of the said PRATT, the
same is admitted to Record
        Recorded the Second day of March 1742 pr. G. L., C. C. W.
              Test GEORGE LEE, C. C. W.

pp.   (On margin: WILLIAM TAYLOR's Deed of Feofment to JOHN OMOHUNDRO)
274-   THIS INDENTURE made the Twenty second day of February in the Sixteenth year
276   of the Reign of our Sovereign Lord George the Second by the grace of God of
        Great Brittain France and Ireland, King, Defender of the faith &c., And in the
year of our Lord one thousand seven hundred and forty two; Between WILLIAM TAY-
LOR and ELIZABETH his Wife of Parish of Cople in County of Westmorland, Planter, of
one part and JOHN OMOHUNDRO of said Parish of Cople in County of Westmorland, Planter, of other part; Witnesseth that WILLIAM TAYLOR and ELIZABETH his Wife in consideration of the sum of Twelve pounds, Ten shillings current money to them in hand
paid by JOHN OMOHUNDRO, the receipt whereof WILLIAM TAYLOR and ELIZABETH his
Wife doth hereby acknowledge, hath and by these presents doth bargain and sell unto
JOHN OMOHUNDRO all that tract of land with appurtenances lying in Parish of Cople in
County of Westmorland containing by estimation Eighty acres of Land be the same more
or less, the Land being bought of WILLIAM SANDERS and the Eighty acres of Land
being bounded; Begining at the mouth of the WOLF PIT SWAMP and runing up the
Swamp to a marked forked white Oak tree, thence from the Swamp along a line to a
marked Chesnutt tree, thence up to the Road, thence down the Road to a marked corner
Chesnutt Stump that divides the Land of RICHARD OMOHUNDRO and WILLIAM SANDERS
Land, thence along said OMOHUNDRO's Line to a corner red Oak, thence along a line
between PHILIP SANDERS and the said WILLIAM SANDERS to the first begining; Together with all houses orchards rights members and appurtenances to the eighty acres of
land belonging; To have and to hold the eighty acres of land and premises unto JOHN
OMOHUNDRO his heirs; and WILLIAM TAYLOR and ELIZABETH his Wife and their heirs
the premises with the appurtenances to JOHN OMOHUNDRO his heirs against WILLIAM

TAYLOR and ELIZABETH his Wife and their heirs shall warrant and forever defend by
these presents; In Witness whereof the parties to these presents have interchangeably
set their hands and seals the day and year first above written
Sealed and delivered in presence of us

    THOS: TEMPLEMAN, JOHN BARNETT,   WILLIAM TAYLOR
    JAMES WHITFIELD

    Memorandum; on the Twenty second day of February 1742 peaceable and quiet pos-
session and seizin was given and delivered to JOHN OMOHUNDRO by WILLIAM TAYLOR by
Turff and Twigg on the land, To have and to hold according to the tenor true form of the
within written Deed In presence of

    THOS: TEMPLEMAN, JOHN BARNETT
    JAMES WHITFIELD

    Westmorland Sct. At a Court held for the said County the 22nd day of February 1742
WILLIAM TAYLOR personally acknowledged this Deed of Feofment for Lands by him
passed to JOHN OMOHUNDRO together with livery of seizin to be his proper act and deed,
And ELIZABETH, Wife of said WILLIAM TAYLOR (she being first privily examined according to Law) relinquished her Right of Dower of in and to the lands by the said Deed
conveyed, all which on motion of the said OMOHUNDRO are admitted to Record

        Recorded the Third day of March 1742, pr. G. L., C. C. W.
            Test   GEORGE LEE, C. C. W.

pp.   (On margin: JOHN CURTIS's Deed for Land to JOHN COMBS)
276-   THIS INDENTURE made the Fifteenth day of March in the year of our Lord
278   Christ one thousand seven hundred and forty two; Between JOHN CURTIS of
        Cople Parish and Westmorland County of one part and JOHN COMBS of the same
Parish and County of other part; Witnesseth Whereas JOHN CURTIS by Indenture
bearing date the fourteenth day of this instant month for the consideration therein
expressed did bargain and sell unto JOHN COMBS all those lands with their appurtenances containing by estimation One hundred and seventy acres (be the same more or
less) scituate in Parish and County aforesaid in LOWER MACHOTICK NECK, and formerly
belonging to Mr. ISAAC ALLERTON as by Pattent may appear; And by Capt. ISAAC
ALLERTON, Grandson to the aforesaid ALLERTON, sold and conveyed unto GERRARD
DAVIES, and by said DAVIES sold unto THOMAS CURTIS, Father of said JOHN CURTIS, party
to these presents; together with all the lands and premises which are scituate as aforesaid; To have and to hold the lands and premises unto JOHN COMBS and assigns during
the term of one year to the intent that by virtue thereof and of the Statute for transfering uses into possession JOHN COMBS might be in the actual possession of the land
and premises and be enabled to accept a release of the inheritance thereof; NOW THIS
INDENTURE WITNESSETH that JOHN CURTIS in consideration of the sum of Ten thousand
pounds of lawfull tobacco to him in hand paid by said COMBS, the receipt whereof he
doth herby acknowledge, hath and doth by these presents bargain and sell the land and
premises with the appurtenances and all claim of said CURTIS in the same; In Witness
whereof the parties to these presents hath interchangeably set their hands and seals
the day and year first above written
Signed Sealed and delivered in presence of

    SPENCER ARISS, SAML. ATTWELL,   JOHN CURTIS
    MARTHA ATTWELL, WM. ASKINS

    March the 15th 1742/3. Received of JOHN COMBS Ten thousnd pounds of tobo: in full
satisfaction for premises by me.

Test   SPENCER ARISS, SAML. ATTWELL,   JOHN CURTIS
    MARTHA ATTWELL, WM: ASKINS

Westmorland Sct. At a Court held for the said County the 29th day of March 1743
JOHN CURTIS personally acknowledged this Deed of Bargain and Sale for Lands by him
passed to JOHN COMBS together with the Receipt endorsed for the consideration to be his
proper act and deed which at the instance of the said COMBS are admitted to Record
Recorded the 11th day of April 1743, pr. G. L., C. C. W.
Test   GEORGE LEE, C. C. W.

(Part of page 278 at the bottom is blank, evidently to permit the insertion of the Plat of WASHING-
TON and WASHINGTON Plat of Land between them &c., that comprises the upper half of page 279).

pp.   (On margin: WASHINGTON and WASHINGTON Plat of Land between them &c.)
279-   (On the sketch of the Plat appears - "BROOKS Patent now AUGUSTINE WASHINGTON's Land;
288   JOHN WASHINGTON's 197 1/2 acres of land; AUGT. WASHINGTON's Land where BEN:
WEEKS lives; JOHN WASHINGTON's Land where JOHN MUSE lives. AUGUSTINE WASHING-
TON's Land where THOS: FINCH LIVES; POPES CREEK to the East of AUGUSTINE WASHINGTON's
largest plat of land; the POTOMACK RIVER to the North; BRIDGE CREEK to the West.)
The Plat or Survey mentioned in the annexed Deed.
A Plat of a Survey made for Capt. AUGUSTINE WASHINGTON and Mr. JOHN WASHINGTON
in Westmorland County, vizt. on the 24th day of August 1742. We begun at (A), the
mouth of BRIDGE CREEK and run S. W. (the course of SISSONs Patent), the dotted line to
(B), the 25th day of August. We began at (C) a corner of BROOKS PATENT proved by Capt.
JOHN ELLIOTT and WILLIAM BROWN on the side of POPES CREEK, and run W. N. W. 60
poles to a Stake in MUSE's Cornfield; then N. W. 1.2 W. 140 poles to s Stake in the South
East Branch of BRIDGE CREEK, then N. 68d. W. 140 poles to (F), in the North West Branch
of said Creek, that being the distance of BROOKS's Patent, crossing the first line 14 poles,
then we went to (E) a Locust Stump shewn by ALEXANDER SIMS for a Corner of CUL-
LOM's and run the dotted line to (F); N. 68d. W. and at about 20 poles went half a chain to
the left hand of a Dogwood said to be CULLOM's Old line and about 80 poles went 8 poles
on the left hand of a white Oak likewise said to be CULLOM's Old line, from (D) to (E) is
nigh or on a line of old marked trees, then we went to (D) and run W. N. W. 260 poles
added to the 60 poles from POPES CREEK makes 320 poles the distance of HILLS PATENT,
and struck the Limbs of a Poplar at (G), said to be an old line tree of SISSON's;. The 26th
day of August we went to (F) and run down the meanders of the North West Branch of
BRIDGE CREEK to the Fork of the Creek, then run up the several courses of the South
East Branch of said Creek to the Stake aforesaid in the said Branch above (E), the Locust
Stump. The figure within the Fork of the Creek and the black line from (F) to the Stake
contains 197 1/2 acres, the figures between the dotted line F, E, D. and the black lines F.
D. contains 25 acres and the figures between the lines F, D., B contains 202 acres.
Surveyed by JOSEPH BERRY
Westmorland Sct. At a Court held for the said County the 29th day of March 1743
This Plat, Survey and Report under the hand of JOSEPH BERRY of KING GEORGE County,
Gentleman, of and concerning certain lands belonging to AUGUSTINE WASHINGTON and
JOHN WASHINGTON, Gent. being presented into Court, which at the joint prayer of the
said WASHINGTONs are ordered to be recorded
Recorded the 12th day of April 1743 pr. G. L., C. C. W.
Test   GEORGE LEE, C. C. W.

(On margin: WASHINGTON and WASHINGTON Referees Award inter them)
Whereas AUGUSTINE WASHINGTON of Parish of Brunswick in County of KING GEORGE,
Gent., and JOHN WASHINGTON of Parish of Washington in County of Westmorland, also

Gent., did on the day of the date of these presents enter into Bond with the penalty of One thousand pounds Sterling to each other to refer all differences that had arisen or were then subsisting between them on or about the Titles and Bounds of their respective lands in MATTOX NECK in Parish of Washington, and final award of us RICHARD BERNARD of Parish of Saint Pauls in County of STAFFORD and DANIEL McCARTY of Parish of Washington in County of Westmorland, Gentlemen, not only in and upon the same, but also concerning any and every other matter and thing that sho'd be offered by either of the parties tending towards the benefit or advantage of themselves or of each other either by swap, exchange, sale or otherwise relation being thereunto had will more at large appear; And we the said RICHARD BERNARD and DANIEL McCARTY having been on and surveyed the Lands in difference and agreed on the several bounds between them, the said AUGUSTINE WASHINGTON and JOHN WASHINGTON, and likewise having perambulated viewed and judged of the several parcels of land proposed by each party in exchange have come to the following determination; (that is to say) that JOHN WASHINGTON having produced a Deed from BROOKS to COATE and ANDERSON to JOHN WASHINGTON the Great Grand Father of said JOHN WASHINGTON, And Whereas the said One hundred acres layeth part on one side of a Branch of BRIDGE CREEK and the other on the other side the said Branch, now as that part which lays on the lower side of the S. E. Branch described in the Surveyor's Plat hereunto annexed that is contiguous to AUGUSTINE WASHINGTON's Land that he claims under BROOKS PATENT, We do adjudge the same to the said AUGUSTINE; And Whereas the Land on the upper side of the said S. E. Branch and on the S. E. side of the N. W. Branch containing 197 1/2 acres bounded by by the black line from (F) where there is now a Locust Post, then down the several meanders of the N. W. Branch to the S. E. Branch, then up the several meanders of the S. E. Branch to a corner in the back line near (E), then up the said Branch till it Entersects HILLs line, then along HILLs line till it Intersects SISSONs line where we began at to be the bounds of JOHN WASHINGTONs Land on BRIDGE CREEK; And Whereas there is in the said bounds between the black lines runing N. 68d. W. 140 poles to (F), then down the meanders to the Fork, thence up the Branch to the said line contains 97 1/2 acres more then is JOHN WASHINGTONs due of BROOKS PATTENT, Therefore we adjudge and allott the land belonging at present to JOHN WASHINGTON bounded from (D) runing W. N. W. 320 poles to the S. E. Branch, thence down the Branch to the black line near (E), thence along the black line which is BROOKS the place first mentioned for this part containing 69 acres unto AUGUSTINE WASHINGTON in part for the 97 1/2 acres; And Whereas there is an ancient line of mark'd trees described by the prick'd lines said to be BROOKS line and in that there is contained 25 acres, we adjudge 12 1/2 acres thereto to belong to JOHN WASHINGTON, but in consideration of there not being land sufficient in the lines between (D) and the Branch to the black line near (E), We do adjudge and allott that likewise to and for AUGUSTINE WASHINGTON; And Whereas there is still a deficiency of 16 acres, we adjudge that JOHN WASHINGTON pay AUGUSTINE WASHINGTON the sum of Eleven pounds, Sixteen shillings current money for the same. In Witness whereof we have hereunto sett our hands and seals this Twenty seventh day of September 1742   RICHD: BERNARD
                                                      DANL: McCARTY

   Westmorland Sct. At a Court held for the said County the 29th day of March 1743 This Referrees Report under the hands and seals of RICHARD BERNARD and DANIEL McCARTY, Gentlemen, Arbitrators chosen by and between AUGUSTINE WASHINGTON and JOHN WASHINGTON, Gentlemen, of and concerning certain Lands to them belonging, being presented into Court by the said McCARTY which at the joint prayer of the said WASHINGTONs is admitted to Record

Recorded the 12th day of April 1743,. pr. G. L, C. C. W.
Test   GEORGE LEE, C. C. W\

(On margin: WASHINGTON and WASHINGTON's Deed of Exchange between them)
THIS INDENTURE made the Third day of December in the year of our Lord God one
thousand seven hundred and forty two; Between AUGUSTINE WASHINGTON of Parish of
Brunswick in County of KING GEORGE, Gent., of one part and JOHN WASHINGTON of
Parish of Washington in County of Westmorland, Gent., of other part; Whereas AUGUS-
TINE WASHINGTON is seised in his demesne as of fee in divers lands and hereditaments
situate in County of Westmorland being part of BROOKS's and SISSON's Pattents; And
Whereas JOHN WASHINGTON is likewise seized in his demesne as of fee tail in divers
other lands and hereditaments situate in MATTOX NECK contiguous and adjoining to the
lands of AUGUSTINE WASHINGTON, And whereas several differences have arisen and
were like to arise between AUGUSTINE WASHINGTON and JOHN WASHINGTON as well
touching & concerning the Titles as the Bounds of their several lands, for settling and
composing thereof as well as to prevent all such happening in the time to come, the
parties mutually entered into and executed Bonds each to the other in the penal sum of
One thousand pounds Sterling to stand to and abide the Arbitrators award and judgment
of RICHARD BERNARD of Saint Pauls Parish in County of STAFFORD, Gent., and DANIEL
McCARTY of Parish of Washington in County of Westmorland, Gent., not only touching
and concerning the settling and establishing the metes and bounds of the said lands but
also as to selling or exchanging such of the said lands as should appear to be advanta-
geous to the parties to be sold or exchanged in order to settle & establish their natural
metes and bounds between the lands as might for the future prevent any disputes between the several Tenants thereof; And Whereas RICHARD BERNARD and DANIEL
McCARTY having undertaken the burthen of the Arbitrement and Award did on the
twenty fourth, twenty fifth and twenty sixth days of August last past in presence of the
said parties, perambulate lay out and survey the several lands of AUGUSTINE WASHING-
TON and JOHN WASHINGTON touching the bounds of which the difference had arisen
and finding that JOHN WASHINGTON was intitled to One hundred acres of land out of
BROOKS PATENT by virtue of a Deed from the said BROOKS to COATE and ANDERSON, who
assigned the same to JOHN WASHINGTON, Gent., deced, the Great Grand Father of JOHN
WASHINGTON (party to these presents) part of which hundred acres JOHN WASHINGTON
held in the Fork of BRIDGE CREEK and the other part thereof on the East side of the
mouth of the said Creek adjoyning to the Land of AUGUSTINE WASHINGTON and not
separated therefrom by any known or certain lines or bounds, and having adjudged
that JOHN WASHINGTON was also intitled to Eighty one acres and an half of land lying in
a triangle between the line of BROOKS (which appeared to be uncertain) and the line of
HILL, which also adjoyned to that part of AUGUSTINE WASHINGTON's land held under
BROOKS PATENT, the Arbitrators in order to fix and establish known certain and natural
boundaries between the parties lands did by and with their full and entire approbation
and consent, arbitrate, award and adjudge that One hundred acres of land claimed by
and belonging to JOHN WASHINGTON out of BROOKS PATENT (instead of being laid off on
both sides of BRIDGE CREEK should for the future should be laid off and accordingly be
held by JOHN WASHINGTON and those claiming under him the intail wholly in the Fork
of BRIDGE CREEK, and there being Ninety seven acres and an half of Land belonging to
AUGUSTINE WASHINGTON (part of BROOKS PATENT and part of SISSONs PATENT) lying in
the Fork of said Creek over and above JOHN WASHINGTONs One hundred acres, the Arbitrators did award and adjudge that AUGUSTINE WASHINGTON should give and convey the
same in exchange to JOHN WASHINGTON and those claiming under the intail, And that

JOHN WASHINGTON should give and convey in exchange to AUGUSTINE WASHINGTON and his heirs the Eighty one acres and an half of land between the lines of BROOKS and HILL belonging to JOHN WASHINGTON; And there being a deficienty of sixteen acres to make up the quantity of Ninety seven acres and an half so to be given in exchange by AUGUSTINE WASHINGTON, the Arbitrators did further adjudge and award that JOHN WASHINGTON should pay AUGUSTINE WASHINGTON the sum of Eleven pounds, Sixteen shillings current money of Virginia in full satisfaction of and for the deficiency as by the Award under the hands and seals of RICHARD BERNARD and DANIEL McCARTY bearing date the twenty seventh day of September last past may more fully appear; NOW THIS INDENTURE WITNESSETH that for the better establishing and confirming the Award and Exchange and Testifying the consent and agreement of AUGUSTINE WASHINGTON and JOHN WASHINGTON thereto, (this very long Indenture continues repeating the award of the Arbitrators to AUGUSTINE WASHINGTON and to JOHN WASHINGTON in manner as all the foregoing, so as to effect the exchange as well as the warrants and covenants found in such Indentures) In Witness whereof the parties to these presents have hereunto set their hands and seals the day and year first before written
Sealed and delivered in the presence of us
      RICHD: BERNARD,   LAW: BUTLER,   AUGUST: WASHINGTON
      ROBT: ELLIOTT,   JOHN STORK   JOHN WASHINGTON
   Westmorland Sct. At a Court held for the said County the 29th day of March 1743 This Deed of Exchange for Land reciprocally passed from by and between AUGUSTINE WASHINGTON and JOHN WASHINGTON, Gentlemen, to each other being presented into Court, which at the joint prayer of the said WASHINGTONs is admitted to Record
      Recorded the 12th day of April 1743; pr. G. L., C. C. W.
         Test   GEORGE LEE, C. C. W.

pp.   (On margin: GEORGE BALL's Will)
288-   IN THE NAME OF GOD, Amen. I GEORGE BALL of Westmorland County do make
289   this my Last Will and Testament in manner and form following;
      Imprimis. I give and bequeath to my Brother, EMANUEL BALL, my bay Horse Saddle and Bridle with Housen, my best sute of Close and two thousand pounds of tobacco to him and his heirs;
   Itom. I give and bequeath to my Brother, SAMUEL BALL, my land whare I now live, it being one hundred and seven acres be the same more or less to him and his heirs forever;
   Itom. I give and bequeath to my Brother, SAMUEL BALL, the remainder of my personal Estate be it of what nature or kind soever to him and his heirs, And I doe heareby nominate and appoint my said Brother, SAMUEL BALL, my hole and sole Executor of this my Last Will and Testament; As Witness hereof I have set my hand and seal this Fifteenth day of February Anno Domini 1742-3
Signed Sealed and delivered in the presence of us
      PETER RUST,   his mark
      JOHN CRITCHER,   SARAH CRITCHER   GEORGE BALL
   Westmorland Sct. At a Court held for the said County the 29th day of March 1743 This Last Will and Testment of GEORGE BALL, deceased, was presented into Court by SAMUEL BALL, his Brother and Executor, who made Oath thereto and being proved by the Oaths of JOHN CRITCHER and PETER RUST, two of the witnesses thereto, is admitted to Record; And upon the motion of the said Executor and his performing what is usual in such cases, Certificate is granted him for obtaining a Probate thereof in due form
      Recorded the 13th day of April 1743, pr. G. L., C. C. W.
        Test   GEORGE LEE, C. C. W.

pp.   (On margin: FRENCH & Wife Release to McCARTY)
289-   THIS INDENTURE made the Sixteenth day of March in the year of our Lord God
292   one thousand seven hundred and forty three; Between HUGH FRENCH of County
         of RICHMOND, Planter, and MARGARET his Wife, of one part and DANIEL McCAR-
TY of County of Westmorland, Gent., of other part; Whereas DANIEL FIELD, late of the
County of Westmorland, Planter, deced., by his Last Will and Testament in Writing
bearing date the Second day of February in the year of our Lord one thousand seven
hundred and thirty two (among other things) did give and devise unto the said MAR-
GARET (party to these presents) by the name of MARGARET GERVISE, and to the heirs of
her body lawfully begotten, the Plantation and all the land thereto belonging where
DANIEL FIELD then lived and his Land at the head of POPES CREEK and for want of such
heirs to MARY BECKWORTH & the heirs of her body lawfully begotten, and for want of
such heirs to the his next heir at Law, as by the said Will now remaining in the Court of
the County of Westmorland may appear; And Whereas MARGARET GERVISS intermarried with HUGH FRENCH and HUGH FRENCH and MARGARET his Wife in right of said
MARGARET were seized of the lands with the appurtenances so as aforesaid devised by
DANIEL FIELD in Fee Tail; And whereas by an Inquisition taken before THOMAS CHIL-
TON, Gent., Sheriff of County of Westmorland the Sixteenth day of September in the year
one thousand seven hundred and forty one by virtue of a Writ in the nature of an ad
quod damnum to him directed pursuant to the Act of General Assembly in such cases
made and provided, it was found that the Plantation and all the land thereto belonging
where DANIEL FIELD lived (the same containing by estimation Three hundred acres)
were of the value of One hundred and Eighty pounds Sterling and no more; and that the
same were a separate parcel & not parcel of or contiguous to other intailed lands in the
possession and seisen of HUGH FRENCH and MARGARET his Wife or either of them; as by
the Inquisition now remaining in the Secretary's Office of this Colony may appear;
And Whereas HUGH FRENCH and MARGARET his Wife by their Deed of Bargain and Sale
bearing date the twenty ninth day of September in the year one thousand seven hundred and forty one in consideration of the sum of One hundred and eighty pounds Sterling did bargain sell and release unto DANIEL McCARTY his heirs all that Plantation
where DANIEL FIELD formerly lived and all the Land thereto belonging; containing by
estimation Three hundred acres be the same more or less situate on POPES CREEK in the
Parish of Washington in County of Westmorland and bounded between the land DANIEL
McCARTY purchased of WILLIAM LORD, the land of HUMPHRY POPE, the land of THOMAS
and WILLIAM CHAMBERS, other land of said DANIEL McCARTY purchased of WILLIAM
BRIDGES and the said POPES CREEK, with all rights priviledges & appurtenances thereunto belonging; NOW THIS INDENTURE WITNESSETH that for the better confirming and
conveying the bargained and sold land unto DANIEL McCARTY his heirs according to
the true intent of the recited Deed of Bargain & Sale as well in consideration of the sum
of One hundred and Eighty pounds Sterling already paid as for the further sum of
Twenty shillings Sterling to HUGH FRENCH in hand paid by DANIEL McCARTY, the receipt whereof HUGH FRENCH doth hereby acknowledge, HUGH FRENCH and MARGARET
his Wife have and by these presents do bargain sell and release unto DANIEL McCARTY
(in his actual possession now being by virtue of the before recited Deed of Bargain and
Sale) and to his heirs the Plantation where DANIEL FIELD formerly lived and all the
land thereunto belonging containing by estimation Three hundred acres, Together
with all houses orchards profits and appurtenances to the same belonging; To have and
to hold the land and premises with appurtenances unto DANIEL McCARTY his heirs free
and clear from all incumbrances and HUGH FRENCH and MARGARET his Wife and their
heirs shall warrant & forever defend; In Witness whereof the parties to these presents

have hereunto interchangeably set their hands and seals the day and year first before written

Sealed and Delivered in the presence of us

The within mentioned Twenty Shillings

Sterling being first paid

JONA: SYDENHAM,   HUGH FRENCH

RICHD: BOWMAN, ROBT. VAULX   MARGARET FRENCH

Westmorland Sct. At a Court held for the said County the 29th day of March 1743 HUGH FRENCH and MARGARET his Wife personally acknowledged this Deed of Release of Right for lands by them passed to DANIEL McCARTY, Gentleman, to be their proper act and deed and the said MARGARET (being first privily examined according to Law) relinquished her right of Dower and Inheritance of in and unto the lands by the said Deed conveyed, all which at the instance of the said McCARTY are admitted to Record

Recorded the 13th day of April 1743, pr. G. L. C. C. W.

Test   GEORGE LEE, C. C. W.

pp.   (On margin: REMEY's Bond to REMEY)
292-   KNOW ALL MEN by these presents that I JAMES REMY of Westmorland County
293   and Parish of Cople am held and firmly bound unto DANIEL REMY of Parish of
        Cople in County of Westmorland in the full and just sum of Six thousand pounds of lawfull Tobacco to the which payment well and truly to be made I bind myself my heirs firmly by these presents; Sealed with my Seal and dated the Twenty ninth day of March in the Sixteenth year of the Reign of our Sovereign Lord George the Second by the grace of God of Great Brittain France and Ireland, King, Defender of the faith &c., Annoq: Domini 1743

THE CONDITION of the above obligation is such that if the above bound JAMES REMY his heirs shall perform and keep all the Covenants which on his or their part ought to be performed and kept for a certain parcel of land lying in the BACK FORREST &c. of Westmld. and bounded on the line of JOHN BAKER, which parcel of land was given him by his Father, WILLIAM REMY, deced., in his Last Will and Testament, which parcel of land JAMES REMY hath bargained and sold unto DANIEL REMY his heirs and that if JAMES REMY do warrant the parcel of land from the claims of his heirs or any other persons that shall by legal title or recover the same of DANIEL REMY his heirs which if so be yt: they do not, Then this obligation to be void and of none effect, otherwise to be and remain in full force power and virtue

Signed Sealed and delivered in the presence of us

AUGUSTINE SANFORD,   JAMES REMY

HUGH FRENCH, ASBURY REMY

Westmorland Sct. At a Court held for the said County the 29th day of March Annoq: Dom: 1743   JAMES REMY of the County of Westmorland personally acknowledged this Bond for performance of Covenants by him passed to DANIEL REMY, to be his proper act and deed, which at the instance of the said DANIEL REMY is admitted to Record

Recorded the 14th day of April 1743; pr. G. L., C. C. W.

Test   GEORGE LEE, C. C. W.

p.   (On margin: CARR's Deed of Gift to THOMAS)
293   THIS INDENTURE made this twenty ninth day of March in the year of our Lord
        Christ one thousand seven hundred and forty three; Between JOSEPH CARR of Cople Parish and County of Westmorland of one part and HUGH THOMAS of same Parish and County of other part; Witnesseth that JOSEPH CARR for the consideration and

natural love which he hath and bears to his Sister, MARY, the Wife of said HUGH, doth
by these presents give unto HUGH THOMAS and MARY his Wife their heirs that place or
Plantation with one hundred acres of land joining to it where JOHN FORSIGH formerly
lived unto said THOMAS his heirs and MARY his Wife and her heirs; To have and to hold
the One hundred acres of land to them and their heirs peaceably and quietly; In Witness whereof the said CARR hath hereunto set his hand and seal the day and year first
above written
Signed Sealed and Delivered in presence of
    JAMES THOMAS, DANIEL LANDMAN,   JOSEPH CARR
    JOHN RICHARDSON, KATHERINE L/F THOMAS
    Westmorland Sct. At a Court held for the said County the 29th day of March 1743
JOSEPH CARR personally acknowledged this Deed of Gift for land by him passed to HUGH
THOMAS and MARY his Wife to be his proper act and deed, which at the instance of the
said THOMAS is admitted to Record
        Recorded the 14th day of April 1743, pr. G. L., C. C. W.
           Test   GEORGE LEE, C. C. W.

pp.   (On margin: WADDEY's Deed of Bargain & Sale to LEE, Esqr. (Further proved
293-   folio 319)
294   THIS INDENTURE made the Twenty sixth day of March in the fifteenth year of
        the Reign of our Sovereign Lord George the Second by the grace of God of Great
Brittain France and Ireland, King, Defender of the faith &c., And in the year of our
Lord MDCCXXXXIII; Between JEANE WADDEY of County of NORTHUMBERLAND, Widdow of
the late BENJA: WADDEY of said County deced., of one part and THOMAS LEE of County of
Westmorland Esqr. of other part; Witnesseth that JEAN WADDEY in consideration of the
sum of Twenty shillings currency to her in hand paid by THOMAS LEE, the Receipt
whereof JEAN WADDEY doth hereby acknowledge, hath and by these presents doth bargain and sell unto THOMAS LEE his heirs all that parcel of Land containing One acre
scituate in County of Westmorland and at both ends of an Old Mill Dam near said LEE's
Landing and bounding on the dividing line between the said parties (that is to say) half
an acre at each end to be marked and bounded by the Patents hereafter in the most convenient manner for a Mill, Together with all commons, profits and advantages to the
premises belonging; To have and to hold the premises with appurtenances unto THO-
MAS LEE his heirs and JEAN WADDEY for her and her heirs the premises against every
person to THOMAS LEE his heirs shall warrant and forever defend by these presents; In
Witness whereof JEAN WADDEY hath hereunto set her hand and seal the day and year
first above written
Signed Sealed and delivered in the presence of
    JOSEPH McADAM,   JEAN her mark   WADDEY
    JOHN his mark+++COAN,
    WILLIAM BLACK
    Westmorland March the 26th 1743. Received Twenty shillings Virga. currency being
the consideration within mentioned
    JOSEPH McADAM   JEAN her mark   WADDEY
    JOHN his mark/+++COAN,
    WILLIAM BLACK
    Westmorland Sct. At a Court held for the said County the 29th day of March 1743
This Deed of Bargain and Sale for Land from JANE WADDEY, Widow,. to THOMAS LEE
Esquire, together with the Receipt for the consideration endorsed were this day proved
in open Court by the Oaths of JOSEPH McADAM and WILLIAM BLACK, two of the wit-

nesses thereto, which on motion of the said LEE are admitted to Record
                Recorded the 14th day of April 1743, pr. G. L., C. C. W.
                    Test   GEORGE LEE, C. C. W.

pp.   (On margin: BUSHROD's Deed of Feofment to LEE)
294-   THIS INDENTURE made the Twenty sixth day of April in the Sixteenth year of
297   the Reign of our Sovereign Lord George the Second by the grace of God of Great
           Brittain France and Ireland, King, Defender of the faith &c., And in the year of
our Lord one thousand seven hundred and forty two, Between RICHARD BUSHROD of
Parish of Cople in County of Westmorland, Gent., of one part and HENRY LEE of the same
Parish and County, also Gent., of other part; Witnesseth that RICHARD BUSHROD in consideration of the sum of Four Pistoles in Gold to him in hand paid by HENRY LEE, the
Receipt whereof RICHARD BUSHROD doth hereby acknowledge, hath and by these presents doth bargain and sell unto HENRY LEE his heirs all that parcel of land containing
by estimation One acre and half an acre scituate in Parish of Cople and County of Westmorland, which Land was at the special instance and by the mutual consent and desire
of RICHARD BUSHROD and HENRY LEE surveyed by ELIAS DAVIS, and is on the Eastermost side and next adjoyning upon TURKS RUN or Branch, bounded, Begining at a white
Oak near the Road and said Run side, runing thence North fifty four degrees East two
chains fifty links to an Ivie Bush, thence up a Branch making into said Run South
seventy degrees East four chains and fifty links to a small white Oak near the said
Branch, thence South thirty degrees West four chains to a bare place near a small
Hiccory, thence North fifty one degrees West five chains and fifty links to the first
begining; the one acre and half an acre of land being part of One hundred acres by
CHARLES DUNKIN and HENRY DUNKIN sold and conveyed to ROBERT SMITH, Weaver, by a
Deed of Feofment bearing date the twenty sixth day of April one thousand seven hundred and eight, the one hundred acres being the one moiety of Two hundred acres of
land granted and conveyed to HENRY DUNKIN by Deed from the Proprietor of the Northern Neck of Virginia, and ROBERT SMITH sold and conveyed the One hundred acres of
the land to JOHN BUSHROD, Gentleman, deceased, Father of said RICHARD BUSHROD, by a
Deed of Feofment bearing date the twenty second day of November one thousand seven
hundred and twelve; which one hundred acres of land JOHN BUSHROD in and by his Last
Will and Testament bearing date the twenty sixth day of January one thousand seven
hundred and nineteen gave and devised among other things to his Sons, THOMAS BUSH-
ROD, JOHN BUSHROD and said RICHARD BUSHROD, which THOMAS BUSHROD departed this
life without issue by means whereof the hundred acres by survivorship and con-
struction on the bequests in the said Will descended to and became the proper inheritance of said RICHARD BUSHROD, all which may more fully appear by the several writings aforesaid on Records of County of Westmorland; Together with all commodities
and appurtenances to the one acre and one half an acre belonging; and the rents issues
and profits thereof; To have and to hold the one acre and half acre of land and other
the premises with appurtenances unto HENRY LEE his heirs and RICHARD BUSHROD his
heirs the land with the appurtenances unto HENRY LEE his heirs against the claim of
all persons shall warrant and forever defend by these presents; In Witness whereof
the parties first above named to these present Indentures have interchangeably set
their hands and seals the day and year first above written
Sealed and delivered in the presence of
        JAMES STEPTOE, SAML: OLDHAM,   RICHARD   BUSHROD
        JNO: SORRELL

Received the 26th day of April Anno Domini one thousand seven hundred and forty three of HENRY LEE four Pistoles in Gold being the consideration within mentioned
Witness   JAMES STEPTOE,   RICHARD BUSHROD
     SAML. OLDHAM,   JNO: SORRELL
Westmorland Sct. At a Court held for the said County the 26th day of April 1743 RICHARD BUSHROD, Gent., personally acknowledged this Deed of Feofment for Land by him passed to HENRY LEE, Gent., together with the Receipt for the consideration there-on endorsed to his his proper act and deed which on the motion of the said LEE are admitted to Record
          Recorded the 29th day of April 1743. pr. G. L., C. C. W.
               Test   GEORGE LEE, C. C. W.

(On margin: BUSHROD's Bond to LEE)
KNOW ALL MEN by these presents that I RICHARD BUSHROD of Cople Parish in County of Westmorland, Gent., and held and firmly bound unto HENRY LEE of the same Parish and County, Gent., in the sum of Fifty pounds Sterling money, to which payment well and truly to be made I bind myself my heirs firmly by these presents; Sealed with my Seal and dated the 26th day of April in the Sixteenth year of the Reign of our Sovereign Lord George the Second by the grace of God of Great Brittain France and Ireland, King, Defender of the faith &c., And in the year of our Lord one thousand seven hundred and forty three
THE CONDITION of this obligation is such that if the above bound RICHARD BUSHROD his heirs shall perform and keep all the covenants which on his or their part ought to be performed and kept expressed in one Deed of Feofment for onee acre and half an acre of land made between RICHARD BUSHROD and HENRY LEE according to the true intent of the Deed, Then this obligation to be void and of none effect, otherwise to be and remain in full force power and virtue
Sealed and delivered in the presence of
     JAMES STEPTOE,   RICHARD BUSHROD
     SAML: OLDHAM,   JNO: SORRELL
Westmorland Sct. At a Court held for the said County the 26th day of april 1743 RICHARD BUSHROD, Gent., personally acknowledged this Bond for performance of Cove-nants by him passed to HENRY LEE, Gent., which on the motion of the said LEE is admitted to Record
          Recorded the 29th day of April 1743; pr. G. L., C. C. W.
               Test   GEORGE LEE, C. C. W.

pp.   (On margin: WILLIAMS's Deed of Feofment to WELCH. (further proved folio 316)
297-   THIS INDENTURE made the 9th day of April in the Sixteenth year of the Reign
299   of our Sovereign Lord George the Second by the grace of God of Great Brittain
          France and Ireland, King, Defender of the faith &c., And in the year of our Lord one thousand seven hundred and forty three; Between JOHN WILLIAMS of Parish of Cople in County of Westmorland, Planter, of one part and WILLIAM WELCH of said Parish and County, also Planter, of other part; Witnesseth that JOHN WILLIAMS in con-sideration of the sum of Twelve hundred pounds of tobacco to him in hand paid by WILLIAM WELCH, the Receipt whereof JOHN WILLIAMS doth hereby acknowledge, hath and by these presents doth bargain and sell unto WILLIAM WELCH his heirs all that Plantation or parcel of land whereon JOHN WILLIAMS now liveth, scituate in YEOCOMO-CO FORREST in Parish and County aforesaid and bounded, Begining at an IRON MINE STONE, corner Stone to the land formerly RICHARD LEE Esquire, deced., now belonging

to Capt. GEORGE LEE, thence runing upon the line of the land of said deced., South forty four degrees West ninety nine poles to a white Oak, corner to said Decedents line, thence South fifty and a half degrees East ninety one poles to a white Oak, corner tree. to Old ROBERT SELF standing by the Main Road, thence 1/2d. West one hundred twenty nine poles to the first departure containing by estimation twenty eight acres be the same more or less, the land being formerly granted to JOHN WILLIAMS, deceased, Father of JOHN WILLIAMS, party to these presents, by a Proprietors Deed dated the Ninth day of April 1698, and said deced. JOHN WILLIAMS in and by his Last Will and Testament bearing date the twenty seventh day of May one thousand seven hundred and two gave and devised the land to JOHN WILLIAMS, party to these presents; Together with all houses profits and advantages unto the Plantation or parcel of land belonging (Except a Burying Place there already twenty foot square) and JOHN WILLIAMS party hereunto shall have the liberty of the Mansion House for his own use two years from the date of these presents (if he shall so long live); To have and to hold the Plantation or parcel of land unto WILLIAM WELCH his heirs (except as before excepted), and JOHN WILLIAMS his heirs against every person to WILLIAM WELCH his heirs shall warrant and forever defend by these presents: In Witness whereof JOHN WILLIAMS, party hereunto hath put his hand and fixed his seal the day and year first above written

Signed Sealed and delivered in the presence of

WILLOUGHBY NEWTON   JNO: his mark $\digamma$ WILLIAMS
JOHN McCULLY. JNO: LELAND.
MICHAEL BRANANAM

Memorandum: That on the 9th day of April 1743, JOHN WILLIAMS delivered unto WILLIAM WELCH peaceable and quiet possession and seizin of the within granted Land and premises by the delivery of Turff and Twigg unto WILLIAM WELCH on the land, To have and to hold the same unto WILLIAM WELCH his heirs according to the tenor form and effect of the within written Deed in presence of

WILLOUGHBY NEWTON,   JOHN McCULLY,
JNO: LELAND.   MICHAEL BRANAM

Recd. of WILLIAM WELCH Twelve hundred pounds of tobo. being the consideration within mentioned to be paid by him to me on the perfection hereof

Witness WILLOUGHBY NEWTON,   JOHN McCULLY   JNO: his mark $\digamma$ WILLIAMS
       JNO: LELAND.   MICHAEL BRANAM

Westmorland Sct. At a Court held for the said County the 26th day of April 1743 This Deed of Feofment for Lands sold and conveyed from JOHN WILLIAMS to WILLIAM WELCH was this day proved in open Court by the Oaths of WILLOUGHBY NEWTON, Gent., and MICHAEL BRANAM (also the Livery of Seizen and Receipt for consideration endorsed were proved by the said NEWTON and BRANAM, two of the witnesses thereto), which on motion of the said WELCH is admitted to Record

Recorded the 30th day of April 1743, pr. G. L., C. C. W.
       Test   GEORGE LEE, C. C. W.

(On margin: WILLIAMS BOND to WELCH)
KNOW ALL MEN by these presents that I JOHN WILLIAMS of Cople Parish in County of Westmorland, Planter, am held and firmly bound unto WILLIAM WELSH of said Parish and County, also Planter, in the sum of Three thousand pounds of tobacco to which payment well and truly to be made I bind myself my heirs firmly by these presents; Sealed with my seal this 9th day of April 1743

THE CONDITION of this obligation is such that if the above bound JOHN WILLIAMS his heirs shall perform and keep all the covenants which on his or their part ought to be

performed and kept particularly expressed in one Deed of Feofment for a parcel of Land
containing Twenty eight acres made between JOHN WILLIAMS and WILLIAM WELCH, in
all things according to the true intent of the said Deed, Then this obligation to be void
and of none effect, else to be in full force
Signed Sealed and delivered in the presence of
     WILLOUGHBY NEWTON, JOHN McCULLY   JOHN his mark **7** WILLIAMS
     JNO: LELAND, MICHAEL BRANNAM
   Westmorland Sct. At a Court held for the said County the 26th day of April 1743
This Bond for performance of Covenants from JOHN WILLIAMS to WILLIAM WELCH was
this day proved in open Court by the Oaths of WILLOUGHBY NEWTON, Gent., and
MICHAEL BRANNAM, two of the witnesses thereto which on the motion of the said
WELCH is admitted to Record
       Recorded the 30th day of April 1743, pr. G. L., C. C. W.
          Test   GEORGE LEE, C. C. W.

pp.   (On margin: DUREN's Lease to BROWN)
299-   THIS INDENTURE made the Twenty sixth day of April in the year of our Lord God
303   one thousand seven hundred and forty three, Between GEORGE DURIN of Parish
       of Truro in County of FAIRFAX, Planter, of one part and JOHN BROWN of Parish of
Cople in County of Westmoreland, Planter, of other part; Witnesseth that GEORGE DURIN
in consideration of the sum of Five shillings Sterling to him in hand paid by JOHN
BROWN, the receipt whereof is hereby acknowledged, hath and by these presents doth
bargain and sell unto JOHN BROWN all that parcel of land containing One hundred acres
be the same more or less scituate in Parish of Cople and County of Westmoreland being
the half of Two hundred and fifteen acres of land formerly granted by Pattent to
GEORGE BROWN bearing date the Twenty second day of November one thousand seven
hundred and Six, and bounded, Begining at a white Oak being the Eastermost corner
tree of Five hundred acres of Land now belonging to the heirs of WILLIAM ROBERTSON
and RICHARD SUTTON and extending from thence along the said ROBERTSON's line South
West to the Main Road, thence down the Main Road to the line that divides this land and
the land of JAMES HAZELRIGG, thence along said line to the Great Swamp, so along the
Swamp North West to the first begining; And all houses orchards profits and appurtenances to the same belonging; To have and to hold the land and premises with appurtenances unto JOHN BROWN and assigns during the term of one whole year paying
therefore the Rent of one Pepper Corn upon the Feast of Saint Michael the Archangel if
demanded; to the intent that by virtue of these presents and by force of the Statute for
transferring of uses into possession JOHN BROWN may be in the actual possession of the
premises and thereby be enabled to take a release of the inheritance thereof to him and
his heirs; In Witness whereof GEORGE DURIN hath hereunto set his hand and seal the
day month and year first above written
Sealed and delivered in the presence of us
The above mentioned five shillings Sterling
being first paid   WILLIAM CAMPBELL,   GEORGE DURIN
      RICHD: DOZER, PRESLEY NEALE
   Westmorland Sct. At a Court held for the said County the 26th day of April 1743
GEORGE DURIN personally acknowledged this Deed of Lease by him passed to JOHN
BROWN to be his proper act and deed, which at the motion of the said BROWN is admitted
to Record   Recorded the Second day of May 1743, pr. G. L., C. C. W.
         Test   GEORGE LEE, C. C. W.

(On margin: DUREN's Release to BROWN)

THIS INDENTURE made the Twenty sixth day of April in the year of our Lord God one thousand seven hundred and forty three, Between GEORGE DURIN of Parish of Truro in County of FAIRFAX, Planter, of one part, and JOHN BROWN of Parish of Cople and County of Westmoreland, Planter, of other part; Witnesseth that GEORGE DURIN in consideration of the sum of Forty five pounds current money to him in hand paid by JOHN BROWN the receipt whereof GEORGE DURIN doth hereby acknowledge and for divers other good considerations him thereunto moving, hath and by these presents doth bargain sell and release unto JOHN BROWN in his actual possession now being by virtue of a Bargain and Sale to him thereof made for one year and by force of the Statute for transferring of uses into possession, all that parcell of land containing One hundred acres be the same more or less scitaute in Parish of Cople and County of Westmorland being the half of two hundred and fifteen acres of land formerly granted by Pattent to GEORGE BROWN bearing date the twenty second day of November one thousand seven hundred and six, and bounded, Begining (the bounds of the land repeated as in the Lease); To have and to hold the land and premises with appurtenances unto JOHN BROWN his heirs free and clear from all incumbrances, the rents and services due for the premises to the Lord of the Fee or Fees thereof only excepted; In Witness whereof GEORGE DURIN hath hereunto set his hand and seal the day month and year first above written

Sealed and delivered in the presence of

WILLIAM CAMPBELL,   GEORGE DUREN
RICHD: DOZER, PRESLY NEALE

Received of JOHN BROWN the sum of Forty five pounds current money be the consideration mentioned in the within Deed to be paid by him to me on the perfection thereof, Witness my hand this Twenty seventh day of April 1743

                                        GEORGE DUREN

Westmorland Sct. At a Court held for the said County the 26th day of April 1743 GEORGE DUREN personally acknowledged this Deed of Release by him passed to JOHN BROWN together with Receipt for the consideration endorsed to be his proper act and deed which on motion of the said BROWN is admitted to Record

Recorded the Second day of May 1743, pr. G. L., C. C. W.
Test GEORGE LEE, C. C. W.

(On margin: DUREN's Bond to BROWN)

KNOW ALL MEN by these presents that I GEORGE DURIN of the Parish of Truro in the County of FAIRFAX am held and firmly bound unto JOHN BROWN of Parish of Cople in County of Westmorland in the sum of Ninety pounds current money, to the which payment well and truly to be made I bind myself my heirs firmly by these presents; Sealed with my Seal and dated the Twenty sixth day of April in the Sixteenth year of the Reign of our Sovereign Lord George the Second by the grace of God of Great Brittain France and Ireland, King, Defender of the faith &c., Annoq: Domini 1743

THE CONDITION of this obligation is such that if the above bound GEORGE DURIN his heirs shall perform and keep all the covenants which on his or their part ought to be performed and kept particularly expressed in one Indenture of Release made between GEORGE DURIN and JOHN BROWN in all things according to the true intent of the said Indenture, Then this obligation to be void, otherwise to be and rmain in full force and virtue

Sealed and delivered in the presence of us

WILLIAM CAMPBELL,   GEORGE DUREN
RICHD: DOZER, PRESLY NEALE

Westmorland Sct. At a Court held for the said County the 26th day of April 1743 GEORGE DUREN personally acknowledged this Bond for performance of Covenants by him passed to JOHN BROWN to be his proper act and deed which on the motion of the said BROWN is admitted to Record
Recorded the Second day of May, 1743, pr. G. L., C. C. W.
Test   GEORGE LEE, C. C. W.

p.   (On margin: THOMAS CHAMBERS's Will)
303   IN THE NAME OF GOD, Amen, I THOMAS CHAMBERS being sick and weak but of
perfect sense and memory, praised by Almighty God for it, do make this my Last Will and Testment hereby revoaking all other Wills heretofore by me made;
Imprimis. I commit my Sole into the hands of Almighty God and my body to the Earth from whence it came &c. I give my Loveing Wife, MARY CHAMBERS, all my Estate both within Dores and without to her and to her disposal forever.
Item. I appoint my Loveing Wife whole Executrix of this my Will and Testament; In Witness whereof I have hereto sett my hand and seale this 7th day of January 1742
Test   HUMPHRY POPE,   THOMAS his mark JC CHAMBERS
JUDITH her mark Ɫ CHAMBERS,
WILLIAM his mark X CHAMBERS
Westmorland Sct. At a Court held for the said County the 26th day of April 1743 This Last Will and Testament of THOMAS CHAMBERS, deceased, was presented into Court by MARY his Relict and Executrix who made Oath thereto and being proved by the Oaths of HUMPHRY POPE and WILLIAM CHAMBERS, two of the witnesses thereto, is admitted to Record. And upon the motion of the said Executrix and her performing what is usual in such cases, Certificate is granted her for obtaining a Probate thereof in due form
Recorded the Second day of May 1743, pr. G. L., C. C. W.
Test   GEORGE LEE, C. C. W.

pp.   (On margin: NATHANIEL GRAY's Will)
303-   IN THE NAME OF GOD, Amen. I NATHANIEL GRAY, SENR., of County of Westmor-
305   land & Parish Washington being sick and weak but of perfect mind and memory
do make and ordain this my Last Will and Testment in manner and form following.
Imprs. I give and bequeath my Soul into the hands of Almighty God not doubting but at the General Resurrection to same to receive again by Almighty power, And my body I give to the Earth to be buryed at the discretion of my Executors hereafter mentioned, And as for my worldly Estate, I give in manner following;
Imprimis. I give to my Son, NATHANIEL GRAY, all my Land in STAFFORD County and to the male heirs of his body lawfully to be begotten, in failour of such heir, the said Land to be and remain at his my said Son's disposal; And all the rest of my Estate in STAFFORD County of what kindsoever that am in any wise Intitled to, I give unto my said Son, NATHANIEL GRAY, and to his disposal. I give unto my Son, NATHANIEL GRAY, one fourth part of the new goods and that to be his full part or portion of my Estate;
Imprs. I give to my Son, GEORGE GRAY, half that land in the IRISH NECK that he now lives in his own possession to be divid by the Old Road;
Imprs. My will and pleasure is that my said Son, GEORGE GRAY, shall have the use and occupation of that Land where he now liveth bounded as followeth; Begining at WASHINGTON's MILL along the Main Road to the Land of Old JOHN WHITE, deceased, thence to the Land of BERNARD and along BERNARD's line to WHITE's MILL, thence from the said Mill along Dam to the corner tree, THOMAS CHANCELLER, along CHANCEL-

LER's line to the aforesaid WASHINGTON's MILL for him my said Son, GEORGE GRAY, to occupy and possess during his natural life and then to fall to my Grandson, NATHANIEL GRAY, and to the heirs of his body lawfully to be begotten and in failour of such heirs to fall to the next male heir of my Son, GEORGE GRAY, lawfully to be begotten, and in failour of such heirs to fall to the right heir of me, NATHANIEL GRAY;

Imprs. I give to my said Son, GEORGE GRAY, all that part of that personal Estate that is now possessed with thats to say seven Negroes, Sam, Aaron, Joe, Little Peter, Old Cate, Young Cate and Old Peter; I give to my Son, GEORGE GRAY, one fourth part of the new Goods, and that to be his full part or claim to any part of my Estate;

Imprs. I give unto my Daughter, SARAH STROTHER, Five thousand pounds of Crop Tobacco to be paid her immediately after my decease;

Imprs. My Will and pleasure is that my Daughter, SARAH, shall be no ways disturb'd nor mislested of or from that place where she now dwell during her natural life;

Imprs. I give and bequeath unto my Daughter, MARGARET GRAY, all the furniture thats down at the New House in what kindsoever. I give to my Daughter, MARGARET, two new father beds and furniture with eight cows and calfs and one persil of new pewter called Peggy's Puter, and one Chest of Draws, one Horse call'd Spright & Saddle. My Will and pleasure that she may be paid fifty pounds cash formerly given by Deed to uses; I give to my Daughter, MARGARET, fifty pounds cash more. I give to my Daughter, MARGARET, one Negroe girl called Nan, and one Negroe Boy called Ben, when they can be spared by or from my Wife and that to be her full part of my Estate, excepting a fourth part of the new Goods.

Imprs. I give to my Son, FRANS: GRAY, that part of Land in the IRISH NECK from the Old Road to the River to him and his lawfull disposal if he departs life before he arive to the age of twenty one years or in failour of male heirs lawfully to be begotten, the said Land to fall to my Son, GEORGE GRAY, and the male heir of his body lawfully to be begotten;

Imprs. I give to my Son, FRANCIS GRAY, all this part land where I now dwell from the corner tree of THOMAS CHANCELLER to WASHINGTON's MILL so along the Main Road to WHITE's line (alias BLACKMORE), along the said line to antien corner tree of THOMAS BOYCE, from thence along the line of WILLIAM TYLER and JARRTT. FOARD, along FOARD's line to include all the land bought of JOB SYMS and every part and persil, thence up ROSIERS CREEK several courses and meanders of the said Creek to the begining Corner; I give to my Son, FRANCIS GRAY, Nine Negroes, thats to say, Negroe Mingoe, Teany, Team, Tom, Jackes, Winny and her three Children, wch: is Prince, Doll and Will.

Imprs. I give to my Son, FRANCIS GRAY, the rest of my personall Estate not already mentioned in my Will, Horses, Hoggs, Cattle & house furniture of all kind, old pewter and new pewter as it now stands he paying my Daughter, MARGARET, that is already mentioned to her (two feather beds and furniture & eight cows and calves and One hundred pounds cash). My Will and pleasure is the Cash and Cash Debts is safly to be kept under the care of my Loveing Wife and my Son, FRANCIS GRAY, for the support of her my Loveing Wife, provided she makes use of any but towards her own maintainance or support. My Will and pleasure is that my Loving Wife may not be hindered or debarr'd of an handsom maintainance according to her own likeing and that she may have the use and command of every thing belonging to this Plantation where she now lives dureing her natural life and after her decease every part and persil to fall to my Son, FRANCIS GRAY, as aforementioned;

Imprs. I appoint my Loving Friend, WILLIAM STROTHER, whole & sole Executor to this my Will and Testment; As Witness my hand and seal this Twenty six day of March Anno Domini one thousand seven hundred and forty three

Sign'd Seal'd & delivered in the presence of
        G. BLACKMORE,   SAML. DAVIS,   NATHANIEL GRAY
        JEAMES his mark   MARSHALL
    Westmorland Sct. At a Court held for the said County the 26th day of April 1743
This Last Will and Testament of NATHANIEL GRAY, deceased, was presented into Court by
WILLIAM STROTHER, his Executor in the said Will named who made Oath thereto, and
being proved by the Oaths of GEORGE BLACKMORE, SAMUEL DAVIS and JAMES MAR-
SHALL, witnesses thereto, is admitted to Record; And upon the motion of the said Executor and his performing what is usual in such cases, Certificate is granted him for obtaining a Probate thereof in due form
        Recorded the Third day of May 1743, pr. G. L, C. C. W.
            Test   GEORGE LEE, C. C. W.

pp.   (On margin: KATHERINE BUTLER's Will)
305-   IN THE NAME OF GOD, Amen. I CATHERINE BUTLER of Westmorland County in
306   Washington Parish being very sick but of perfect sense and memory do make
        and ordain this my Last Will and Testament in manner and form following;
    Item. I give and bequeath unto my Son, JAMES BUTLER, my Negroe girl to him & his
heirs and if she proves a Breeder, my Will is that second Child that she brings shall be
given unto my Son, JOHN BUTLER, at the age of two years old, And the third Child if she
brings so many shall be given to my Son, THOMAS BUTLER, at the age of two years old.
My Will is that all the rest of her increase shall remain my Son, JAMES BUTLERs
    Item. I give and bequeath unto my two Sons, JOHN and JAMES, two Chests, two small
potts and one large brass kittle and one Table to be equally divided between them;
    Item. I give and bequeath unto my Cuzin, SARAH ANDERSON, one heiffer to be paid
unto her at the day of marriage;
    Item. I give and bequeath unto my Cuzin, THOMAS PRICE, one young Sow. I give all
the remaining part of my Estate unto my three Sons, THOMAS, JOHN and JAMES equally
to be divided in quantity and quallity amongst them. I do make (long blank) to fore made
by me. Given under my hand and seal this (blank) day of November 1730. I leave my two
Brothers, WILLIAM BUTLER & JAMES BUTLER, my sole Executors of my Estate. Given
under my hand and seal
        WILLIAM SMITH,   CATHERINE BUTLER
        SAMUEL WHEELER   CATHER her mark /︶ BUTLER
    Westmorland Sct. At a Court held for the said County the 26th day of April 1743
This Writing purporting to be the Last Will and Testament of KATHERINE BUTLER, deceased, was at July Court last, presented into Court by JAMES BUTLER, JUNIOR, in order
to be proved, which was objected to by THOMAS BUTLER the Elder who then entered a
caveat against such proof, And thereupon the said Will was ordered to be lodged for the
Court and the parties concerned in and about the said Will to consider the same; which
Will hath been from time to time continued til March Court last, when a summons issued
for JAMES BUTLER the Elder who was an Executor therein named to know if he would
undertake the burthen of the execution of the said Will, And for that it being suggested
to this Court that the said JAMES BUTLER the Elder although summoned, as appears by
the Sheriff's return, renounced to have anything to do with the said Will. On motion of
the said THOMAS BUTLER, who now made Oath thereto, and it being proved at March
Court aforesaid by the Oath of SAMUEL WHEELER, the surviving witness thereto, is admitted to Record; And upon the further motion of the said THOMAS BUTLER and his performing what is usual in such cases, Certificate is granted him for obtaining Letters of

Administration thereupon with the said Will annexed in due form
Recorded the Third day of May 1743 pr. G. L. C. C. W.
Test   GEORGE LEE, C. C. W.

pp.   (On margin: POWNALL & Wife;s Lease for Dower to MOTHERSHEAD &c.)
306-   THIS INDENTURE made the Twenty fifth day of April in the year of our Lord one
307   thousand seven hundred and forty three, Between JOHN POWNALL and his Wife,
         ELIZABETH POWNALL, both of the Parish of Overwharton in County of STAFFORD
of one part and CHRISTOPHER MOTHERSHEAD and JOHN CLAYTOR of the Parish of
Washington in County of Westmorland of other part; Witnesseth that JOHN POWNALL
and ELIZABETH POWNALL his Wife in consideration of the sum of Eleven pounds current money of Virginia to them in hand paid by CHRISTOPHER MOTHERSHEAD and JOHN
CLAYTOR, the receipt whereof JOHN and ELIZABETH POWNALL do hereby acknowledge,
have and by these presents do bargain and sell unto CHRISTOPHER MOTHERSHEAD and
JOHN CLAYTOR a certain parcel of land scituate in Parish of Washington in County of
Westmorland bounded by the land of DANIEL McCARTY, Gent., JOHN BUTLER, an Orphan,
JOSEPH BUTLER and JOHN HAZELL, containing by estimation thirty acres being ELIZA-
BETH POWNALL's third part descended to her by her former Husband, JOHN BUTLER,
deceased, To have and to hold the parcell of land and premises hereby sold unto
CHRISTOPHER MOTHERSHEAD and JOHN CLAYTOR their heirs during the life of ELIZA-
BETH POWNALL party to these presents; And JOHN and ELIZABETH POWNALL for them-
selves do agree with CHRISTOPHER MOTHERSHEAD and JOHN CLAYTOR their heirs by
these presents that they shall warrant and forever defend the land against the claim of
JOHN and ELIZABETH POWNALL; In Witness whereof JOHN and ELIZABETH POWNALL
have to this present Indenture set their hands and seals the day and year first above
written
Signed Sealed & Delivered in the presence of
         HUMPHRY POPE, B. WEEKS   JOHN POWNALL
         JNO: signed ⨍ MURPHY   ELIZABETH her mark X POWNALL
    Westmorland Sct At a Court held for the said County the 26th day of April 1743
JOHN POWNALL who intermarryed with ELIZABETH, the Relict of JOHN BUTLER, deceased
together with the said ELIZABETH personally acknowledged this Deed for the said
ELIZABETH's Dower of the said BUTLER's Land by them passed and conveyed to CHRISTO-
PHER MOTHERSHEAD and JOHN CLATOR to be their proper act and deed (she the said
ELIZABETH being first privily examined as the Law directs) which upon the motion of
the said Donees are admitted to Record
         Recorded the Third day of May 1743, pr. G. L., C. C. W.
             Test   GEORGE LEE, C. C. W.

pp.   (On margin: SMITH's Lease to SMITH)
308-   THIS INDENTURE made the Twenty seventh day of March in the Fifteenth year
310   of the Reign of our Sovereign Lord George the Second by the grace of God of
         Great Brittain France and Ireland, King, Defender of the faith &c., And in the
year of our Lord one thousand seven hundred and forty three; Between THOMAS SMITH
of Parish of (blank) in ORANGE County of one part and JOHN SMITH of Parish of
Washington in County of Westmorland of other part; Witnesseth that THOMAS SMITH in
consideration of five shillings of good and lawfull money of England paid to him in
hand by JOHN SMITH, the receipt whereof he doth hereby acknowledge, hath and by

these presents doth bargain and sell unto JOHN SMITH a certain tract of land containing Two hundred acres lying in County of Westmorland on the head of MATTOX CREEK as by Patent bearing date the Tenth of December Sixteen hundred fifty three will more fully appear; and bound with the line of JOHN VAUGHAN, running North along the line of said VAUGHAN three hundred and twenty poles, thence West to a Box Oak, thence South three hundred and twenty poles to the Creek, thence down the Creek to the first begining; Together with all houses priviledges and advantages belonging; and the rents issues and profits thereof; To have and to hold the land and premises with appurtenances unto JOHN SMITH his heirs during the term of one whole year paying therefore the Rent of one Ear of Indian Corn on the Birthday of our Lord God next ensuing if demanded to the intent that by virtue of these presents and of the Statute for transferring uses into possession, JOHN SMITH may be in the actual possession of the premises and be thereby enabled to accept a release of the inheritance thereof to him and his heirs; In Witness whereof THOMAS SMITH to this present Indenture hath set his hand and seal the day and year first above written
Signed Sealed and Delivered in presence of
    ORIGINAL BROWN,   JOHN JETT,   THOMAS SMITH
    ISAAC KINGTON, JOSEPH SMITH
    Westmorland Sct. At a Court held for the said County the 31st day of May 1743
This Deed of Lease for Land passed and conveyed from THOMAS SMITH to JOHN SMITH was proved in open Court by the Oaths of ORIGINAL BROWN, JOHN JETT and ISAAC KINGHTON, three of the witnesses thereto, which on the motion of the said JOHN SMITH is admitted to Record
        Recorded the Eighth day of June 1743, pr. G. L., C. C. W.
           Test   GEORGE LEE, C. C. W.

(On margin: SMITH's Release to SMITH)
    THIS INDENTURE made the Twenty eighth day of March in the fifteenth year of the Reign of our Sovereign Lord George the Second by the grace of God of Great Brittain France and Ireland, King, Defender of the faith &c. And in the year of our Lord one thousand seven hundred forty and three; Between THOMAS SMITH and ELIZABETH his Wife of Parish of (blank) in ORANGE County, and MARY SMITH of the Parish of Washington in County of Westmorland of one part and JOHN SMITH of Washington Parish in County of Westmorland of other part; Witness that THOMAS SMITH and ELIZABETH his Wife and MARY SMITH in consideration of the sum of Seventy five pounds current money to him in hand paid by JOHN SMITH, the receipt whereof he doth hereby acknowledge, hath and by these presents doth bargain sell and release unto JOHN SMITH being in actual possession of the premises by virtue of a Lease thereof made and of the Statute for transferring uses into possession, Two hundred acres of land lying in Parish of Washington in County of Westmorland on the head of MATTOX CREEK as by Patent bearing date the Tenth of December Sixteen hundred fifty three will more fully appear; Bounded (bounds repeated as in the Lease); To have and to hold the Two hundred acres of land with all premises and their right members & appurtenances unto JOHN SMITH his heirs; And THOMAS SMITH and ELIZABETH his Wife and MARY SMITH for themselves their heirs do warrant and forever defend the land and premises unto JOHN SMITH his heirs against the claim of every person; In Witness whereof the parties to these presents have interchangeably set their hands & seals the day and year first above written
Signed Sealed and delivered in presence of
    ORIGINAL BROWN, ISAAC KINGHTON,   THOS: SMITH,
    JOHN JETT,   ELIZABETH SMITH
    JOSEPH SMITH   MARY SMITH

Received of JOHN SMITH seventy five pounds current money being the consideration money within mentioned to be paid by said JOHN SMITH to me.   L. 75.

    ORIGINAL BROWN,   ISAAC KINGHTON   THOS: SMITH
    JOHN JETT,   JOSEPH SMITH

Westmorland Sct. At a Court held for the said County the 31st day of May 1743 This Deed of Release for Land from THOMAS SMITH and MARY SMITH, Mother of said THOMAS, to JOHN SMITH was this day proved in open Court by the Oaths of ORIGINAL BROWN, JOHN JETT and ISAAC KINGHTON, three of the witnesses thereto, who also proved the Receipt for the consideration endorsed, And the said MARY in open Court relinquished her right of Dower of in and to the Land by the said Deed conveyed, all which on the motion of the said JOHN SMITH are admitted to Record

    Recorded the Eighth day of June 1743, pr. G. L., C. C. W.
        Test   GEORGE LEE, C. C. W.

pp.   (On margin: SMITH's Sale for Life to SMITH)
310-   THIS INDENTURE made the Twenty third day of May in the fifteenth year of the
312   Reign of our Sovereign Lord George the Second by the grace of God of Great
        Brittain France and Ireland, King, Defender of the faith &c., Between JOHN SMITH of Parish of Washington in County of Westmorland of one part and MARY SMITH of the Parish and County aforesaid of other part; Witnesseth that JOHN SMITH in consideration of Twenty pounds current cash in hand paid by MARY SMITH, the receipt whereof JOHN SMITH doth hereby acknowledge, hath and by these presents do bargain and sell unto MARY SMITH her heirs &c., during the natural life of MARY SMITH, the Plantation whereon MARY SMITH now dwelleth with about Two hundred acres of Land thereunto adjoyning be the same more or less and bounded, Begining at COVENTRY RUN and runing Easterly to CRADENHILL RUN, thence up the Run to a marked red Oak saplin, thence Westerly to a marked Maple standing in COVENTRY RUN, thence down the Run to the first begining; Together with all houses advantages and appurtenances to the same belonging; To have and to hold the land and premises to MARY SMITH her heirs &c. during the natural life of MARY SMITH, And JOHN SMITH for himself his heirs doth warrant and defend the premises from the claims of all manner of persons; the Rent of the Chief Lord of the Fees only excepted; In Witness whereof JOHN SMITH hath hereunto set his hand and seal the day and year first above written

Signed Sealed & delivered in the presence of

    ORIGINAL BROWN,   ISAAC KINGHTON   JOHN SMITH
    JOSEPH SMITH

Westmorland Sct. At a Court held for the said County the 31st day of May 1743 JOHN SMITH personally acknowledged this Deed of Bargain and Sale for Land by him passed and conveyed for Life to MARY SMITH to be his proper act and deed, which on motion of the said MARY is admitted to Record

    Recorded the 8th day of June 1743, pr. G. L., C. C. W.
        Test   GEORGE LEE, C. C. W.

pp.   (On margin: JAMES's Lease to PRICE)
312-   THIS INDENTURE made the Twenty fifth day of April in the Sixteenth year of
315   the Reign of our Sovereign Lord George the Second by the grace of God of Great
        Brittain France and Ireland, King, Defender of the faith &c., And in the year of our Lord one thousand seven hundred forty three; Between FRANCIS JAMES of Parish of Washington and in Westmorland County of one part and JOHN PRICE of aforesaid Parish and County of other part; Witnesseth that FRANCIS JAMES in consideration of

Five shillings current money to him in hand paid by JOHN PRICE, the receipt whereof
FRANCIS JAMES doth hereby acknowledge, hath and by these presents doth bargain and
sell unto JOHN PRICE all that parcel of Land lying part in KING GEORGE County & part in
Westmorland and commonly called the FORREST OLD FIELD, & bounded, Begining at a
post, corner to a parcell of land now in the possession of JOHN EDRINGTON and JOHN
JAMES, extending thence E:N:E: 160 poles to another post standing by or near JETT's line,
thence N. 17.0. W. 105 poles to a red Oak saplin near a Branch, thence Northerly down
the Branch crossing JETT's line to a crooked Maple standing on the Edge of the Run, it
being a parcel of Land that FRANCIS JAMES sold the said PRICE out of JETT's Patent,
thence from the crooked Maple S. 65d. W 31 1/2 poles to a Chesnut standing in JETT's
line thence along JETT's line S. 43 W. 64 poles to Majr. UNDERWOODs line, thence South
South East 45 poles to a white Oak standing by a Branch, thence up the Branch Westerly
to a red Oak yt: stands by the Main Road yt: leads to KING GEORGE COURT commonly called
the RIDGE ROAD; from thence S. 17d. E. to the first mentioned post including One hundred and twenty acres & twenty nine poles, be the same more or less, one part One hundred and five acres formerly belonging to Old FRANCIS TRIPLETT and the other part
fifteen acres and twenty nine poles part of JETT's Patent sold by the said JAMES to the
said PRICE; Together with all advantages and appurtenances belonging; and the rents
issues and profits thereof; To have and to hold the land and premises with appurtenances unto JOHN PRICE his heirs during the full term of one whole year paying therefore the Rent of one Ear of Indian Corn on the Birthday of our Lord God next ensuing if
lawfully demanded, to the intent that by virtue of these presents and by force of the
Statute for transferring uses into possession JOHN PRICE may be in the actual possession of the premises and thereby enabled to take a release of the inheritance thereof to
him and his heirs; In Witness whereof FRANCIS JAMES hath hereunto set his hand and
seal the day and year first above written
Sealed and Delivered in presence of
    ORIGL: WROE,
    GEORGE HALES,   EDWD. NOWLES
                             FRANCIS his mark JAMES
   Westmorland Sct. At a Court held for the said County the 31st day of May 1743
FRANCIS JAMES personally acknowledged this Deed of Lease for Land by him passed to
JOHN PRICE to be his proper act and deed, which on the motion of the said PRICE is ad-
mitted to Record
       Recorded the Ninth day of June 1743, pr. G. L., C. C. W.
           Test   GEORGE LEE, C. C. W.

(On margin: JAMES's Release to PRICE)
   THIS INDENTURE made the Twenty sixth day of April in the Sixteenth year of the
Reign of our Sovereign Lord George the Second by the grace of God of Great Brittain
France and Ireland, King, Defender of the faith &c., And in the year of our Lord one
thousand seven hundred and forty three; Between FRANCIS JAMES of Parish of
Washington in Westmorland County of one part and JOHN PRICE of Parish and County
aforesaid of other part; Witnesseth that FRANCIS JAMES in consideration of the sum of
Fifty pounds current money to him in hand paid by JOHN PRICE, the receipt whereof
FRANCIS JAMES doth hereby acknowledge, hath and by these presents doth bargain sell
and release unto JOHN PRICE and his heirs, JOHN PRICE being in actual possession of the
premises by virtue of a Lease thereof made and of the Statute for transferring uses into
possession all that parcel of land lying part in KING GEORGE County and part in Westmorland & commonly called the FORREST OLD FIELD, & bounded; (bounds repeated as in the
Lease); To have and to hold the land and premises with every of their rights members &

appurtenances unto JOHN PRICE his heirs; And FRANCIS JAMES for himself his heirs doth warrant and forever defend the said Land unto JOHN PRICE his heirs against the claims of all manner of persons; In Witness whereof FRANCIS JAMES hath hereunto set his hand and seal the day and year first above written

Sealed and Delivered in the presence of
    ORIGL. WROE,   FRANCIS his mark ∮ JAMES
    GEORGE HALES, EDWD. NOWLES
    Westmorland Sct. At a Court held for the said County the 31st day of May 1743 FRANCIS JAMES personally acknowledged this Deed of Release for Lands by him passed to JOHN PRICE to be his proper act and deed; And MARY, Wife of the said JAMES (being first privily examined according to Law) relinquished her right of Dower of in and to the Lands by the said Deed conveyed, all which on motion of the said PRICE are admitted to Record   Recorded the Ninth day of June 1743, pr. G. L., C. C. W.
        Test   GEORGE LEE, C. C. W.

p.   (On margin: STEEL's Gift of Land to STEEL)
315   TO ALL CHRISTIAN PEOPLE to whome these presents shall come, KNOW YE that I MARGARET STEEL of Parish of Washington in County of Westmorland, Relict and Executrix of JOHN STEEL of the same Parish and County, deced., as well for the natural love which I have and do bare unto my well beloved Son, THOMAS STEEL, as also for divers other good causes and considerations to me at this present time especially moving, have and by these presents do give and make over unto THOMAS STEEL, my Son, and his heirs all my right title and property of all the Land that my former Husband, JOHN STEEL, ever held as his own property, except the Plantation whereon I now live, and the Plantation whereon JOHN PRICE, JUNIOR now lives on, called and known by the name of KENNEDAYs; To have and to hold the land from me or any person claiming under me to THOMAS STEEL and his heirs without any matter of price or demand of me MARGARET STEEL or of any other person under me; In Witness whereof I have set my hand and seal this Thirtieth day of May Annoq: Domini 1743

Signed Sealed and delivered in presence of
    B. WEEKS, JAMES THOMPSON   MARGARET her mark ⫲ STEEL
    JOHN STEEL
    Westmorland Sct. At a Court held for the said County the 31st day of May 1743 MARGARET STEEL personally acknowledged this Deed of Gift for Land by her passed to her Son, THOMAS STEEL, to be her proper act and deed, which on the motion of the said THOMAS is admitted to Record
        Recorded the Ninth day of June 1743; pr. G. L. C, C. W.
        Test   GEORGE LEE, C. C. W.

pp.   (On margin: SPENCE's Deed to MOXLEY)
315-   THIS INDENTURE made this 31st day of May in the year of our Lord one thou-
316   sand seven hundred and forty three, And in the Sixteenth year of the Reign of our Sovereign Lord George the Second, by the grace of God of Great Brittain France and Ireland, King, Defender of the faith &c., Between THOMAS SPENCE of County of Westmorland of one part and JOHN MOXLEY of same County of other part; Witnesseth that THOMAS SPENCE in consideration of the sum of Four thousand five hundred pounds of lawfull tobacco to him in hand paid by JOHN MOXLEY, hath and by these presents doth bargain and sell unto JOHN MOXLEY a certain parcel of land scituate in County of Westmorland containing by estimation Thirty acres be the same more or less and boun-ded, Begining at a white Oak dividing the Lands of ROBERT SANFORD, deceased, and

JOSEPH MOXLEY, deceased, thence Westerly bounded by the said ROBERT SANFORD's line to the head of a vally that makes from a Nole called STONEY NOLE, thence down the Valley to the head of a Branch, thence down the Branch bounded by the Land of PATRICK SPENCE, Gent., to a white Oake standing on West side of said Branch, thence Southerly bounded by PATRICK SPENCE's land to the Main Swamp, thence up the Swamp to JOHN MOXLEY's line, thence bounded by the line of JOHN MOXLEY and JOSEPH MOXLEY deceased, to the begining white Oak, it being the reversion of what Land THOMAS SPENCE holds in a Pattent that was granted to one WHETSONE; Together with all houses orchards profits and emoluments to the same belonging; To have and to hold the parcel of land to JOHN MOXLEY and THOMAS SPENCE and any person claiming any right thereto shall warrant and forever defend by these presents; In Witness whereof the parties have hereunto set their hands and fixed their seals the day and year first above mentioned

Signed Sealed & delivered in the presence of

    THOS: TEMPLEMAN,   THOS: SPENCE
    JOHN SANFORD, JACOB SUTTON

    Westmorland Sct. At a Court held for the said County the 31st day of May 1743 THOMAS SPENCE personally acknowledged this Deed of Bargain and Sale for Land by him passed to JOHN MOXLEY to be his proper act and deed, which on motion of the said MOXLEY is admitted to Record

        Recorded the Ninth day of June 1743; pr. G. L., C. C. W.
                Test GEORGE LEE, C. C. W.

p.   (On margin: WILLIAMS's Sale to WELCH further proved; Deed Recorded folio
316   297 in this Book)
    Westmorland Sct. At a Court held for the said County the 31st day of May 1743 A Deed of Feofment for Lands sold and conveyed by JOHN WILLIAMS to WILLIAM WELCH together with Livery of Seizen and Receipt endorsed were this day further proved by the Oaths of JOHN McCULLEY and JOHN LELAND, the other witnesses thereto subscribed which is ordered to be recorded

        Recorded the Ninth day of June 1743, pr. G. L., C. C. W.
                Test GEORGE LEE, C. C. W.

pp.   (On margin: STEEL's Arbitration Bond to STEEL)
316-   KNOW ALL MEN by these presents that I JOHN STEEL of the Parish of Washing-
317   ton in County of Westmorland, Planter, am held and firmly bound unto
    RICHARD STEEL of the aforesaid Parish and County in the sum of Five hundred pounds current money of Virignia, to which payment well and truly to be made I bind myself my heirs firmly by these presents. Sealed with my seal and dated this Seventh day of May AD. 1743

    THE CONDITION of the above obligation is such that if the above bound JOHN STEEL his heirs shall in all things perform and keep the determination of JOHN ELLIOTT, JOHN WATTS, JOHN MARTIN, THOMAS SHAW and HUMPHRY QUESENBURY, Gentlemen, (or any three of them) of the aforesaid Parish and County indifferently chosen & named as well on the behalf of the above bounden JOHN STEEL as of RICHARD STEEL to determine all manner of actions suits and demands depending by and beween the said parties so that the determination of the Arbitrators or any three of them upon the premises be made or drawn up in writing under their hands & seals and delivered or ready to be delivered to said parties or such of them as shall desire the same on or before the twenty third day of this instant, Then this obligation to be void and of none effect, But if it should

happen that default be made contrary to the true intent & meaning of these presents;
Then this obligation to stand & remain in full force power and virtue
Signed Sealed and delivered in presence of
  THOS: SHAW, R. VAULX   JOHN STEEL
 Westmorland Sct. At a Court held for the said County the 31st day of May 1743
This Award Bond from JOHN STEEL to RICHARD STEEL was presented into Court by the
said RICHARD, which on motion of the said RICHARD is admitted to Record
   Recorded the Tenth day of June 1743, pr. G. L., C. C. W.
    Test GEORGE LEE, C. C. W.

pp. (On margin: JAMES THOMAS's Will)
317- IN THE NAME OF GOD Amen, the first day of December in the year of our Lord
318 Christ one thouand seven hundred and forty two, I JAMES THOMAS of County of
  Westmorland in Colony of Virginia being of sound and perfect mind and memory thanks be to God Almighty for the same, do make this my Last Will and Testament in
manner and form following; revoking and absolutely annulling all and every Will or
Wills heretofore by me made either by word or writing and this only to be my Last Will
and Testament and none other;
 First, I give my Soul to God that gave it, my body to the Earth from whence it came, to
be buried in such decent and Christian manner as my Exrs. hereafter named shall see
convenient, trusting through the merits of my blessed Saviour Jesus Christ to find free
pardon for all sins.
 I give bequeath and devise to my Son, JAMES THOMAS, all the tract of land I
bought of JOSEPH CARR and JOHN RUST, to him and his heirs forever, on condition he
make over and convey Two hundred acres of Land I gave him on the SUGAR LAND RUN
in PRINCE WILLIAM County to my Son, GEORGE THOMAS, and pay what fees is due from
me to the COLLEGE of SURVEYS made. It is also my Will that if my Son, GEORGE THOMAS,
should die without lawfull issue of his body, then the said Two hundred acres of land to
be and descend to my Daughter, WINIFRED THOMAS, and her heirs forever; I also give
to my Son, JAMES THOMAS, all my books and surveying Instruments.
 I give bequeath and devise to my DAughter, ELIZABETH THOMAS, One hundred
acres of Land adjoining to WILLIAM BUCKLEY in PRINCE WILLIAM County together
with three Negroes (vizt.) Lucey, Will and Daniel; to her and the heirs of her body
lawfully begotten and for want of such issue then I give the Land and Negroes to my
Son, JOHN THOMAS, and his heirs forever;
 I give bequeath and devise to my Grandson, WILLIAM THOMAS, the Son of my
Daughter, KATHERINE, One hundred acres of land (adjoining to the land before given to
my Daughter, ELIZABETH, in PRINCE WILLIAM County) to him the said WILLIAM & his
heirs.
 I give bequeath and devise to my Daughter, HANNAH THOMAS, the remaining part of
my tract of Land in PRINCE WILLIAM County to her and the heirs of her body lawfully
begotten and for want of such issue, then I give the said Land to my Daughter, WINI-
FRED THOMAS and her heirs forever;
 I give to my Son, GEORGE THOMAS, my Negro boy, Frank, to him and his heirs forever.
What I have given to my Son, GEORGE, is in lieu of a Bond I passed to the Honble. THO-
MAS LEE on his Accot.
 I give to my Daughter, WINIFRED THOMAS, one Negro girl named Jenney to her and
her heirs forever;
 I give bequeath and devise to my Daughter, SARAH JENKINS, one two year old
heiffer;

I also give bequeath and devise to my Son, JOHN THOMAS, six Negroes, (vizt.) Cathcart, Frank, Archy, Scipio, Anthony & Jack together with all the rest of my Estate be it of what nature soever to him and his heirs for ever he paying all my just Debts (excepting the College Fees above mentioned) and taking care and maintaining my Loving Wife, SARAH THOMAS, his Mother, for and during her natural life;

And Lastly I make ordain constitute and appoint my Son, JOHN THOMAS, whole & sole Executor of this my Last Will and Testament. In Witness whereof I have hereunto set my hand & seal the day and year above written

Signed Sealed & delivered in the presence of

WILLOUGHBY NEWTON,   JAMES THOMAS
ANDREW McAULAY,   JOS: SMITH

Westmorland Sct. At a Court held for the said County the 31st day of May 1743 This Last Will and Testament of JAMES THOMAS, deceased, was presented into Court by JOHN THOMAS, his Executor, who made Oath thereto and being proved by the Oaths of WILLOUGHBY NEWTON, Gent., and ANDREW McAULAY, two of the witnesses thereto is admitted to Record; And upon the motion of the said Executor and his performing what is usual in such cases, Certificate is granted him for obtaining a Probate thereof in due form   Recorded the Tenth day of June 1743, pr. G. L., C. C. W.

Test   GEORGE LEE, C. C. W.

pp.   (On margin: BUNCH ROE's Nuncupative Will)
318-   BUNCH ROE's Will Feby. 10th 1742/3. Item. I give to BUNCH ROE, my Nephew,
319   my Ne. Dick. Item. I give to my Nephew, HENRY ROE, one Negro named Prince.
Item. I give (blank).
Item. I give W. E. FRANK my Negro, Jemmy; He farther said that WILLIAM TAYLOR and THOMAS WHITING should have part of his Estate and that he thought he must give his Sister some small matter by way of a token or words to that effect.

This day, ANDREW MONROE made Oath before me that the above Writing was delivered him from the mouth of BUNCH ROE, deceased, and that he was in disposing sense and memory. Given under my hand this 11th Feby. 1742/3

JAS: BANKHEAD

Westmorland Sct. At a Court continued and held for the said County the first day of June 1743   This Last Will and Testament of BUNCH ROE, deceased, was presented into Court by BUNCH ROE, and being proved by the Oath of ANDREW MONROE, Gent., is admitted to Record; And for that the said Decedent omitted nominating an Executor, Upon the motion of the said BUNCH ROE and giving WILLIAM MONROE for his security and performing what is ususal in such cases, Certificate is granted him for obtaining Letters of Administration with the Will annexed in due form

Recorded the Tenth day of June 1743, pr. G. L., C. C. W.

Test   GEORGE LEE, C. C. W.

p.   (On margin: WADDEY's Deed of Bargain and Sale to LEE Esqr., further proved;
319   Deed recorded folio 293)
Westmorland Sct. At a Court held for the said County the 28th day of June 1743

A Deed of Bargain and Sale for Land from JANE WADDEY, Widow, to THOMAS LEE, Esquire, together with the Receipt for the consideration endorsed was this day further proved by the Oath of JOHN COAN, the other witness thereto, which on the motion of the said LEE is admitted to Record

Recorded the Fourth day of July 1743, pr. G. L., C. C. W.

Test   GEORGE LEE, C. C. W.

pp.   (On margin: PAYTON's Lease to PAYTON)
319-   THIS INDENTURE made this Twenty eighth day of January in the Sixteenth year
321   of the Reign of our Sovereign Lord George the Second by the grace of God of
          Great Brittain France and Ireland, King, Defender of the faith &c., And in the
year of our Lord one thousand seven hundred forty and two; Between ANTHONY PAY-
TON of County of KING GEORGE, Planter, of one part and JOHN PAYTON of County of Westmorland, Planter, of other part; Witnesseth that ANTHONY PAYTON in consideration of
the sum of Five shillings current money of Virginia to him in hand paid by JOHN PAY-
TON, the Receipt whereof he doth hereby acknowledge, hath and by these presents doth
bargain and sell unto JOHN PAYTON a certain parcel of land containing by estimation
Fifty four acres be the same more or less scituate in County of Westmorland, it being a
parcel of land that was granted to ANTHONY PAYTON by his Father, ANTHONY PAYTON,
late of County of Westmorland, deceased, which parcel of land is bounded and included
between the line of JOHN PAYTON, WILLIAM PAYTON and HENRY WASHINGTON; And all
houses orchards profits and appurtenances to the parcel of land belonging; To have
and to hold the land and premises with appurtenances unto JOHN PAYTON and assigns
during the term of one whole year paying therefore the rent of one ear of Indian Corn
upon the last day of the term if lawfully demanded to the intent that by virtue of these
presents and for the Statute for transferring uses into possession JOHN PAYTON may be
in the actual possession of the premises and thereby be enabled to accept a release of
the inheritance thereof to him and his heirs; In Witness whereof the parties to these
presents have interchangeably set their hands and seals the day and year first above
written
Sealed and delivered in presence of us
          FRANCIS JETT, WILLIAM PAYTON   ANTHONY *A* PAYTON
                                                                    signed

     Westmorland Sct. At a Court held for the said County the 30th day of August 1743
ANTHONY PAYTON personally acknowledged this Deed of Lease for Lands by him passed
to JOHN PAYTON to be his proper act and deed which on the motion of the said JOHN is
admitted to Record
          Recorded the Sixth day of September 1743, pr G. L. C. C. W.
               Test GEORGE LEE, C. C. W.

     (On margin: PAYTON's Release to PAYTON)
     THIS INDENTURE made the Twenty ninth day of January in the Sixteenth year of the
Reign of our Sovereign Lord George the Second by the grace of God of Great Brittain,
France and Ireland, King, Defender of the faith &c., And in the year of our Lord one
thousand seven hundred forty and two; Between ANTHONY PAYTON of County of KING
GEORGE, Planter, of one part and JOHN PAYTON, of County of Westmorland, Planter, of
other part; Witnesseth that ANTHONY PAYTON in consideration of the sum of Twelve
pounds current money of Virginia to ANTHONY PAYTON in hand paid by JOHN PAYTON,
the receipt whereof he doth hereby acknowledge, hath and by these presents doth bargain sell and release unto JOHN PAYTON (in his actual possession now being by virtue
of a bargain and sale to him thereof made for one whole year and by force of the
Statute for transferring uses into possession) and to his heirs all that parcel of Land
containing Fifty four acres (be the same more or less) scituate in County of Westmorland and bounded included between the lines of said JOHN PAYTON, WILLIAM PAYTON
and HENRY WASHINGTON; To have and to hold the land and premises with appurtenances unto JOHN PAYTON his heirs free and clear from all incumbrances; In Witness
whereof the parties to these presents have interchangeably set their hands and seals
the day month and year first above written

Sealed and delivered in the presence of us
    FRANCIS JETT, WILLIAM PAYTON   ANTHONY A PAYTON
                                                      signed

    Westmorland Sct. At a Court held for the said County the 30th day of August 1743 ANTHONY PAYTON personally acknowledged this Deed of Release for Land by him passed to JOHN PAYTON to be his proper act and deed, which on the motion of the said JOHN, is admitted to Record
        Recorded the Sixth day of September 1743, pr. G. L., C. C. W.
            Test   GEORGE LEE, C. C. W.

pp.   (On margin: THOS: BROWN's Deed of Feofment to COLEMAN READ)
322-   THIS INDENTURE made September the 23rd and in the Seventeenth year of the
325   Reign of our Sovereign Lord George the Second by the grace of God of Great
Brittain France and Ireland, King, Defender of the faith &c., And in the year of
our Lord one thousand seven hundred and forty three; Between THOMAS BROWN and
ELIZABETH his Wife of Parish of Cople in County of Westmorland of one part and COLE-
MAN READ of aforesaid Parish and County of other part; Witnesseth that THOMAS
BROWN and ELIZABETH his Wife in consideration of the quantity and sum of Fifty
pounds current money to him in hand paid by by COLEMAN READ, the receipt whereof
THOMAS BROWN and ELIZABETH his Wife doth hereby acknowlege, hath and by these
presents doth bargain and sell unto COLEMAN READ his heirs all that Plantation and
parcel of land containing by estimation One hundred and Thirty acres be the same
more or less together with a right of a parcel of land held by a Pattent granted WIL-
LIAM OVEREIT now in the possession of said COLEMAN REID with the priviledges and
appurtenances a half an acre of land only excepted for the use of a burying place and
for no other use, the Hundred and thirty acres of land lying in the Parish of Cople in
County of Westmorland and lying on the South West side of a Creek and is bounded on
the North West and North East by the land of said COLEMAN READ and on the South by
the River, which hundred and thirty acres is part of a greater tract formerly granted to
THOMAS HAWKINS and hath been by sundry conveyances legally conveyed down and
became the right of JOHN WALKER, who died siezed with the said land and leaving no
heir behind him, and not disposing of the land by Will, it was then escheated for THO-
MAS BROWN and his Brother, GEORGE BROWN, the said GEORGE BROWN dying also, and
THOMAS BROWN being his heir is now lawfully vested with the hundred and thirty
acres of land, Together with all houses orchards priviledges and appurtenances to the
Plantation and parcel of land belonging; To have and to hold the hundred and thirty
acres of land with appurtenances unto COLEMAN REID his heirs; And THOMAS BROWN
and ELIZABETH his Wife the land and premises hereby granted unto COLEMAN REID his
heirs against all persons shall warrant and forever defend by these presents (the
Rents from henceforth to become due and payable to the Chief Lord or Lords of the fee
to the premises only excepted and foreprized); In Witness whereof the partys first
aforementioned to these present Indentures have interchangeably set their hand & fixt
their seal the day and year first above written
Signed Sealed and delivered in presence of
    GERARD HUTT, RICHD: HOLLIDAY,   THOMAS BROWN
    EDWARD mark V GILL
    Memorandum; that on the 23rd day of September in the year of our Lord 1743, THO-
MAS BROWN delivered peaceably actual and quiet possession and seizen of the within
granted land and premises by the delivery of Turff and Twigg on the land unto COLE-
MAN REID in the name and token of the possession of the whole land and premises;

In presence of GERARD HUTT,
    RICHD. HALLIDAY, EDWARD his mark ⟩ GILL

    I do hereby acknowledge to have had and received of COLEMAN READ the full quantity of Fifty pounds current money being the consideration to be paid me by him and thereof and of every part and parcel thereof do hereby acquit release and discharge the said COLEMAN READ his heirs; As Witness my hand the day and year first within written

Test   GERARD HUTT,   THOMAS BROWN
        RICHD: HALLIDAY,
        EDWARD his mark ʃ GILL

    Westmorland Sct. At a Court held for the said County the 25th day of October 1743 This Deed of Feofment for Lands from THOMAS BROWN to COLEMAN READ together with the Livery of Seizen and receipt for the consideration endorsed were proved in open Court by the Oaths of the witnesses thereto, which on the motion of the said READ are admitted to Record

        Recorded the 5th day of November 1743, pr. G. L., C. C. W.
                Test   GEORGE LEE, C. C. W.

    (On margin: THOS: BROWN's Bond to COLAMAN READ)

    KNOW ALL MEN by these presents that I THOMAS BROWN of Cople Parish in County of Westmorland, Planter, am held and firmly bound unto COLEMAN READ of the Parish and County aforesaid, Planter, in the just sum of One hundred pounds current money, to the which payment well and truly to be made I bind myself my heirs firmly by these presents; Sealed with my Seal and dated the 23rd day of September in the Seventeenth year of the Reign of our Sovereign Lord George the Second of Great Brittain France and Ireland King, Defender of the faith &c., Annoq: Domini 1743

    THE CONDITION of the above obligation is such that if the above bounden THOMAS BROWN his heirs shall truly perform and keep all the covenants which on his or their part ought to be performed and kept contained in a certain Deed of Feofment made between THOMAS BROWN and COLEMAN READ and in all things according to the purport of the said Deed, then this Obligation to be void and of none effect, otherwise to stand remain and be in full force power and virtue

Signed Sealed and deliveredin presence of
        GERARD HUTT,   THOMAS BROWN
        RICHD: HOLLIDAY, EDWARD his mark Ϲ GILL

    Westmorland Sct. At a Court held for the said County the 25th day of October 1743 This Bond for performance of Covenants from THOMAS BROWN to COLEMAN READ was proved in open Court by the Oaths of the witnesses thereto, which on motion of the said READ is admitted to Record

        Recorded the 5th day of November 1743, pr. G. L., C. C. W.
                Test   GEORGE LEE, C. C. W.

p.   (On margin: KIRK & Others Division of Land &c.)
325   ARTICLES of AGREEMENT upon dividing of a tract of land lying in the County of Westmorland and formerly belonging to JOSEPH HARDWITCH, deceased, and by Will left the land to be equally divided among his Children, And now this 29th day of September 1743, division being agreed upon and lines run before evidence between ANN KIRK his said Wife and us the said Children for the same and as we shall interchangeably set our hands to the said Agreement that us nor neither of us shall oppose or impose each other in each others parts; As Witness our hands the day and year above written

ANN mark _A_ KIRK.   GEORGE ASBURY
WILLIAM MOON   JAMES HARDWICH
                         HAZEL HARDWICH

Signed in the presence of us
   HENRY his mark _H_ ASBURY,
   THOMAS his mark _T_ WILLIAMS,
   JNO: GUTHRIE, JUNR., SAMUEL WALKER
   Westmorland Sct. At a Court held for the said County the 25th day of October 1743
This Writing purporting to be a Division of Land between ANN KIRK, GEORGE ASBURY,
WILLIAM MOON and JAMES HARDWICH was personally acknowledged in Court by the
said parties, at whose motion the same is admitted to Record
   Recorded the 5th day of November 1743 pr. G. L., C. C. W.
      Test GEORGE LEE, C. C. W.

pp.   (On margin: HARDWICH's Deed of Feofment to ASBURY)
325-   THIS INDENTURE made the 25th day of October in the Seventeenth year of the
328   Reign of our Sovereign Lord George the Second by the grace of God of Great
      Brittain France and Ireland, King, Defender of the faith; And in the year of our
Lord one thousand seven hundred and forty three; Between JAMES HARDWICH of
Parish of Cople in County of Westmorland, Planter, of one part and GEORGE ASBURY of
the aforesaid Parish and County of other part; Witnesseth tht JAMES HARDWICH in consideration of the quantity or sum of Five pounds current money of Virginia and Nine
hundred pounds of tobacco in one Hogshead to him in hand paid by GEORGE ASBURY,
the receipt whereof JAMES HARDWICH doth hereby acknowledge, hath and by these
presents doth bargain and sell unto GEORGE ASBURY his heirs all that plantation parcel
of land containing Thirty five acres of land more or less scitaute in Parish of Cople in
County of Westmorland being aprt of a tract of land whereon JOSEPH HARDWICH, Father
of said JAMES HARDWICH, party to these presents, which land JOSEPH HARDWICH willed
part to said JAMES HARDWICH as may appear by the Records of the County Court of
Westmorland, which land is part of a Division now vested lawfully in JAMES HARDWICH
his Son; Together with all houses orchards and appurtenances to the parcel of land belonging; To have and to hold the Thirty five acres of land with appurtenances unto
GEORGE ASBURY his heirs; And JAMES HARDWICH his heirs against every person shall
warrant and forever defend by these presents; And that ISABEL, the Wife of JAMES
HARDWICH, shall personally appear at the next Court held for the said County and then
and there in open Court relinquish her right and title of Dower and Thirds at the Common Law in the premises hereby conveyed by her Husband to GEORGE ASBURY his
heirs; In Witness whereof the parties first above named to these presents Indentures
have interchangeably set their hands and affixed their seals the day and year first
above written
Signed Sealed and delivered in the presence of
   SAML; WALKER,   JAMES HARDWICH
   JOS: READ, HAR: WALKER   ISABELL her mark _H_ HARDWICH
   Memorandum; That on the 25th day of October in the year of our Lord 1743, JAMES
HARDWICH delivered peaceable and quiet possession and seizin of the within granted
land and premises by delivery of Turff and Twigg on the land unto GEORGE ASBURY in
the name and token of the possession of the whole land and premises within granted;
In presence of   JOS: READ
        SAML: WALKER, HAR: WALKER

I do hereby acknowledge to have had and received of GEORGE ASBURY the full quantity of five pounds current money of Virginia and Nine hundred pounds of tobacco in one hogshead being the consideration within mentioned to be paid me by him; As Witness my hand the day and year first within written

      (no witnesses recorded)   (no signature recorded)

Westmorland Sct. At a Court held for the said County the 25th day of October 1743 JAMES HARDWICH personally acknowledged this Deed of Feofment for Lands by him passed to GEORGE ASBURY together with livery of seizin and receipt for the consideration endorsed to be his proper act and deed, and ISABELLA, Wife of the said JAMES (being first privily examined according to Law), relinquished her right of Dower of in and to the lands by the said Deed conveyed, all which on motion of the said ASBURY are ordered to be recorded

      Recorded the 7th day of November 1743; pr. G. L., C. C. W.
          Test GEORGE LEE, C. C. W.

    (On margin: HARDWICH's Bond to ASBURY)

KNOW ALL MEN by these presents that I JAMES HARDWICH of Parish of Cople in County of Westmorland, Planter, am held and justly indebted unto GEORGE ASBURY of the Parish and County aforesaid, Planter, in the just sum of Ten pounds current money and Eighteen hundred pounds of tobacco, to the which payment well and truly to be made I bind myself my heirs firmly by these presents; Sealed with my Seal and dated this 25th day of October in the Seventeenth year of the Reign of our Sovereign Lord George the Second of Great Brittain France and Ireland, King, Defender of the faith &c., Annoq: Domini 1743

THE CONDITION of the above obligation is such that if the above bounden JAMES HARDWICH his heirs shall truly perform and keep all Covenants which on his or their part ought to be performed and kept contained in a certain Deed of Feofment made between JAMES HARDWICH and GEORGE ASBURY and by all things according to the purport of the said Deed, Then this Obligation to be void and of none effect, otherways to stand remain and full force power and virtue

Signed Sealed and delivered in presence of

      SAML: WALKER,   JAMES HARDWICH
      JOS: READ,   HAR: WALKER

Westmorland Sct. At a Court held for the said Coutny the 25th day of October 1743 JAMES HARDWICH personally acknowledged this Bond for performance of Covenants by him passed to GEORGE ASBURY, to be his proper act and deed, which on motion of the said ASBURY is admitted to Record

      Recorded the 7th day of November 1743, pr. G. L., C. C. W.
         Test   GEORGE LEE, C. C. W.

pp.   (On margin: JOHN STEEL's Will)
328-   IN THE NAME OF GOD, Amen. I JOHN STEEL of Westmorland County being sick
329   and weak but of perfect memory thanks be to God, but calling to mind that all
       mankind is mortall, I do hereby make and ordain this my Last Will and Testament as follows, (vizt.)

First and principally, I give my Soul into the hands of Almighty God that gave it me nothing doubting but to have everlasting life.

I give unto MARY STEEL alias WEEKS, Daughter of young MARGT. STEEL, that Plantation that RICHARD STEEL now lives on thats now in dispute;

Item. I give unto THOMAS STEEL that part of land which comes from the Old House where JOHN CUZENS now lives on to the Branch that line that THOMAS SHAW and HUMPHRY QUESENBURY made tho' against my consent;

Item. I give the Plantation where HOPKIN MATTHEWS now lives to SARAH FINCH with the Plantation with the Plantation called CANNADAY's that JOHN RICE now lives on.

Item. I give unto THOS. STEEL all my wearing cloaths;

Item. I give SARAH FINCH my Riding Horse and the remainder of my Estate to be divided equally among my Sisters. I do appoint BENJAMIN WEEKS my hole and sole Executor of this my Last Will and Testment revoking and disannulling all other Wills by me made. In Witness my hand and seal this third day of October in the year of our Lord God 1743

THOMAS HUGHS,   JOHN STEEL.
THOMAS KING

Westmorland Sct. At a Court held for the said County the 29th day of November 1743 This Last Will and Testament of JOHN STEEL, deceased, was presented into Court by BENJAMIN WEEKS his Executor who made Oath thereto and being proved by the Oaths of the witnesses thereto is admitted to Record; And upon the motion of the said Executor and his performing what is usual in such cases, Certificate is granted him for obtaining a Probate thereof in due form

Recorded the Seventh day of December 1743; pr. G. L., C. C. W.
Test   GEORGE LEE, C. C. W.

p.   (On margin: ELIZABETH BROWN's Relinquishment of Dower to Land by her
329   Husband, THOS: BROWN, sold to COLEMAN READ. Deed Recorded
                       folio 322)

Westmoreland Sct. At a Court held for the said County the 29th day of November 1743   ELIZABETH BROWN, Wife of THOMAS BROWN (she being first privily examined according to Law) relinquished her Right of Dower of in and to certain Lands by her said Husband sold and conveyed unto COLEMAN READ as by a Deed thereof bearing date the twenty third day of September one thousand seven hundred and forty three, which said Deed is recorded in this Book; And on motion of the said COLEMAN, this Certificate is ordered to be recorded

Recorded the Seventh day of December 1743, pr. G. ., C. C. W.
Test   GEORGE LEE, C. C. W.

pp.   (On margin: ESKRIDGE's Relinqushmt. of Dower to RUST &c.)
329-   Westmoreland Sct. George the Second by the Grace of God of Great Brittain
330   France and Ireland, King, Defender of the faith &c., To HENRY LEE, JAMES
          STEPTOE and PRESLY COX of County aforesd. Gentlemen, Greeting. We do hereby authorise and impower you or any two or more of you at such time and place as you shall appoint (some time before the next Court to be held for the County aforesaid) to take the privy examination of JANE, Wife of SAMUEL ESKRIDGE, of said County, Gent., apart from her Husband touching her willingness and unconstrained consent and assent to the passing a certain Deed of Feofment for conveying her right of Dower to a certain parcel of land scituate in Parish of Cople in County afsd., containing fifty acres unto PETER RUST (the Commission for the privy examination of JANE, the Wife of SAMUEL ESKRIDGE); herein you are not to fail; Witness GEORGE LEE, Clerk of the said County Court the 14th day of January in the 17th year of our Reign

GEORGE LEE, C. C. W.

Westmorland Sct. Pursuan to the Commission to us directed we have examined the within JANE ESKRIDGE privately and apart from her Husband, SAMUEL ESKRIDGE (the return of the execution of the privy examination of JANE ESKRIDGE); Given under our hands and Seals this 24th day of January 1743/4.

JAMES STEPTOE
PRESLY COX

Westmorland Sct. At a Court held for the said County the 31st day of January 1743 This Commission for the privy examination of JANE, the Wife of SAMUEL ESKRIDGE, Gentleman, concerning the said JANE's Right of Dower to fifty acres of land by the said SAMUEL sold to PETER RUST being returned executed as appears by a Certificate under the hands and seals of JAMES STEPTOE and PRESLY COX, two of the Gentlemen in the Commission named, all which are admitted to Record

Recorded the Sixth day of February 1743, pr. G. L., C. C. W.
Test   GEORGE LEE, C. C. W.

pp.   (On margin: ESKRIDGE's Relinquishmt. of Dower to RUST &c.)
330-   Westmorland SCt. George the Second by the grace of God of Great Brittain
331   France and Ireland, King, Defender of the faith &c., to HENRY LEE, JAMES
           STEPTOE and PRESLY COX of County aforesaid, Gent., Greeting. We do hereby authorise and impower you or any two of you at such time as you shall appoint (some time before the next Court to be held for the County aforesaid) to take the privy examination of JANE, Wife of SAMUEL ESKRIDGE, of said County, Gentleman, apart from her said Husband touching her willingness and unconstrained consent and assent to the passing a certain Deed of Feofment for conveying her right of Dower to a certain parcel of land scituate in Parish of Cople in County aforesaid, containing One hundred acres be the same more or less unto PETER RUST (the Commission for the privy examination of JANE, the Wife of SAMUEL ESKRIDGE); herein you are not to fail; Witness GEORGE LEE, Clerk of the said County Court the xivth day of January in the xviith year of our Reign

GEORGE LEE, C. C. W.

Westmorland Sct. Pursuant to the Commission of us directed we have examined the within named JANE ESKRIDGE privately and apart from her Husband, SAMUEL ESKRIDGE, (the return of the execution of the privy examination of JANE ESKRIDGE); Given under our hands and seals this 24th day of January 1743/4

JAMES STEPTOE
PRESLY COX

Westmorland Sct. At a Court held for the said County the 31st day of January 1743 This Commission for the privy examination of JANE, the Wife of SAMUEL ESKRIDGE, Gentleman, concerning the said JANE's Right of Dower to one hundred acres of Land by said SAMUEL sold to PETER RUST being returned executed as appears by a Certificate under the hands and seals of JAMES STEPTOE and PRESLY COX, two of the Gentlemen in the said Commission named, all which are admitted to Record

Recorded the Sixth day of February 1743, pr. G. L., C. C. W.
Test   GEORGE LEE, C. C. W.

pp.   (On margin: BAKER and BAKER's Plat and Division of Land &c.)
331-   (Near the top of page 331 is a sketch of the Division of the Land showing in part,
332   Figure 1, 129 acres Mr. BUTLER BAKER's part; which shows ROSIERS CREEK to the North and North West; Figure 2 for 164 acres Mr. JOHN BAKER's part).

A Platt of Two hundred ninety three acres of Land surveyed and divided for Mr. BUTLER BAKER and Mr. JOHN BAKER of Westmorland County lying on ROSIERS CREEK alias ATTOPIN CREEK being a tract of land give to the said BUTLER and JOHN BAKER by their Father, JOHN BAKER, late of the said County, deceased, bounded as follows; Begining at

(A), the mouth of a small Valley and runing down the several courses of the said Creed vizt., N. 76 E. 28 po., N. 20 W. 26 po; N. 41 1/2 E. 76 po., S. 85 E. 124 po: S. 68 E. 30 po. to (B), a large white Oak standing at the mouth of a small Branch opisite to a small Island in the Marsh, then S. 47 1/2 E. 137 po. to (C), w white Oak stump in a Swamp then S. 49 W. 222 po: to a red Oak by Mr. DAVIS's Fence, then N. 32 W. 33 po. to a red Oak standing by the Road to Mr. LOVEL's FERRY at (E), then N. 39 E. 37 po> to (F), a Walnut tree standing by the said Road, then N. 35 W. 60 po., N. 55 W. 38 po. N. 41 1/2 W. 34 po. to the begining;

The Division Lines is described from (H) a white Oak fallen down in the Marsh to (G) a white Oak Stump by the Road, then along the Road, being described in the Plat by dotted lines to (F), the said Walnut standing by the said Road. Figure the first contains 129 acres is the Mansion Plantation laid of for Mr. BUTLER BAKER; Figure the second contains 164 acres and laid off for Mr. JOHN BAKER.

Surveyed and divided the 11th February 1742 p. JOSEPH BERRY

Westmorland Sct. At a Court held for the said County the 31st day of January 1743 This Plat and Report for the Division of Lands between BUTLER BAKER and JOHN BAKER was presented into Court by the said parties which at their joint prayer are admitted to Record   Recorded the Seventh day of February 1743, pr. G. L., C. C. W.

Test   GEORGE LEE, C. C. W.

(On margin: BAKER and BAKER's Award between &c., about Division of Land)

Westmorland Sct. We the Subscribers being mutually chosen and appointed by Mr. BUTLER BAKER and Mr. JOHN BAKER of the County aforesaid to arbitrate and determine a matter of controversy between about a tract of land containing Two hundred and ninety three acres lying on the lower side of ROSIERS CREEK and given by the Last Will and Testament of their Father, JOHN BAKER, late of said County, deceased, to be equally divided between them. Now being desirous as much as in us lies to settle the said controversy, we have made the division after the most equitable manner we in our Judgment could, And considering the Manor Plantation for its scituation and improvements and quality of Land to be preferrable to the other part; we have laid of for the said JOHN BAKER thirty five acres more in his part than to the said BUTLER BAKER, the said BUTLER BAKER to have the Mannor Plantation where he now lives and JOHN BAKER to have the other part, it being where he now lives; and as for the several bounds quantitites of the dividents with the discription of the division lines, we refer to the Surveyors Plat hereunto annexed; We also award that BUTLER BAKER have Rail Timber of the said JOHN BAKER's part sufficient to make one thousand Rails, and the wood of the tree whence they are taken on demand and that JOHN BAKER have that Wheat which he sowed, it being on said BUTLER's part; and the Fence thereabout to be carryed to the Division Line. Given under our hands this 23rd day of March 1742/3

ROBT. LOVELL
THOS: CHANCELLOR
JOHN WHITE

Westmorland Sct. At a Court held for the said County the 31st day of January 1743 This Award and Division of Land between BUTLER BAKER and JOHN BAKER was by them presented into Court at whose joint motion the same is admitted to Record

Recorded the Seventh day of February 1743, pr. G. L., C. C. W.

Test   GEORGE LEE, C. C. W.

pp.   (On margin: SHOTWELL's Lease to BERRYMAN)
332-   THIS INDENTURE made the Sixteenth day of February in the year of our Lord
335   one thousand seven hundred forty three; Between JOHN SHOTWELL of Washington Parish in County of Westmorland, Taylor, of one part and WILLIAM BERRY-

MAN of the same Parish and County of other part; Witnesseth that JOHN SHOTWELL in consideration of the sum of Five shillings to him in hand paid have lett and to farm lett unto WILLIAM BERRYMAN one parcel of land scituate in Parish of Washington in County of Westmorland containing by estimation Two hundred acres of land being part of a Patent granted to WILLIAM WEBB bearing date the twenty sixth day of September in the year of our Lord one thousand six hundred sixty eight; out of which Patent, PETER SKINNER, late of the said Parish and County, bought Two hundred acres bounded, Begining at DANIEL WHITE's MILL DAMM at the corner of PETER SKINNER's Dividend of land, runing North North West two hundred twenty eight poles, then North West twenty poles, then South seventy two poles, then South East twenty poles, then South South East two hundred and twenty eight poles, then East North East to the begining; To have and to hold the leased premises with all houses orchards and gardens to WILLIAM BERRY-MAN his heirs during the term of one whole year from the Twenty fifth day of December last past paying unto JOHN SHOTWELL his heirs one Ear of Indian Corn on or before the twenty fifth day of December one thousand seven hundred and forty four if lawfully demanded, to the intent that WILLIAM BERRYMAN his heirs may be enabled by virtue of this Lease and by force of the Statute for transferring uses into possession to take a Deed of Release of the abovesaid Leased premises to him and his heirs; In Witness whereof JOHN SHOTWELL have hereunto set his hand and seal the day and year first above mentioned

Signed Sealed and delivered in the presence of us

WILLIAM HARRISON,   PETER BAILLEUL,   JOHN SHORTWILL
JOHN WELCH,   SAMUEL WHEELER,
SAMUEL his mark S SIMS

Received the day of the date within mentioned five shillings Sterling being the consideration money within mentioned 0...5...0.

WILLIAM HARRISON,   PETER BAILLEUL,   JOHN SHOTWILL
JOHN WELCH,   SAMUEL WHEELER
SAMUEL his mark S SIMS

Westmorland Sct. At a Court held for the said County the 28th day of February 1743 JOHN SHOTWELL personally acknowledged this Deed of Lease for Land by him passed to WILLIAM BERRYMAN, Gentleman, together with a Receipt for the consideration endorsed to be his proper act and deed, which on motion of the said BERRYMAN are admitted to Record

Recorded the Sixth day of March 1743; pr. G. L., C. C. W.
Test   GEORGE LEE, C. C. W.

(On margin: SHOTWELL's Release to BERRYMAN)

THIS INDENTURE made the Seventeenth day of February in the year of our Lord one thousand seven hundred forty three; Between JOHN SHOTWELL of Washington Parish in County of Westmorland, Taylor, of one part and WILLIAM BERRYMAN of the same Parish and County of other part; Witnesseth that JOHN SHOTWELL in consideration of Nine thousand pounds of tobacco to him in hand paid by WILLIAM BERRYMAN, the receipt whereof he doth hereby acknowledge, hath and by these presents doth bargain sell and set over unto WILLIAM BERRYMAN his heirs one parcel of land scituate in Washington Parish in County of Westmorland containing by estimation Two hundred acres be the same mor or less being part of a Patent for Four hundred acres of Land granted to WILLIAM WEBB which JOHN SHOTWELL bought of WILLIAM WHITEING and being the remainder of said Pattent after Two hundred acres which was sold out of the Pattent to PETER SKINNER late of said Parish and County was laid out to him, bounded;

Begining the bounds of the land repeated as in the Lease); To have and to hold the premises with all houses gardens with all profits and commodities to the same belonging unto WILLIAM BERRYMAN his heirs; And JOHN SHOTWELL will warrant and defend the premises sold unto WILLIAM BERRYMAN his heirs from all persons; In Witness whereof JOHN SHOTWELL have hereunto set his hand and seal the day and year first above mentioned

Signed Sealed and delivered in the presence of

WILLIAM HARRISON,	JOHN SHOTWELL
PETER BAILLEUL, JOHN WELCH	
SAMUEL WHEELER; SAMUEL his mark _S_ SIMS	

Reced. of WILLIAM BERRYMAN the day of the date within mentioned Nine thousand pounds of tobacco being the consideration within mentioned, I say rec'd;

Test WILLIAM HARRISON,	JOHN SHORTWELL
PETER BAILLEUL. JOHN WELCH,	
SAMUEL WHEELER, SAMUEL his mark _S_ SIMS	

Westmorland Sct. At a Court held for the said County the 28th day of February 1743 JOHN SHOTWELL personally acknowledged this Deed of Release for Land by him passed to WILLIAM BERRY, Gentleman, together with Receipt for consideration endorsed, to be his proper act and deed, which on motion of said BERRYMAN are admitted to Record

Recorded the Sixth day of March 1743, pr. G. L., C. C. W.

Test   GEORGE LEE, C. C. W.

p.   (On margin: THOMAS's Bond to THOMAS)
335   KNOW ALL MEN by these presents that I JAMES THOMAS the Elder of Westmorland County, Gentleman, am held and firmly bound unto GEORGE THOMAS (my third Son) of said County in the full and just sum of One hundred pounds Sterling, to the which payment well and truly to be made I bind myself my heirs firmly by these presents; Sealed with my Seal and dated this Twenty second day of February Anno Domini 1741/2

THE CONDITION of the above obligation is such that if the above bound JAMES THOMAS his heirs &c. shall make over and confirm by good and sufficient Deeds unto GEORGE THOMAS and to his heirs at any time within two years from the date hereof a parcel of land in the County of PRINCE WILLIAM of the full value of Fifty pounds Sterling at this time, Then the above obligation to be void otherwise to remain effectual in the Law

Signed Sealed and delivered in the presence of

JOSEPH McADAM, ALEXR. WHITE,	JAMES THOMAS
DAVID DOAK, WILLIAM BLACK	

Westmorland Sct. At a Court held for the said County the 28th day of February 1743 This Bond from JAMES THOMAS, deceased, to his Son, GEORGE THOMAS, for and concerning making over and confirming unto the said GEORGE THOMAS by good and sufficient Deeds, a tract or parcel of land in the County of PRINCE WILLIAM, was proved by the Oath of WILLIAM BLACK, one of the witnesses thereto, which is ordered to be recorded

Recorded the Sixth day of March 1743, pr. G. L., C. C. W.

Test   GEORGE LEE, C. C. W.

pp.   (On margin: MINOR's Lease of Lives to RICE
335-   THIS INDENTURE made this 27th day of July in the year of our Lord one thou-
337   sand seven hundred and forty three; Between NICHOLAS MINOR, JUNIOR of the County of Westmorland, Gent., of one part and ZOROBABLE RICE of said County, Planter, of other part; Witnesseth that NICHOLAS MINOR, JUNIOR in consideration of

the Rents and Covenants hereafter reserved on part of ZOROBABLE RICE to be paid and performed hath and by these presents doth demise and to farm lett one parcel of land containing One hundred and forty nine acres scituate in County of Westmorland and bounded; Begining at a red Oak on the head of a Branch, thence North 17d. East 52 pole to a Hiccory and Chesnutt, thence down a Branch reduced to a right line East 98 pole to a small red Oak, thence along a line of marked trees South 10d. West 184 pole to a large Chesnutt, thence North West 47 pole to a small red Oak, thence 59d. West 35 pole to a small red Oak, thence North 40d. West 174 poles, thence North 28d. East 53 pole to the MATTOX ROAD, thence South 52d. East 92 pole to the begining; with all houses orchards profits and appurtenances to the same belonging; To have and to hold the parcel of land and premises with all appurtenances unto ZOROBABLE RICE his heirs during the term of the natural lives of said ZOROBABLE RICE and SARAH his Wife and THOMAS RICE, Son of said ZOROBABLE RICE, paying unto NICHOLAS MINOR, JUNIOR his heirs every year on the Feast of St. Luke being the Eighteenth of October the neat sum and quantity of Five hundred pounds of tobacco and cask, the tobacco to be made upon the said land, thence rolled to such convenient Rolling Houses or Warehouses on the Water as the Law from time to time shall appoint; as also at the time four hens, capons or pulletts, And ZOROBABLE RICE his heirs shall within three years from the date hereof plant upon the premises fifty Apple trees and take care of secure and improve and sufficient-ly repair and keep all houses upon the premises repaired; and during the term of the Lease pay the Quit Rents of the land held thereby to the Chief Lord of the Fee and save NICHOLAS MINOR, JUNIOR his heirs harmless and indemnified from the same; And if ZOROBABLE RICE his heirs shall make over his Lease to any person he or they will pay to NICHOLAS MINOR, JUNIOR his heirs one whole years Rent over and above what he was before obliged to pay; In Witness whereof the parties above named have hereunto interchangeably set their hands and seals the day and year first above written
Sealed and Delivered in presence of us

    THOS: SORRELL,   WILLIAM RICE   NICHOLAS MINOR, JR.
    JOHN SPENCE

Westmorland Sct. At a Court held for the said County the 28th day of February 1743 NICHOLAS MINOR, JUNIOR personally acknowledged this Deed of Lease for Land for life by him passed to ZOROBABLE RICE to be his proper act and deed, which is ordered to be recorded   Recorded the Seventh day of March 1743, G. L., C. C. W.
          Test   GEORGE LEE, C. C. W.

pp.   (On margin: THOMAS's Lease to TEBBS)
337-   THIS INDENTURE made the Twenty sixth day of February in the Seventeenth
341   year of the Reign of our Sovereign Lord George the Second by the grace of God
       of Great Brittain France and Ireland, King, Defender of the faith &c., And in the year of our Lord 1743; Between JOHN THOMAS of County of Westmorland, Planter, and DANIEL TEBBS of said County; Witnesseth that JOHN THOMAS in consideration of the sum of Five shillings current money of Virginia to JOHN THOMAS in hand paid, the receipt whereof is hereby acknowledged, hath and by these presents doth bargain and sell unto DANIEL TEBBS all that parcel of land containing Two hundred and eighty acres or thereabouts scituate in Parish and County aforesaid, near unto YEOCOMOCO CHURCH, being all the Land adjacent to the Plantations whereon JAMES THOMAS the Elder, lately lived in right of his Wife, whether the same was bought by said JAMES of JOSEPH CARR deceased or any other person; And also all the Land whereon JAMES THOMAS the Younger, also deceased, lived, together with all Land adjacent thereunto or in way be-longing unto the last mentioned JAMES whether the same was given unto said JAMES by

his Father by Will, Deed of Gift, taken up by said JAMES or otherwise; to both whom the said JOHN is now heir at Law; And all right title claim and demand of JOHN THOMAS in any Lands thereunto adjacent; And all houses orchards profits and appurtenances to the same belonging; To have and to hold the land and premises unto DANIEL TEBBS and assigns during the term of one whole year paying therefore the Rent of Ear of Indian Corn upon the last day of the term (if the same shall be demanded) to intent that by virtue of these presents and of the Statute for transferring uses into possession DANIEL TEBBS may be in the actual possession of the premises and thereby be enabled to take a release of the inheritance thereof to him and his heirs; In Witness the parties to these presents have interchangeably set their hands and seals the day and year first above written
Sealed and delivered in presence of
    JOHN BUSHROD, WILLOUGHBY NEWTON   JOHN THOMAS
    WILLIAM CAMPBELL
    Westmorland Sct. At a Court held for the said County the 28th day of February 1743 JOHN THOMAS personally acknowledged this Deed of Lease for Land by him passed to DANIEL TEBBS to be his proper act and deed, which on the motion of the said TEBBS is admitted to Record
        Recorded the Eighth day of March 1743, pr. G. L., C. C. W.
          Test GEORGE LEE, C. C. W.

    (On margin: THOMAS's Release to TEBBS)
    THIS INDENTURE made the Twenty eighth day of February in the Seventeenth year of the Reign of our Sovereign Lord George the Second by the grace of God of Great Brittain France and Ireland, King, Defender of the faith &c., And in the year of our Lord 1743; Between JOHN THOMAS of the Parish of Cople in County of Westmorland, Planter, of one part and DANIEL TEBBS of said Parish and County of other part; Witnesseth that JOHN THOMAS in considertion of the sum of One hundred and fifty pounds to JOHN THOMAS in hand paid, the receipt whereof JOHN THOMAS doth hereby acknowledge, hath and by these presents doth bargain sell and release unto DANIEL TEBBS (in his actual possession now being by virtue of a Bargain and Sale to him thereof made for one whole year and by force of the Statute for transferring uses into possession) and to his heirs all those parcels of land containing Two hundred and eighty acres or thereabouts lying in Parish and County aforesaid near unto YEOCOMOCO CHURCH, being (this release repeats the lands of JAMES THOMAS the Elder and JAMES THOMAS the Younger) To have and to hold the land and premises unto DANIEL TEBBS his heirs; And JOHN THOMAS and his heirs the parcels of land released unto DANIEL TEBBS his heirs against all persons shall warrant and forever defend by these presents; In Witness whereof the parties to these presents have interchangeably set their hands and seals the day and year first above written
Sealed and delivered in the presence of
    JNO: BUSHROD, WILLOUGHBY NEWTON,   JOHN THOMAS
    WILLIAM CAMPBELL
    February 28th day 1743. Then recd. of DANIEL TEBBS the sum of One hundred and fifty pounds current money of Virginia being the consideration money within mentioned, reced. by
    JNO: BUSHROD, WILLOUGHBY NEWTON,   JOHN THOMAS
    WILLIAM CAMPBELL
    Westmorland Sct. At a Court held for the said County the 28th day of February 1743 JOHN THOMAS personally acknowledged this Deed of Release for Lands by him passed to

DANIEL TEBBS together with Receipt for the consideration endorsed to be his proper act and deed, which on motion of the said TEBBS are admitted to Record
Recorded the Eighth day of March 1743, pr. G. L., C. C. W.
Test   GEORGE LEE, C. C. W.

(On margin: THOMAS's Bond to TEBBS)
KNOW ALL MEN by these presents that I JOHN THOMAS of Parish of Cople in County of Westmorland am held and firmly bound unto DANIEL TEBBS of the Parish and County aforesaid in the full and just sum of Four hundred pounds current money of Virginia, to the which payment well and truly to be made I bind myself my heirs firmly by these presents; Sealed with my Seal dated this Twenty eighth day of February Anno Domini 1743   THE CONDITION of the above obligation is such that if the above said JOHN THOMAS his heirs shall well and truly perform and keep all the Covenants which on his or their part ought to be performed and kept mentioned in certain Indentures of Lease and Release made between JOHN THOMAS and DANIEL TEBBS according to the true intent thereof, then the above obligation to be void else to be and remain in full force power and virtue
JNO: BUSHROD, WILLOUGHBY NEWTON,   JOHN THOMAS
WILLIAM CAMPBELL
Westmorland Sct. At a Court held for the said County teh 28th day of February 1743 JOHN THOMAS personally acknowledged this Bond for performance of Covenants by him passed to DANIEL TEBBS to be his proper act and deed, at whose motion the same is admitted to Record
Recorded the Eighth day of March 1743, pr. G. L., C. C. W.
Test   GEORGE LEE, C. C. W.

pp.   (On margin: CARR's Deed of Feofment to TEBBS)
341-   THIS INDENTURE made the 24th day of February in the Seventeenth year of the
344   Reign of our Sovereign Lord George the Second by the grace of God of Great
         Brittain France and Ireland, King, Defender of the faith &c., And in the year of
our Lord God one thousand seven hundred and forty three; Between JOSEPH CARR of Cople Parish and Westmorland County of one part and DANIEL TEBBS of same Parish and County of other part; Witnesseth that JOSEPH CARR in consideration of the sum of Four thousand punds of lawfull crop tobacco and Twenty four pounds current money to him in hand paid by DANIEL TEBBS, the receipt whereof JOSEPH CARR doth hereby acknowledge, hath and by these presents doth bargain and sell unto DANIEL TEBBS his heirs all that tract of land containing One hundred and twenty acres which was given to me the said JOSEPH CARR by the Last Will and Testament of my Father, JOSEPH CARR, deced., scituate in Parish and County aforesaid and is bounded; Joining upon the land of Captain DANIEL McCARTY and JAMES THOMAS and bounden on TUCKERS RUN with all its rights members and appurtenances together with all houses orchards profits and appurtenances to the same belonging; To have and to hold the One hundred and twenty acres of Land unto DANIEL TEBBS his heirs and JOSEPH CARR his heirs and all other persons lawfully claiming under him shall warrant and forever defend by these presents; In Witness whereof the parties to these presents have interchangeably set their hands and seals the day and year first above written
Signed Sealed and delivered in presence of
CHARNOCK COX, JUNR.,   JOSEPH CARR
ARCHABLE his mark X GARNER
JOHNSON his mark (X JONES

Memorandum; That on the 24th day of February in the year of our Lord one thousand seven hundred forty and three JOSEPH CARR made livery and seizen of the lands and appurtenances within mentioned by delivery of Turff and Twigg and the Ring of the Door of the Chief Mansion House on the lands unto DANIEL TEBBS in the name of the whole lands and appurtenances within sold according to the tenor and effect of the Deed; And also HUGH THOMAS, Tenant thereon, did attorn and became Tenant to DANIEL TEBBS in presence of us

CHARNOCK COX, JUNR. ARCHABLE his mark X GARNER
JOHNSTON his mark / JONES

Received of DANIEL TEBBS the sum of Four thousand pounds of lawfull crop tobacco and twenty four pounds current money in full payment for the consideration within mentioned; Witness my hand this Twenty fourth day of February Annoq: Domini 1743
Testes CHARNOCK COX, JUNR.   JOSEPH CARR
ARCHABLE his mark X GARNER
JOHNSON his mark / JONES

Westmorland Sct. At a Court held for the said County the 28th day of February 1743 JOSEPH CARR personally acknowledged this Deed of Feofment for Lands by him passed to DANIEL TEBBS together with Livery of Seizen and Receipt for the consideration thereon endorsed to be his proper act and deed, all which on motion of the said TEBBS is admitted to Record

Recorded the Ninth day of March 1743, pr. G. L., C. C. W.
Test   GEORGE LEE, C. C. W.

(On margin: CARR'S Bond to TEBBS)

KNOW ALL MEN by these presents that I JOSEPH CARR of Cople Parish in County of Westmorland do owe and justly stand indebted and am by these presents firmly bounden and obliged unto DANIEL TEBBS of the same Parish and County in the penal sum of Eight thousand pounds of good lawfull tobacco and Forty eight pounds current money to the which payment well and truly to be made I bind myself my heirs firmly by these presents; Sealed with my Seal and dated this Twenty fourth day of February in the Seventeenth year of the Reign of our Sovereign Lord George the Second by God's grace of Great Brittain France and Ireland, King, Defender of the faith &c., Annoq: Domini 1743

THE CONDITION of the above obligation is such that if the above bounden JOSEPH CARR his heirs shall perform and keep all the Covenants which on his or their part ought to be performed and kept mentioned in one Indenture of Bargain and Sale made between JOSEPH CARR and DANIEL TEBBS according to the true meaning of the Indenture, That then the above obligation to be void and of none effect, othewise to stand remain and be in full force power strength and virtue
Signed Sealed and delivered in presence of

CHARNOCK COX, JUNR.   JOSEPH CARR
ARCHABLE his mark X GARNER
JOHNSON his mark (JONES

Westmorland Sct. At a Court held for the said County the 28th day of February 1743 JOSEPH CARR personally acknowledged this Bond for performance of Covenants by him passed to DANIEL TEBBS to be his proper act and deed which on motion of the said TEBBS is admitted to Record

Recorded the Ninth day of March 1743; pr. G. L., C. C. W.
Test   GEORGE LEE, C. C. W.

pp.   (On margin: LEE & Others about a Banquetting House &c.)
344-   WHEREAS there is a mutual Agreement signed sealed and delivered by and
345   between the parties whose names are hereunder written, the which Writing
          bears date with these presents for the marking of each persons bounds; NOW
KNOW YEE that the said parties do agree that there be a House erected where Mr. ALLER-
TON and Mr. GERRARD shall think fit for the continuance of good Neighbourhood, and
to be built by the direction of said Mr. ALLERTON and Mr. GERRARD and every person to
bear an equal charge to the building thereof; and Ten pounds Sterling to be allowed Mr.
LEE for the building of said House, said Mr. LEE bearing his proportion of the charge
and each man or his heirs yearly according to his due course to make and honourable
treatment fit to entertain the undertakers thereof, their Wives, Misters and Friends
yearly and every year and to begin upon the 29th day of May which will be in the year
one thousand Six hundred seventy and one. Mr. CORBIN to make the first treatment,
Mr. LEE the next, Mr. GERRARD the next and Mr. ALLERTON the next after that and so
round. Witness our hands this 30th day of March 1670.

                        HENRY CORBIN.   J. LEE,
                        THOS: GERRARD   ISAAC ALLERTON
    Westmorland Sct. At a Court held for the said County the 27th day of March 1744
GEORGE LEE, Gent., Son and heir of RICHARD LEE, Gent., deceased, who was Son of
RICHARD LEE, also Gent., deced., and Brother of JOHN LEE, likewise Gent., deced., pre-
sented into Court this Ancient Instrument of Writing concerning a Banquetting House
formerly erected by the said JOHN LEE and others on the Land now belonging to the said
GEORGE LEE, whoch on motion of the said GEORGE LEE is admitted to Record
          Recorded the Fifth day of April 1744, pr. G. L., C. C. W.
          Test   GEORGE LEE, C. C. W.

    (On margin: LEE and Others about Land Bounds &c.)
    WHEREAS it is Enacted that once every four years there shall be a procession of the
Neighbourhood to every mans land for the plain marking and bounding out by line
trees or other convenient boundaries to every particular persons divident or seat in
which no course hath ever been taken by the County Court of Westmorland. It is
therefore mutually consented to and agreed upon by and between all and every one of
us and for the better preservation of that Friendness which ought to be between
Neighbours that each man's line whereon any one of us is bounded one upon the other
be remarked and plainly set forth by sufficient bound trees and that in presence of
each of us four or our Substitutes between this present day and the last of September
next ensuing; Witness our hands and seals this 30th of March 1670
                        THOS: GERARD Seal HENRY CORBYN Seal
                        ISAAC ALLERTON, Seal   J. LEE, Seal
    Westmorland Sct. At a Court held for the said County the 27th day of March 1744
GEORGE LEE, Gent., Son and heir of RICHARD LEE, Gent., deced., who was Son of RICHARD
LEE also Gent., deced., and Brother of JOHN LEE, likewise Gent, deceased, presented into
Court this Ancient Instrument of Writing concerning the bounds and lines of the land
of the said JOHN LEE and others, which on motion of the said GEORGE LEE is admitted to
Record   Recorded the 5th day of April 1744, pr. G. L., C. C. W.
              Test   GEORGE LEE, C. C. W.

    (On margin: LEE's Deposition about LEE's Land &c.)
    The Deposition of THOMAS LEE, Esqr. above 50 years of age and sworn sayeth that he
has been informed by persons of Credit that lived before the year 1670, that there was a

Banquetting House erected in PECKATOWNS FIELD by HENRY CORBYN Esqr., Capt. JOHN LEE, THOMAS GERRARD Esqr. and Mr. (afterwards Coll:) ISAAC ALLERTON, in order to perpetuate the bounds of their lands and this Deponent has been told by his Father, (who was Brother to the said Capt. JOHN LEE, and marryed the Eldest Daughter of HENRY CORBYN Esqr.) that he had been at an Entertainment in the said Banquetting House and this Deponent's Father has mentioned to this Deponent some particulars that are in an ancient paper now produced in Court which ancient paper this Deponent believes to be the Original Agreement for building the said Banquetting House, for he has been shewn the hands of CORBYN, LEE and ALLERTON, and does believe the names subscribed to the said ancient paper is their hand writing. This Deponent was told by the late Colo: GEORGE ESKRIDGE that he had the Agreement about the Banquetting House in his possession, he was then Attorney to JOHN GERRARD, who as this Deponent has heard and believes was the Grandson and heir of THOMAS GERRARD, Esqr. and further this Deponent sayeth not

THOMAS LEE

Westmorland Sct. At a Court held for the said County the 27th day of March 1744 This Deposition of the Honourable THOMAS LEE, Esquire, being by the said LEE sworn to in open Court concerning the validity of the two preceding Instruments of Writing, is on motion of GEORGE LEE, Gent., admitted to Record

Recorded the Fifth day of April 1744, pr. G. L., C. C. W.
Test   GEORGE LEE, C. C. W.

pp.   (On margin: HARRIS's Feofment to HEABURN)
345-   THIS INDENTURE made the Twenty sixth day of March in the Seventeenth year
348   of the Reign of our Sovereign Lord George the Second by the grace of God of
        Great Brittain France and Ireland, King, Defender of the faith &c., And in the
year of our Lord God one thousand seven hundred forty and four; Between ARTHUR HARRIS of Parish of Cople and County of Westmorland of one part and JAMES HEABURN of the same Parish and County of other part; Witnesseth that ARTHUR HARRIS in consideration of the sum of One thousand pounds of tobacco to him in hand paid by JAMES HEABURN, the receipt whereof ARTHUR HARRIS doth hereby acknowledge, hath and by these presents doth bargain and sell unto JAMES HEABURN his heirs all that parcel of land containing One hundred acres be the same more or less scituate in the Parish and County aforesaid and was formerly a purchase made by ARTHUR HARRIS, Grand Father to said ARTHUR HARRIS, of ROBERT SMITH may more fully appear, it fell by heirship to ARTHUR HARRIS by the death of his Father, WILLIAM HARRIS, and is bounded, Begining at a marked red Oak standing by or upon the Road leading from the Plantation of GEORGE LAMKIN, deced., to the Plantation of ROBERT SMITH, runing up a line of marked trees dividing the land of ROBERT SMITH and RICHARD DUNAHAW, deced., North East to a marked red Oak standing by a Branch, thence runing down the Branch North West to a marked black Gum standing in the mouth of a small Branch by another line of marked trees to a marked red Oak standing by the dividing paths that lead to the Plantations of ROBERT SMITH and JOHN BAILEY, deced., in the Road above mentioned, and so runing down the same Road to the place where it first began containing by estimation One hundred acres more or less with all its rights members and appurtenances and all houses orchards and profits to the same belonging; To have and to hold the One hundred acres of land and other the premises with appurtenances unto JAMES HEABURN his heirs; And ARTHUR HARRIS for himself his heirs &c. the premises with appurtenances unto JAMES HEABURN and his heirs against every person lawfully claiming under him and against the claim of any other person shall warrant and forever defend by these presents; In Witness whereof the parties to these presents have interchange-

by these presents; In Witness whereof the parties to these presents have interchangeably set their hands and seals the day and year first above written
Signed Sealed and delivered in presence of
     DANL: TEBBS, JOHN COOMBS   ARTHUR HARRIS
   Memorandum; That on the Twenty sixth day of March in the year of our Lord God one
thousand seven hundred and forty four ARTHUR HARRIS made livery and seizen of the
lands and appurtenances within mentioned by delivering Turff and Twigg and the
Ring of the Chief Mansion House on the lands unto JAMES HEABURN in the name of the
whole lands and appurtenances within sold according to the tenor form and effect of
the Deed; In presence of us
        (no witnesses recorded)
   Received of JAMES HEABURN the sum of One thousand pounds of lawfull tobacco in
full payment for the consideration within mentioned; Witness my hand this twenty
sixth day of March Annoq: Domini 1744
Test   DANL: TEBBS, JOHN COOMBS   ARTHUR HARRIS
   Westmorland Sct. At a Court held for the said County the 27th day of March 1744
ARTHUR HARRIS personally acknowledged this Deed of Feoment for Land by him passed
to JAMES HEABURN together with Livery of Seizin and Receipt for consideration endorsed to be his proper act and deed, which on motion of the said HEABURN are admitted
to Record   Recorded the 5th day of April 1744, pr. G. L., C. C. W.
        Test   GEORGE LEE, C. C. W.

  Truly Transcribed (from page 242 to 348 by W: BUTLER for
                JOHN W. R. WATTS

Westmoreland County Deeds & Wills, No. 8 1738-1744.   End.

WESTMORELAND COUNTY, VIRGINIA
DEEDS & WILLS No. 10
1744-1748·

p. (At the top of page 1 of this book, is a sketch for land with an explanation on the left
1 hand side as follows: A. is the beginning division line between this Land and the
Land of JAMES WHITE; B., is a red Oak corner tree; C., is a Spanish Oak corner
tree; D., is a corner to this Land and in the land of WILLIAM EDWARDS; E., is a corner to
the said EDWARDS; F. is the end of twenty poles. (No landmarks shown in the sketch except
the BRYERY BRANCH which divides one part for 140 acres; the other part for 135 acres, no indica-
tion which part belongs to whom)

October 17th 1743. Then surveyed a certain parcel of land lying in Washington
Parish in County of Westmoreland containing Two hundred and seventy five acres the
courses & distances as appear by the above plat for and in behalf of Mr. LAWRENCE
BUTLER and JAMES WHITFIELD, and by a mutual agreement between themselves have
divided it into two parts which division is by a Branch called the BRYERY BRANCH, and
that within the aforesaid Branch and dotted lines is and allotted Mr. LAWRENCE BUTLERs
part and that within the aforesaid Branch and black lines is and allotted the aforesaid
JAMES WHITFIELDs part; surveyed the day and year abovesaid
p me JAMES HORE

Westmd. Sct. At a Court held for the said County the 27th day of March 1744
This Platt, survey and division of land between LAWRENCE BUTLER and JAMES WHIT-
FIELD was presented into Court by the said parties, which on motion of the said WHIT-
FIELD, is admitted to Record
Test GEORGE LEE, C. C. W.

pp. (On margin: SHOTWELL's Relinquishment of Dower to BERRYMAN)
1- Westmd. Sct. George the Second by the grace of God of Great Brittain France
2 and Ireland, King, Defender of the faith &c., to WILLIAM TYLER, JOHN WATTS
and JOHN MARTIN of County aforesaid, Gentlemen, Greeting; We do authorise
and impower you or any two of you at such time and place as you shall appoint (some
time before the next Court to be held for the County aforesaid) to take the privy examination of ANNE SHOTWELL, Wife of JOHN SHOTWELL apart from her Husband touching
her willingness and unconstrained consent and assent to the passing of a certain Deed
of Lease and Release for conveying her right of Dower to a certain parcel of land lying
in the Parish of Washington in County of Westmorland containing by estimation Two
hundred acres unto WILLIAM BERRYMAN of the County aforesaid, Gent., (the Commission
for the privy examination of ANNE, the Wife of JOHN SHOTWELL); herein you are not to fail;
Witness GEORGE LEE, Clerk of the said County Court the 31st day of March and in the 17th
year of our Reign
GEORGE LEE, C. W. C.

By virtue of the within Commission to us directed, we have privately examined ANNE
SHOTWELL, Wife of JOHN SHOTWELL (the return of the execution of the privy examination of
ANNE SHOTWELL); Certified this 31st day of March 1744
WILLIAM TYLER
JNO: WATTS

Westmd. Sct. At a Court held for the said County the 24th day of April 1744
This Commission for the privy examination of ANNE, the Wife of JOHN SHOTTWELL, concerning the said ANNE's right of Dower of in and two Two hundred acres of Land by the
said JOHN SHOTWELL sold and conveyed to WILLIAM BERRYMAN, being returned duly
executed as appears by a Certificate under the hands of WILLIAM TYLER and JOHN

WATTS, two of the Gent: in the said Commission named, all which are admitted to Record
Test   GEORGE LEE, C.W.C.

pp.   (On margin: COLEMAN to TEBBS)
2-   THIS INDENTURE made this 14th day of May in the Seventeenth year of the
7   Reign of our Sovereign Lord George the Second by the grace of God of Great
         Brittain France and Ireland, King, Defender of the faith &., And in the year of
our Lord God 1744; Between RICHARD COLEMAN of Truro Parish and FAIRFAX County of
one part and DANIEL TEBBS of Cople Parish and County of Westmoreland of other part;
Witnesseth that RICHARD COLEMAN in consideration of the sum of Twenty pounds current money of Virginia to him in hand paid by DANIEL TEBBS, the receipt whereof
RICHARD COLEMAN doth hereby acknowledge, hath and by these presents doth bargain
and sell unto DANIEL TEBBS his heirs all that parcel of land containing Fifty four acres
be the same more or less situate in Parish of Cople in County of Westmoreland being
bounded on the Land of JAMES THOMAS, deceased, and on the land of JOSEPH CARR deceased, and JOHN GARNER may more fully appear; and by JOSEPH CARR, deceased, conveyed unto RICHARD COLEMAN; with all its rights members and appurtenances, together with all houses orchards profits and hereditaments to the same belonging; To
have and to hold the Fifty four acres of land unto DANIEL TEBBS his heirs without any
lawfull interruption of RICHARD COLEMAN his heirs and freely and clearly acquitted of
all incumbrances; In Witness whereof the parties to these presents have interchangeably set their hands and seals the day and year first above written
Sealed and delivered in the presence of
         JOHN COLVILL, JNO: PAGAN,   RICHARD COLEMAN
         JOHN MINOR
    Memo, That on the 14th day of May in the year of our Lord 1744, RICHARD COLEMAN
made Livery and Seizen of the lands and appurtenances within mentioned by delivering Turff and Twigg and the Ring of the Door of the Chief Mansion House on the
lans unto DANIEL TEBBS in the name of the whole lands and appurtenances sold according to the tenor form and effect of the within Deed; And also HUGH DUNAHAW, Tenant
thereon, did attorn and became tenant to DANIEL TEBBS in presence of us
         (no witnesses recorded)
    Received of DANIEL TEBBS the sum of Twenty pounds current money of Virginia in
full payment for the consideration within mentioned; Witness my hand the 14th day of
May Anno Domini 1744
Teste   JOHN PAGAN, JNO: COLVILL,   RICHARD COLEMAN
        JNO: MINOR
    Westmd. Sct. At a Court held for the said County the 29th day of May 1744
RICHARD COLEMAN personally acknowledged this Deed of Feofment for Lands by him
passed to DANIEL TEBBS, together with Livery & Seizen and Receipt for the consideration endorsed to be his proper act and deed, and ELEANOR, Wife of the said RICHARD, by
virtue of a Commission relinquished her right of Dower of in and to the lands by the
said Deed conveyed, all which on motion of the said DANIEL TEBBS are admitted to
Record   Test GEORGE LEE, C.C.W.

    (On margin: COLEMAN's Bond to TEBBS)
    KNOW ALL MEN by these presents that I RICHARD COLEMAN of (blank) Parish in Coun-
ty of FAIRFAX doe owe and justly stand indebted and am by these presents firmly bound
and obliged unto DANIEL TEBBS of Parish of Cople in County of Westmorland in the
penal sum of Forty pounds current money of Virginia to the which payment well and

truly to be made I bind myself my heirs firmly by these presents; Sealed with my Seal
and dated this 14th day of May in the Seventeenth year of the Reign of our Sovereign
Lord George the Second by God's grace of Great Britain France and Ireland, King, Defender of the faith &c.

THE CONDITION of the above obligation is such that if the above bounded RICHARD
COLEMAN his heirs shall perform and keep all the Covenants which on his or their part
ought to be performed and kept mentioned in one Indenture of bargain and sale made
between RICHARD COLEMAN and DANIEL TEBBS according to the true meaning of the
said Indenture, That then the above obligation to be void and of none effect, otherwise
to stand remain and be in full force power strength and virtue
Signed Sealed and delivered in the presence of

    PETER RUST, HUGH THOMAS   RICHARD COLEMAN

Westmd. County Sct. George the 2nd by the Grace of God of Great Brittain France and
Ireland, King, Defender of the faith &c., to JOHN COLVILL, JOHN MINOR, DANIEL
FRENCH and RICHARD OSBORNE of FAIRFAX County Gent., Greeting; We do hereby
authorise and impower you or any two of you at such time and place as you shall appoint (some time before the next Court to be held for the County of Westmoreland in
May next) to take the privy Examination of ELLINNOR the Wife of RICHARD COLEMAN, of
the aforesaid County of FAIRFAX apart from her Husband (the Commission for the privy
examination of ELLINNOR, Wife of RICHARD COLEMAN); herein you are not to fail; Witness
GEORGE LEE, Clk, of the said County Court of Westmoreland and the 3rd day of April in
the 17th year of our Reign   GEORGE LEE, C. W. C.

FAIRFAX May 24th 1744. Pursuant to the above, we have privately examined ELINOR
COLEMAN, Wife of RICHARD COLEMAN (the return of the execution of the privy examination of
ELINOR COLEMAN); and which we accordingly certify under our hands
                    JOHN COLVILL
                    JOHN MINOR

Westmd. Sct. At a Court held for the said County the 29th day of May 1744
The aforegoing Deed of Bargain and Sale from COLEMAN & Wife to TEBBS, together with
a Commission for the examination of ELINOR COLEMAN returned duly executed, also a
Bond for the performance of Covenants returned acknowledged, and ordered to be
recorded   Teste   GEORGE LEE, C. W. C.

pp.   (On margin: TURNER to GARNER)
7-   THIS INDENTURE made the 26th day of May in the year of our Lord 1744 And in
8   the 17th year of the Reign of our Sovereign Lord George the Second by the
    grace of God of Great Brittain France and Ireland, King, Defender of the faith
&c., Between WILLIAM TURNER of Parish of Cople in County of Westmoreland, Planter,
of one part and HENRY GARNER, JUNR. of the same Parish and County, Planter, of other
part; Witnesseth that WILLIAM TURNER in consideration of the sum of Eleven pounds,
Five shillings current money of Virginia to him in hand paid by said HENRY GARNER,
hath and by these presents doth bargain and sell unto HENRY GARNER his heirs (there
appears to be line missing) being all the parcel of land situate in Parish and County aforesaid containing fifteen acres of land more or less being part of the land now in the
possession of and belonging to WILLIAM TURNER bounded at or upon the North side of a
Branch between said HENRY GARNER and the land of Captain GEORGE LEE, And all
houses orchards and advantages to the parcel of land belonging; To have and to hold
the parcel of land and premises with appurtenances unto said HENRY GARNER his heirs
And WILLIAM TURNER and his heirs against all persons shall warrant and forever defend by these presents; In Witness whereof the parties above named have hereunto
interchangeably set and put their hands and seals

Signed Sealed and deld. in the presence of
      THOS: GARNER, CLEMENT ARLADGE,   WM. TURNER
      VINCENT Q. GARNER

    Memo; That on the 26th day of May Anno 1744; WILLIAM TURNER gave and delivered unto HENRY GARNER peacible and quiet possession and seizen of the land and premises by the delivery of Turff and Twigg unto HENRY GARNER on the said land, To have and to hold the same unto HENRY GARNER his heirs according to the form & effect of the within written Deed in presence of
      THOS: GARNER, CLEMENT ARLADGE,   WM: TURNER
      VINCENT Q. GARNER

    1744. the 26th day of May. Then received of HENRY GARNER the sum of Eleven pounds Five shillings current money being the full consideration within mentioned to be paid to me
Witnesses THOS: GARNER,   WM. TURNER
      CLEMENT ARLADGE, VINCT. Q. GARNER

    Westmd. Sct. At a Court held for the said County the 29th day of May 1744 WILLIAM TURNER personally acknowledged this Deed of Feofment for Lands by him passed to HENRY GARNER, JUNR., together with Livery of Seizen and Receipt for the consideration endorsed to be his proper act and deed, all which on motion of the said GARNER is admitted to Record
          Teste GEORGE LEE, C. W. C.

pp.   (On margin: THOMAS's to TEBBS)
8-   THIS INDENTURE made the 28th day of May in the 17th year of the Reign of our
$/Z   Sovereign Lord George the Second by the grace of God of Gret Brittain France and Ireland, King, Defender of the faith &c., And in the year of our Lord God 1744, Between HUGH THOMAS and MARY his Wife of Cople Parish and Westmoreland County of one part and DANIEL TEBBS of same Parish and County of other part; Witnesseth that HUGH THOMAS and MARY his Wife in consideration of the sum of Nine thousand pounds of lawfull tobacco and Eight pounds current money of Virginia to them in hand paid by DANIEL TEBBS, the receipt whereof HUGH THOMAS and MARY his Wife doth hereby acknowledge, hath and by these presents doth bargain and sell unto DANIEL TEBBS his heirs all that parcel of land containing One hundred acres siituate in Parish and County aforesaid given to us by a Deed of Gift from JOSEPH CARR may it more fully appear; fell by discent to JOSEPH CARR by the death of his Brother, JAMES CARR, deceased, to whom it was given by JOSEPH CARR, deceased, Last Will and Testament and surveyed and laid off by Mr. WILLO: NEWTON and bounded according to his survey with all rights members and appurtenances, Together with all houses orchards profits and hereditaments belonging; To have and to hold the One hundred acres of land and all other the premises unto DANIEL TEBBS his heirs; And HUGH THOMAS and MARY his Wife their heirs against the claim of any person shall warrant and forever defend by these presents; In Witness whereof the parties to these presents have interchangeably set their hands and seals the day and year first above written
Signed Sealed and delivered in the presence of
      RICHARD COLEMAN,   HUGH THOMAS
      PETER RUST   MARY THOMAS

    Memo: That on the 28th day of May in the year of our Lord 1744; HUGH THOMAS and MARY his Wife made livery and seizen of the lands and appurtenances within mentioned by delivering Turff and Twigg on the land unto DANIEL TEBBS in the name of the whole lands and appurtenances sold according to the form and effect of the Deed

In presence of us   RICHARD COLEMAN
                    PETER RUST
    Received of DANIEL TEBBS the sum of Nine thousand pounds of lawfull tobacco and
Eight pounds current money of Virginia in full payment for the consideration within
mentioned; Witness our hands this (blank) day of (blank) Anno Domini 1744
Teste   RICHARD COLEMAN,   HUGH THOMAS
        PETER RUST

        (On margin: THOMAS's to TEBBS)
    KNOW ALL MEN by these presents that we HUGH THOMAS and MARY THOMAS of
County of Westmoreland and Parish of Cople our heirs &c. do owe & justly stand indebted and am by these presents firmly bound and obliged unto DANIEL TEBBS of the
same place his heirs &c. in the penal sum of Eighteen thousand pounds of lawfull crop
tobacco and Sixteen pounds current money of Virginia to which payment well and
truly to be made we bind ourselves our heirs firmly by these presents; Sealed with our
Seals and dated this 28th day of May in the Seventeenth year of the Reign of our
Sovereign Lord George the Second by God's grace of Great Brittain France and Ireland,
King, Defender of the faith &c. Anno Dom: 1744
    THE CONDITION of the above obligation is such that if the above bounded HUGH THO-
MAS and MARY THOMAS their heirs shall perform and keep all the covenants which on
their part ought to be performed and kept contained in one Indenture of Bargain and
Sale made between HUGH THOMAS and MARY THOMAS and DANIEL TEBBS according to
the true meaning of the same Indenture; That then this obligation to be void and of no
effect otherwise to stand remain and be in full force and virtue
Signed Sealed and delivered in the presence of
        RICHARD COLEMAN,   HUGH THOMAS
        PETER RUST   MARY THOMAS
    Westmd. Sct. At a Court held for the said County the 29th day of May 1744
HUGH THOMAS personally acknd. this Deed of Feoffment for lands by him passed to
DANIEL TEBBS together with Livery of Seizen and Rect. for the consideration endorsed
to be his proper act and deed, and MARY, Wife of the said HUGH (being first privily
examined according to Law) relinquished her right of Dower of in and to the land by
the said Deed conveyed, together with a Bond for the performance of Covenants, all
which on motion of said TEBBS are admitted to Record
                    Teste   GEORGE LEE, C. W. C.

pp.   (On margin: TRIPLETTs to ELMS)
12-   THIS INDENTURE made the 25th day of May in the 17th year of the Reign of our
16   Sovereign Lord George the Second by the grace of God of Great Brittain France
         and Ireland, King, Defender of the faith &c., And in the year of our Lord God
1744; Between JOHN TRIPLETT of the Parish of Hanover in County of KING GEORGE of
one part and EDWARD ELMS of Washington Parish in County of Westmoreland of other
part; Witnesseth that JOHN TRIPLETT in consideration of the sum of Five shillings current money to him in hand paid by EDWARD ELMS, the receipt whereof JOHN TRIPLETT
doth hereby acknowledge, hath and by these presents doth bargain and sell unto ED-
WARD ELMS a certain dividend of land containing by estimation One hundred acres be
the same more or less situate in Washington Parish in the County of Westmoreland and
is bounded; Beginning at a white Oak and running thence Easterly 140 poles to a
marked white Oak near the line of EDWARD KNOWLES, thence E. by S. 71 poles to a small
black Oak, thence Southerly 73 poles to a black Oak saplin, thence Westerly 159 poles to

a large white Oak, thence N. 90 poles to the first beginning; Together with all rents issues and profits thereof; To have and to hold the land and premises with appurtenances unto EDWARD ELMS his heirs during the term of one whole year paying therefore the rent of one Ear of Indian Corn on the Birth day of our Lord God next ensuing if demanded, to the intent that by virtue of these presents and of the Statute for transferring uses into possession, EDWARD ELMS may be in the actual possession of the premises and be thereby enabled to take a release of the inheritance thereof to him and his heirs; In Witness whereof JOHN TRIPLETT to the present Indenture hath set his hand and seal the day month and year first above written
Sealed and delivered in the presence of
    ORIGINAL BROWN, JOS: SMITH   JOHN TRIPLETT
   Westmd. Sct. At a Court held for the said County the 29th day of May 1744
JOHN TRIPLETT personally acknowledged this Deed of Lease for Land by him passed to EDWARD ELMS to be his proper act and deed, which on motion of said ELMS is admitted to Record   Teste GEORGE LEE, C. W. C.

   (On margin: TRIPLETTs to ELMS)
   THIS INDENTURE made the 26th day of May in the 17th year of the Reign of our Sovereign Lord George the Second by the grace of God of Great Brittain France and Ireland, King, Defender of the faith and in the year of our Lord God 1744; Between JOHN TRIPLETT and CATHARINE his Wife of the Parish of Hanover in County of KING GEORGE of one part and EDWARD ELMS of Washington Parish in County of Westmoreland of other part; Witnesseth that JOHN TRIPLETT and CATHARINE his Wife in consideration of the sum of Eighteen pounds, five shillings and six pence current money to them in hand paid by EDWARD ELMS, the receipt whereof JOHN TRIPLETT and CATHARINE his Wife do hereby acknowledge, have and by these presents do bargain and sell unto EDWARD ELMS and his heirs, said EDWARD ELMS being in actual possession of the premises by virtue of a Lease thereof made for one year and by force of the Statute for transfering uses into possession, a certain dividend of land containing by estimation One hundred acres be the same more or less situate in Washington Parish in County of Westmoreland and bounded, Beginning (the bounds of the land repeated as in the Lease) To have and to hold the parcel of land containing One hundred acres unto EDWARD ELMS his heirs freely and clearly discharged from all incumbrances; In Witness whereof the parties to these presents have interchangeably set their hands and seals the day and year first above written
Sealed and delivered in presence of
    ORIGINAL BROWN, JOS: SMITH,   JOHN TRIPLETT
    SAML: RALLINS   CATHARINE TRIPLETT
   Received of the within named EDWARD ELMS this 26th day of May 1744, the sum of Eighteen pounds, five shillings and six pence current money being the consideration money within mentioned to be by the said EDWARD ELMS paid to me
Witness ORIGINAL BROWN   JOHN TRIPLETT
    JOS: SMITH, SAML: RALLINS
   Westmd. Sct. At a Court held for the said County the 29th day of May 1744
JOHN TRIPLETT personally acknowledged this Deed of Release for Land by him and his Wife, CATHARINE, passed to EDWARD ELMS, together with the receipt for the consideration endorsed to be his proper act and deed, all which on motion of the said ELMS are admitted to Record   Teste GEORGE LEE, C. W. C.

pp.   (On margin: TRIPLETT to RALLINS)
16-   THIS INDENTURE made the 19th day of March in the 17th year of the Reign of
21   our Sovereign Lord George the Second by the grace of God of Great Brittain
        France and Ireland, King, Defender of the faith &c., And in the year of our Lord
God 1743/4, Between JOHN TRIPLETT of Parish of Hanover in County of KING GEORGE
and THOMAS SMITH of Parish of Saint Thomas in County of ORANGE of one part and
SAMUEL RALLINS of Washington Parish in County of Westmoreland of other part; Witnesseth that JOHN TRIPLETT and THOMAS SMITH in consideration of the sum of five shillings current money of Virginia to them in hand paid by SAMUEL RALLINS, the receipt
whereof JOHN TRIPLETT and THOMAS SMITH doth hereby acknowledge, hath and by
these presents doth bargain and sell unto SAMUEL RALLINS a certain parcel of land
containing by estimation One hundred and fifty acres be the same more or less, situate
in County of Westmoreland on North side of the head of MATTOX CREEKE, part of the land
being part of a Pattent formerly granted unto WILLIAM SMITH by Pattent bearing date
the 1st day of April 1695 and the other part thereof was given and granted unto
WILLIAM FREEKE by Pattent bearing date the 11th of September 1653, and is bounded;
Beginning at the aforesaid Creeke opposite to the mouth of a branch, thence North to a
live Oak standing by the side of the Branch, thence up a Ridge to the Main Road at a
Slash, thence up the Road to a box Oak standing on the West side of the Road, thence
West to a red Oak at the head of a Glade, thence N. West down the Glade to the line of
JOHN PRICE, thence South with the line of PRICE to the line of REEDS, thence West along
the said line to the WOOLF TRAP RUN, thence down the Run to JOHN JETT's Mill Path,
thence down the Path to a small red Oak, thence S. to the Creeke to a marked Hiccory,
thence down the meanders of the Creeke to the first beginning; Together with all rents
issues and profits thereof; To have and to hold the land and premises with their appurtenances unto SAMUEL RALLINS his heirs during the term of one whole year paying
therefore the rent of one Ear of Indian Corn on the Birthday of our Lord God next ensuing if demanded to the intent that by virtue of tehse presents and of the Statute for
transfering uses into possession, SAMUEL RALLINS may be in the actual possession of
the premises and be thereby enabled to take a release of the inheritance thereof to him
and his heirs; In Witness whereof JOHN TRIPLETT and THOMAS SMITH to this present
Indenture hath set their hands and seals the day month and year first above written
Signed Sealed and delivered in the presence of us
        ORIGINAL BROWN,   JOSEPH SMITH,   JOHN TRIPLETT
        JOHN FERGUSSON,   JOHN PIPER   THOMAS SMITH
     Westmd. Sct. At a Court held for the said County the 29th day of May 1744
JOHN TRIPLETT personally acknowledged this Deed of Lease for Land by him and THO-
MAS SMITH passed to SAMUEL RALLINS, And the same was proved by the Oaths of all the
witnesses thereto (except JOHN PIPER) to have been the proper act and deed as well of
the said SMITH as of the said TRIPLETT, which on motion of the said RALLINS is admitted
to Record   Teste GEO: LEE, C. W. C.

        (On margin: TRIPLETTs &c. Release to RALLINS)
     THIS INDENTURE made the 20th day of March in the 17th year of the Reign of our
Sovereign Lord George the Second by the grace of God of Great Brittain France and Ireland, King, Defender of the faith &c., And in the year of our Lord God 1743/4; Between
JOHN TRIPLETT and CATHARINE his Wife of Parish of Hanover in County of KING GEORGE
and THOMAS SMITH and ELIZABETH his Wife of the Parish of Saint Thomas in County of
ORANGE of one part and SAMUEL RALLINS of Washington Parish in County of Westmoreland of other part; Witnesseth that JOHN TRIPLETT and CATHARINE his Wife and

THOMAS SMITH and ELIZABETH his Wife in consideration of the sum of Fifty pounds current money to them in hand paid by SAMUEL RALLINS, the receipt whereof they do hereby acknowledge, have and by these presents do bargain sell and release unto SAMUEL RALLINS, being in his actual possession now being by virtue of a Lease thereof made for one year and by force of the Statute for transfering uses into possession, a certain parcel of land containing by estimation One hundred and Fifty acres be the same more or less situate in County of Westmoreland and on the North side of MATTOX CREEKE, party of the land being (the previous Patents, the description of the bounds of the land repeated as in the Lease); To have and to hold the parcel of land and premises with appurtenances unto SAMUEL RALLINS his heirs; And JOHN TRIPLETT and CATHARINE his Wife and THOMAS SMITH and ELIZABETH his Wife for themselves their heirs do warrant & forever defend the land and premises against the claims of all persons; In Witness whereof the parties to these presents have interchangeably set their hands and seals the day and eyar first above written
Signed Sealed and delivered in the presence of us
    ORIGINAL BROWN,   JOS: SMITH,   JOHN TRIPLETT
    JOHN FERGUSSON,   JNO: PIPER   CATHARINE TRIPLETT
                                                     THOMAS SMITH
                                                     ELIZA: SMITH
    Received of SAMUEL RALLINS the 20th March 1743 the sum of Fifty pounds current money being the consideration money mentioned to be paid by SAMUEL RAWLINS to us
Teste   ORIGINAL BROWN,   JOS: SMITH   JOHN TRIPLETT
        JNO: FERGUSSON,   JNO: PIPER   THOS: SMITH
    Westmd. Sct. At a Court held for the said County the 29th day of May 1744
JOHN TRIPLETT personally acknowledged this Deed of Release for Lands by him and CATHARINE his Wife, THOMAS SMITH and ELIZABETH his Wife passed to SAMUEL RALLINS, together with receipt for the consideration endorsed, And the same were proved by the Oaths of all the witnesses thereto (except JOHN PIPER) to have been the proper act and deed of the said SMITH and Wife, as of the said TRIPLETT and his Wife, all which on motion of said RALLINS are admitted to Record
                    Teste   GEORGE LEE, C.W.C.

pp.   (On margin: HAZELRIGGs to BROWN)
21-   THIS INDENTURE made the 29th day of May in the 17th year of the Reign of our
24   Sovereign Lord George the Second by the grace of God of Great Brittain France
         and Ireland, King, Defender of the faith &c., And in the year of our Lord 1744;
Between RICHARD HAZELRIG of Parish of HAMILTON in County of PRINCE WILLIAM, Planter, of one part and JOHN BROWN of Parish of Cople in County of Westmoreland, Planter, of other part; Witnesseth that RICHARD HAZELRIG in consideration of the sum of Sixty pounds current money to him in hand paid by JOHN BROWN, the receipt whereof RICHARD HAZELRIG doth hereby acknowledge, hath and by these presents doth bargain and sell unto JOHN BROWN that tenement of land with appurtenances lying in Parish of Cople and County of Westmoreland containing by estimation One hundred and Eighty eight acres of land and part of the One hundred and Eighty eight acres of land was granted to ANTHONY CARPENTER by a Proprietors Deed dated the 27th day of Februaryu 1698/9, for fifty acres of land and bounded; Beginning at a Maple tree in the Swamp near the HORSE BRIDGE extending thence North 82 1/2d. West 112 poles to a marked red Oak in WILLIAM ROBINSONs line, thence N. 41d. E. 178 poles to a marked Poplar, corner tree in said ROBINSONs line, thence up the meanders of the Branch to the before mentioned place containing and being now laid out for fifty acres of land

and likewise part of the said One hundred and eighty eight acres of land was granted JOHN CARPENTER by a Proprietors Deed dated the 8th day of October 1695 for sixty nine acres of land and bounded; Beginning at a marked Maple tree standing in a Branch formerly called COSS COSS, extending thence N. 89d. West 193 poles to a marked Hiccory tree standing in WILLIAM ROBINSONs line being a corner tree to this Land and the land of JAMES HAZELRIGG, thence N. 41d. E. 102 poles to a marked red Oak of said ROBINSONs line being a corner tree to this Land and the Land of WILLIAM KEMP, thence S. 82 degrees and a half E. 112 poles to a marked Maple tree standing in the Swamp between this land and the land of said KEMP, thence up the meanders of the Branch to the first beginning; containing and being now laid out for sixty nine acres of land; Likewise part of the One hundred and eighty eight acres of land was granted to JAMES HAZELRIGG by a Proprietors Deed dated the 8th day of October 1695, for sixty nine acres of land and bounded; Beginning at a marked Gum standing upon West side of a Branch of COSS COSS being a corner tree to this land and the land of THOMAS HARRIS extending thence S. 88d. and a half W. 152 poles to a marked Hiccory corner tree to this land and the land of said HARRIS, thence N. West 38 poles to a marked red Oak standing in the line of WILLIAM ROBINSON, thence N. 41d. E. 40 poles to a marked corner Hiccory in said ROBINSONs line to this land and the land of RICHARD MIDDLETON, thence S. 89d. E. 193 poles to a marked Maple tree in the Branch dividing this land and the land of said MIDDLETON, thence up the meanders of the Branch to the first beginning, containing and being now laid out of sixty nine acres of land; Together the whole one hundred and eighty eight acres of land with all houses orchards rents issues and profits thereof; To have and to hold the one hundred and eighty eight acres of land and premises with the appurtenances unto JOHN BROWN his heirs; And RICHARD HAZELRIG and his heirs the land and premises to JOHN BROWN his heirs against RICHARD HAZELRIG his heirs shall warrant save harmless keep indemnified and forever defend by these presents; In Witness whereof the parties to these presents have interchangeably set their hands and seals the day and year first above written
Sealed and delivered in the presence of us

WM: CAMPBELL, WILLO: NEWTON,   RICHARD HAZELRIG
PRESLY NEALE

Memorandum; On the 29th day of May 1744 peacible and quiet possession and seizen was delivered by RICHARD HAZELRIG to JOHN BROWN by the delivery seizen and turff and twig the said Land, To have and to hold according to the true intent of the within written Deed; In presence of us

PRESLY NEALE   RICHARD HAZELRIG
HESTER her mark   (? SANOY)

(On margin: HAZELRIG's Bond to BROWN)
KNOW ALL MEN by these presents that I RICHARD HAZELRIG of Parish of Hamilton in County of PRINCE WILLIAM am held and firmly bound unto JOHN BROWN of Parish of Cople in County of Westmoreland in the penal sum of One hundred and twenty pounds current money, to the which payment well & truly to be made I bind myself my heirs firmly by these presents; Sealed with my seal and dated this 29th day of May 1744

THE CONDITION of the above obligation is such that whereas the above bound RICHARD HAZELRIG have the day of the date hereof by a certain Deed of Bargain and Sale sold JOHN BROWN his heirs a certain tract of Land, Now if RICHARD HAZELRIG his heirs shall perform and keep all the Covenants on his part to be performed according to the same intent and meaning of the Deed, That then this obligation to be void and of none effect, otherwise to be and remain in full force power and virtue

Signed Sealed and delivered in the presence of us
         WILLO: NEWTON, WM: CAMPBELL   RICHARD HAZELRIG
         PRESLEY NEALE
     Westmd. Sct. At a Court held for the said County the 29th day of May 1744
RICHARD HAZELRIG personally acknowledged this Deed of Feoffment for lands by him
passed to JOHN BROWN, together with Livery of Seizen to be his proper act and deed, also
a Bond for the performance of Covenants, all which on the motion of the said BROWN
are admitted to Record   Teste GEO: LEE, C. W. C.

pp.   (On margin: MINOR, NICHOLAS Will. At July Court 1748, NICHOLAS MINOR, Gent.
24-   was sworn an Exor. to this Will. See Order Book page 87).
26   IN THE NAME OF GOD Amen, I NICHOLAS MINOR of the Parish of Cople in County
         of Westmoreland, Gent., being very sick and weak of body but of sound mind and
memory praised be to Almighty God for the same, and knowing the certainty of death
and uncertainty of the time thereof, do make constitute and appoint this to be my Last
Will and Testament in manner and form as follows;
     Imprimis. I give and bequeath my Soul into the hands of Almighty God that gave it
me with a Christian hope of the pardon of all my sins thro the alone merits of my
Saviour Christ and my body to be decently intered at the discretion of my Exr. herein
after named, and touching such worldly Estate as it hath pleased God to bestow upon me,
I give and bequeath in manner and form as followeth;
     Item. I give unto my Son, WILLIAM STEWART MINOR, ten young Negros whose names
are Jack, Winny, Lucy, Sam, Nan, Dick, Young Jenny, Nan, Charles, Bick, my said
Son WILLIAM, to have the said Negroes when he shall attain to the age of twenty one
years to him and his heirs lawfully begotten and in case that my Son, WILLIAM, aforesaid die without any issue, then the abovesaid Negroes and all their future increase to
return unto my Sons, JOHN, NICHO: and STEWART MINOR, and their heirs forever to be
equally divided;
     Item. I give and bequeath unto my Daughter, ELIZABETH WHERREL, two thousand
pounds of Crop Tobacco over and above what I have already given her, it being the full
part of my Estate to her and her heirs forever;
     Item. I give and bequeath unto my Son, WILLIAM STEWART MINOR, my largest Stil
with one dozen of large Silver spoons to him and his heirs forever at the age of twenty
one years;
     Item. all the rest residue and remainder of my personal Estate not heretofore by me
given I give and bequeath the use and benefit thereof unto my Loving Wife, JEMIMA
MINOR, for and during her natural life, and after her decease, I give and bequeath all
my Negroes not heretofore by me given unto my Son, WILLIAM STEWART MINOR, unto
my Sons, JOHN MINOR, NICHO: MINOR and STEWART MINOR, equally to be divided between them, to them and their heirs forever; and the rest of my personal Estate such as
household goods, stock &c. after the decease of my Loving Wife, JEMIMA, I give and bequeath the same unto my Sons, JOHN, NICHO:, STEWART and WILLIAM STEWART MINOR
equally to be divided between them and to their heirs forever;
     Item. I give and bequeath unto my Son, JOHN MINOR, one tract of Five hundred and
thirty six acres of land situate and lying in the Little Fork of RAPPAHANNOCK which I
bought of JOHN EDY to him and his heirs forever;
     Item. I give and bequeath unto my Son, NICHO: MINOR, one tract of Four hundred and
ninety six acres of land situate and lying in the County of KING GEORGE which I bought
of JOHN EDY as also one other tract of three hundred and thirty acres of land more or
less and lying in the County of Westmoreland and commonly known by the name of THE
WHITE MARSH, to him and his heirs forever;

Item. I give and bequeath unto my Son, STEWART MINOR, one tract of Land I bought of JOSEPH SCOTT being in the County of RICHMOND as also one other tract of one hundred (more or less) acres known by the name of WATTS QUARTER, the Mill Run to be the border between the said STEWART MINOR and my Son, WILLIAM STEWART MINOR, it being part of the tract of land whereon I now live; I give the two tracts aforesaid unto my Son, STEWART MINOR, and the heirs of his body lawfully begotten and for want of such issue I give and bequeath the said land unto the male heirs of my Sons, JOHN MINOR and NICHOLAS MINOR equally to be divided between them and to the heirs of my Son, WILLIAM. I give and bequeath unto my Son, WILLIAM STEWART MINOR, my now dwelling House and the remainder of the tract of land thereunto belonging and the Mill thereon as also one better tract of One hundred and fifty (more or less) acres of land which I bought of GEORGE BLACKMORE, unto him and his heirs lawfully begotten and for want of such issue, I give the abovesaid Land unto the male heirs of my Sons, JOHN, NICHOLAS and STEWART MINOR equally to be divided between them;

Item. I give unto THOMAS TEMPLEMAN fifteen shillings;

Lastly, I constitute and appoint my Loving Wife, JEMIMA, my Son NICHOLAS, and my Son WILLIAM STEWART MINOR with my request WILLIAM JORDAN, Gent., and JOHN MINOR, to be Exors. of this my Last Will and Testament, revoking all other Wills heretofore by me made allowing and confirming this to be my Last Will and Testament; In Witness hereof I have hereunto set my hand and seal this 11th day of October 1743 Sealed and Delivered as his Last Will and Testament
in the presence of us
     THOS: TEMPLEMAN, JNO: BRIDGES,   NICHOLAS MINOR
     WILLIAM KIRKHAM
Westmd. Sct. At a Court held for the said County the 29th day of May 1744
This Last Will and Testament of NICHOLAS MINOR, deceased, was presented into Court by JEMIMA his Relict and one of his Exors. therein named, who made Oath thereto and being proved by the Oaths of all the witnesses thereto is admitted to Record; And upon the motion of the said Exr. and her performing what is usual in such cases, Certificate is granted her for obtaining a Probate thereof in due form
          Teste GEO: LEE, C. W. C.

pp.   (On margin: GARRARD's Lease to WILLIAMS)
26-   THIS INDENTURE made the 28th day of May 1744 Between NATHANIEL GARRARD
27   of Parish of Washington in County of Westmoreland of one part; Planter, and
        THOMAS WILLIAMS and JANE WILLIAMS of Parish of Cople and County aforesaid;
Witnesseth that NATHANIEL GARRARD in consideration of Five hundred pounds of lawfull tobacco and the Quit Rents to him yearly paid after one three years from this present date paid by THOMAS WILLIAMS or JANE WILLIAMS to him his heirs, I NATHANIEL GARRARD have released unto THOMAS WILLIAMS and JANE WILLIAMS his Wife a parcel of land lying in Parish of Cople and County aforesaid in NOMONY and adjoining on the land of HARDWICKs, the which tract of land to contain One hundred acres, And I NATHANIEL GARRARD do release the tract of land to THOMAS WILLIAMS and JANE WILLIAMS to them or either of them during their or either of their lives during which time the Land to be held as their own proper right only the said WILLIAMS not to make any wilfull waste of Timber and must plant One hundred Apple trees on the land and THOMAS WILLIAMS and JANE WILLIAMS performing all and paying the said Five hundred and thirty pounds of tobacco yearly and the quit rents, said THOMAS WILLIAMS nor JANE WILLIAMS is not to be molested on the land; As Witness my hand and seal this day and year above written

Signed Sealed and delivered in presence of
    RICHARD LEE, GEORGE LEE,   NATHL: GARRARD
    CHARLES BEALE
    Westmd. Sct. At a Court held for the said County the 30th day of May 1744
This Deed of Lease for Lives for lands from NATHANIEL GARRARD to THOMAS WILLIAMS
was proved in open Court by the Oaths of GEORGE LEE, CHARLES BEALE and RICHARD
LEE, Gent., three of the witnesses thereto, which on motion of the said WILLIAMS is
admitted to Record   Teste GEO: LEE, C.W.C.

pp.   (On margin: COX, CHARNOCKs Will)
27-   IN THE NAME OF GOD, Amen, I CHARNOCK COX being in perfect sense and memo-
28   ry of body and mind do make this my Last Will and Testament. First, I deliver up
        my Soul to Almighty God and my body to the ground to be decently buried by my
Executor hereinafter mentioned, And as for what Estate it hath pleased Almighty God to
bestow on me, I do dispose of as followeth;
    Item. I give unto my two Sons, PRESLY and CHARNOCK COX, this tract of land which I
purchased of Mr. SAMUEL EARLE, JUNR., containing Two hundred and fifty three acres
to be equally divided between them, and my Son, PRESLY, to have my Dwelling Plantation in his part of the land and my Son, CHARNOCK to have the Plantation where
LASURE HALL did live in his part of the Land,
    Item. I likewise give to my two Sons, VINCENT and JOHN COX, the two Negroes which
shall fall to my beloved Wife as her Dower and after her death to my two Sons, VINCENT
and JOHN, to them and their heirs forever;
    Item. I likewise give the land mentioned above to my two Sons, PRESLY and CHAR-
NOCK to them and their heirs forever;
    Item. I give all the remainder of my Estate before not given after my debts are paid
to be equally divided amongst my four Children and I do appoint my Loving Friend,
DANIEL TEBBS, my Executor of this my Last Will & Testament; As Witness my hand and
seal this 1st day of March Anno Dom: 1743/4
Signed Sealed and delivered in the presence of
    WM: MIDDLETON, STEPHEN BAILEY, JUNR.   CHA: COX, JR.
    JAMES LEWIS, JUNR.
    Westmd. Sxt. At a Court held for the said County the the 26th day of June 1744
This Last Will and Testment of CHARNOCK COX, JR., deceased, was presented into Court by
DANIEL TEBBS, his Exor., who made Oath thereto and being proved by the Oaths of all the
witnesses thereto is admitted to Record; And upon the motion of the said Exor. and his
performing what is usual in such cases, Certificate is granted him for obtaining a Probate thereof in due form
                Teste GEO: LEE, C.W.C.

pp.   (On margin: McCARTY, DANIEL Will)
28-   I DANIEL McCARTY of Westmoreland County, Gent., declare this to be my Last
29-   Will, that is to say, I give unto my beloved Wife the use of all my Estate real and
        personal during her natural life or until my Son, DANIEL, arrives to the age of
twenty one years, she supporting, maintaining and educating him my said Son according to the instructions of my Executor in trust hereinafter named; But if it should
happen that my Wife be alive when my Son, DANIEL, attains to the age of twenty one
years; It is my will that she give and deliver up unto him all my Estate both real and
personal save only the tract of land whereon my now Dwelling House stands and fifteen
slaves her choice which at her decease, together with all my Estate real and personal I

give to my said Son, DANIEL, and his heirs forever; And whereas the several heirs at Law with my Brothers, DENNIS and BILLINGTON McCARTY must of necessity be amply provided for by means of the lands being Intailed by the Will of their Grand Father whilst the others in a great measure destitute of support, It is my will that in case of the death of my Son, DANIEL, without issue before the age of twenty one years or afterwards all and every such part and parcel as may remain unsold by my said Son be equally divided among the several male issue of the said two Brothers that shall be alive at the time (other than the heirs at Law of my said Brothers) and to their respectively. I give unto my Friend, JOSEPH MORTON, a moiety of his debt to me and until my Son, DANIEL, arrives to the age of twenty one years or in the year he would have been so should he die, the use of the other moiety thereof; And to each of my Executors I give fifteen pounds as a token of my regard to buy them a suit of Mourning if they think fit to apply it that way. And Lastly, I constitute and appoint my well beloved Friends, Colo. PRESLEY THORNTON, Mr. JOSEPH MORTON, Mr. AUGUSTINE WASHINGTON and Mr. LAURENCE BUTLER, Gent., Exors. of this my Last Will and Testament. In Testimony whereof I have hereunto set my hand and seal this 16th day of May 1744

Signed Sealed and published in the presence of
     ANTHONY THORNTON, FRANCIS THORNTON,   DANIEL McCARTY
     JAMES CARTER

I DANIEL McCARTY of Westmoreland County calling to mind since the publication of the above will the possibility of my Wifes being with Child, in such case for provision for the same, It is my will that if she be delivered of a Son he have such education and support out of my Estate as my Executors before named shall think fit and at his arrival to twenty one years of age that he be paid out of my Estate eight hundred pounds current money, and that if she should be delivered of a Daughter, at the age of seventeen years or married, she shall be paid out of my Estate five hundred pounds current money provided nevertheless that if my Son, DANIEL, shall die without issue before he arrives to the age of twenty one years, in that case my will is that my said other Child (whatever it happens to be) shall have and be entitled to all the benefits and advantages of my Estate that my said Son, DANIEL, would have had had he lived. My will is that my Friend, Mr. LAURENCE BUTLER, have One hundred pounds current money out of my Estate. In Testimony whereof I have hereunto set my hand and seal this 16th day of May 1744

Signed Sealed and published in the presence of
     ANTHONY THORNTON, FRANCIS THORNTON,   DANIEL McCARTY
     JAMES CARTER

Westmoreland Sct. At a Court held for the said County the 26th day of June 1744 This Last Will and Testament of DANIEL McCARTY, Gent., deceased, together with the Codicil thereon were presented into Court by JOSEPH MORTON and LAURENCE BUTLER, Gent., two of the Exors. in the said Will named, who made Oath thereto and being proved by the Oaths of ANTHONY THORNTON and FRANCIS THORNTON, Gent., two of the witnesses thereto is admitted to Record; And upon the motion of the said Executors and their performing what is usual in such cases, Certificate is granted them for obtaining a Probate thereof in due form   Teste GEO: LEE, C.W.C.

pp.   (On margin: WELCH &c. to BERRYMAN)
29-   THIS INDENTURE made the 18th day of July in the year of our Lord 1744, Be-
33   tween JOHN WELCH of County of Westmoreland, Yeoman, and MARY his Wife, one
    of the Daughters and coheirs of JOHN HUDSON and MARY his Wife, deceased, of
one part and JAMES BERRYMAN of County aforesaid Gent. of other part; Witnesseth that

JOHN WELCH and MARY his Wife in consideration of the sum of Five shillings of lawfull money to them in hand paid by JAMES BERRYMAN, the receipt whereof is hereby acknowledged, have and by these presents doth bargain and sell unto JAMES BERRYMAN all that moiety of land on UPPER MACHODICK CREEKE in Westmoreland County called by the name of LITTLE DICKS, now in the possession of JOHN SETTLES and binding a deep Branch, it being part of a parcel of land purchased of EDWARD HART by WILLIAM BENNETT contained two hundred and seven acres by Deed bearing date the last day of November 1693, and by the Last Will and Testament of WILLIAM BENNETT bearing date the 2nd day of February 1702/3, he bequeathed the Land called LITTLE DICKS to his Eldest Daughter, MARY, who married the said JOHN HUDSON, with all houses orchards profits and appurtenances to the parcel of land belonging and the rents issues and profits thereof; To have and to hold the the land and premises unto JAMES BERRYMAN his heirs during the term of one whole year paying therefore the rent of one Ear of Indian Corn upon the last day of the term (if lawfully demanded) to the intent that by virtue of these presents and of the Statute for transferring uses into possession, JAMES BERRYMAN may be in the actual possession of the premises and thereby be the better enabled to take a release of the inheritance thereof to him and his heirs; In Witness whereof the parties to these presents have interchangeably set their hands and seals the day and eyar first above written
Sealed and delivered in the presence of
    WM: TYLER,   WM: BERRYMAN,   JOHN WELCH
    SAML. WHEELER   MARY WELCH
    Westmd. Sct. At a Court held for the said County the 28th day of Augt. 1744
JOHN WELCH personally acknd. this Deed of Lease for Land by him passed to JAMES BERRYMAN, Gent., to be his proper act and deed, all which on motion of the said BERRYMAN is admitted to Record   Teste GEO: LEE, C. W. C.

(On margin: WELCH & Wifes Release to BERRYMAN)
    THIS INDENTURE made the 19th day of June in the year of our Lord 1744, Between JOHN WELCH of County of Westmoreland, Yeoman, and MARY his Wife, (one of the Daughters and coheirs of JOHN HUDSON and MARY his Wife, deced.) of one part and JAMES BERRYMAN of County aforesaid, Gent., of other part; Witnesseth that JOHN WELCH and MARY his Wife in consideration of the quantity of Two thousand five hundred and fifty pounds of Crop Tobacco in three hogsheads to them in hand paid by JAMES BERRYMAN, the receipt whereof they do hereby acknowledge, have and by these presents do bargain sell and release unto JAMES BERRYMAN (in his actual possession now being by virtue of a bargain and sale to him thereof made for one year and by force of the Statute for transfering uses into possession) and to his heirs all that moiety of land on UPPER MACHODICK CREEKE in Westmld. County called by the name of LITTLE DICKS now in the possession of JOHN SETTLES, (this Release continues as in the Lease with the purchase of the land and the passing by Will &c.) To have and to hold the parcel of land and premises with appurtenances unto JAMES BERRYMAN his heirs, and JOHN WELCH and MARY his Wife and the heirs of the said MARY and against all persons will warrant and forever defend by these presents; In Witness whereof the parties to these presents have interchangeably set their hands and seals the day and year first above written
Sealed and delivered in presence of
    WM: TYLER,   WM: BERRYMAN,   JOHN WELCH
    SAML: WHEELER   MARY WELCH

July the 18th 1744. Received of JAMES BERRY the quantity of Two thousand five hundred and fifty pounds of tobacco and cask being the consideration within mentioned, I say reced. by me

Witness WM.: BERRYMAN,   JOHN WELCH
    SAML: WHEELER

 Westmd. Sct. At a Court held for the said County the 28th day of Augt. 1744 JOHN WELCH personally acknowledged this Deed of Release for land by him passed to JAMES BERRYMAN, Gent., together with Receipt for the consideration endorsed to be his proper act and deed, and MARY, Wife of the said JOHN, by virtue of a Commission relinquished her right of Inheritance in and to the lands by the said Deeds conveyed, which on motion of the said BERRYMAN are admitted to Record

    Teste GEO: LEE, C.W.C.

 Westmd. Sct. George the 2nd by the grace of God of Great Brittain France and Ireland King Defender of the faith &c., to JOHN WATTS, WILLIAM TYLER, JOHN MARTIN, WILLIAM BERRYMAN and ROBERT VAULX (VALX in text) of County aforesaid, Gent., Greeting: We do hereby authorise and impower you or any two of you at such time and place as you shall appoint, (some time before the next Court to be held for the County aforesaid) to take the privy examination of MARY, the Wife of JOHN WELCH, apart from her Husband (the Commission for the privy examination of MARY, the Wife of JOHN WELCH); herein you are not to fail. Witness GEORGE LEE, Clerk of the said County Court the 27th day of June in the 18th year of our Reign   GEORGE LEE, C.C.W.

 Westmd. Sct. By virtue of the within Commission to us directed, we have privately examined MARY, the Wife of JOHN WELCH of aforesaid County (the return of the execution of the privy examination of MARY WELCH): Certified under our hands this 18th day of July 1744

    WM: TYLER
    WM. BERRYMAN

 Westmd. Sct. At a Court held for the said County the 28th day of August 1744 The Commission for the Examination of MARY, the Wife of JOHN WELCH, for relinquishment of her right of Inheritance to lands sold by her Husband to JAMES BERRYMAN, Gent., being returned executed is ordered to be recorded

    Teste GEO: LEE, C.W.C.

pp. (On margin: ASHTONs Lease to ARROWSMITH)
33- THIS INDENTURE made the 21st day of June in the year of our Lord God 1744,
36 Between BURDITT ASHTON of County of Westmoreland and Parish of Washington in the Colony of Virginia of one part and RICHARD ARROWSMITH of County and Parish aforesaid and Colony of Virginia of other part; Witnesseth that BURDITT ASHTON in consideration of the sum of Five shillings Sterling to him in hand paid by RICHARD ARROWSMITH the receipt whereof is hereby acknowledged, hath and by these presents doth bargain and sell unto RICHARD ARROWSMITH all that parcel of land containing by estimation One hundred acres be the same more or less sitaute in Parish of Washington and County of Westmoreland, the land being conveyed by PENELOPE JENNINGS to JOHN ASHTON by Deeds bearing date the second and third days of March 1736, and JOHN ASHTON in and by his Last Will and Testament bequeathed the land to BURDITT ASHTON, party to these presents; the land being bounded in the Last Will and Testament of GEORGE BOWDEN alias HARRIS by a Lease thereof made to one ROBERT LEGG and is now adjoining to the lands of JOSEPH SMITH and RICHARD ARROWSMITH, party to these presents; and all houses orchards profits and appurtenances to the same belonging; To have and to hold the land and premises unto RICHARD ARROWSMITH his heirs during

the term of one whole year paying therefore one Pepper Corn upon the Feast day of Saint Michael the Archangel if demanded to the intent that by virtue of these presents and by force of the Statute for transfering uses into possession, RICHARD ARROWSMITH may be in the actual possession of the premises and be enabled to take a release of the inheritance thereof to him and his heirs; In Witness whereof BURDIT ASHTON hath hereunto set his hand and seal the day month and year first above written
Teste   JOHN SHROPSHIRE,   WM. STROTHER   BURDITT ASHTON
             GEO: GRAY

(On margin: ASHTONs Release to ARROWSMITH)
THIS INDENTURE made the 22nd day of June in the year of our Lord God 1744, Between BURDITT ASHTON of Parish of Washington in County of Westmoreland of one part and RICHARD ARROWSMITH of the Parish and County aforesaid of other part; Witnesseth that BURDITT ASHTON in consideration of the sum of Thirty five pounds current money to him in hand paid by RICHRD ARROWSMITH, the receipt whereof BURDITT ASHTON doth hereby acknowledge, hath and by these presents doth bargain sell and release unto RICHARD ARROWSMITH (in his actual possession now being by virtue of a bargain and sale to him thereof made for one year and by force of the Statute for transfering uses into possession) and to his heirs all that parcel of land containing by estimation One hundred acres be the same more or less (the location and passing of the land repeated as in the Lease): To have and to hold the land and premises with appurtenances unto RICHARD ARROWSMITH his heirs; And BURDITT ASHTON doth covenant for himself and his respective heirs shall warrant and forever defend the granted land and premises against the claims of Mr. RODERICK MACCULLOCK and ST. JOHN SHROPSHIRE and their heirs and that RICHARD ARROWSMITH his heirs shall possess the land and premises clearly acquitted and discharged of all quit rents and arrears of quit rents; In Witness whereof (according to the true intent and meaning of these presents for to make a special conveyance) BURDITT ASHTON hath to this Indenture set his hand and seal the day and year first above written
Signed sealed and acknd. in presence of
          JOHN SHROPSHIRE,   WM. STROTHER,   BURDITT ASHTON
          GEORGE GRAY
     Received of RICHARD ARROWSMITH this 22nd day of June 1744, Thirty five pounds current money being the consideration money within mentioned to be by RICHARD ARROWSMITH paid to me
          (no witnesses recorded)   BURDITT ASHTON
     Westmd. Sct. At a Court held for the said County the 28th day of August 1744 BURDITT ASHTON personally acknowledged this Deed of Lease and Release for Land by him passed to RICHARD ARROWSMITH, Together with the receipt for consideration to be his proper act and deed, which on motion of the said ARROWSMITH is admitted to Record
                    Teste GEO: LEE, C.W.C.

pp.   (On margin: FITZHUGH & Wifes Lease to BUTLER)
36-   THIS INDENTURE made the 16th day of July in the year of our Lord 1744, Be-
40   tween WILLIAM FITZHUGH of the Parish of Cople in County of Westmoreland in
               Colony and Dominion of Virginia, Esqr., and MARTHA his Wife of one part and
LAURENCE BUTLER of the same Parish County and Colony, Gentleman, of other part; Witnesseth that WILLIAM FITZHUGH and MARTHA his Wife in consideration of the sum of five shillings Sterling in hand paid by LAURENCE BUTLER, the receipt whereof is hereby acknowledged, have and by these presents do bargain and sell unto LAURENCE

BUTLER all that undivided moiety or equal half part of all the land situate in County of
Suffolk in Kingdom of Great Brittain which were devised by the Last Will and Testament of MARTHA LEE, late of Mansel Street in Goodmans Fields in the Parish of Saint
Mary Matfellow alias White Chappel in the County of Middlesex in the Kingdom of Great
Brittain, to her two Daughters, MARTHA LEE, party to these presents, and LETTICE LEE
their heirs share and share alike as tenants in common and not as joint tenants,
together with all houses dovehouses orchards and appurtenances to any part thereof
belonging; To have and to hold the moiety of said lands and other the premises during
the term of one whole year paying therefore the Rent of one Ear of Indian Corn on the
Feast of St. Michael the Archangel if lawfully demanded to the intent that by virtue of
these presents and of the Statute for transfering uses into possession LAURENCE BUT-
LER may be in the actual possession of the premises and be thereby enabled to take a
release of the inheritance thereof to him and his heirs; In Witness whereof the parties
to these presents have hereunto interchangeably set their hands and seals the day and
year first above written
Signed and delivered in the presence of

    GEORGE LEE,   WILLIAM FITZHUGH
    SAML: OLDHAM,   CHARLES BEALE   MARTHA FITZHUGH

(On margin: FITZHUGH and Wifes Release to BUTLER)
THIS INDENTURE made the 17th day of July in the year of our Lord 1744, Between
WILLIAM FITZHUGH of Parish of Cople in County of Westmoreland, Esqr., and MARTHA
his Wife of one part and LAURENCE BUTLER of the same Parish and County, Gentleman,
of other part; Whereas MARTHA LEE, late of Mansel Street in Goodman Fields in Parish
of St. Mary Matfellow alias White Chappel in County of Middlesex in Kingdom of Great
Brittain, Widow, deceased, by her Last Will and Testament in Writing bearing date the
26th day of April in the year of our Lord Christ 1725, among other things, did give and
devise all her lands in the County of Suffolk (subject to the payment of Two hundred
and eighty pounds and interest charged thereon by Mortgage and also to the payment
of One hundred pounds to DANIEL WATTS when he attained his age of one and twenty
years, pursuant to the Will of THOMAS MOORE, her former Husband, deced., unto her two
Daughters MARTHA LEE, party to these presents and LETTICE LEE their heirs share and
share alike as tenants in common and not as joint tenants, provided always the said
Tetatrix declared her mind and will to be that in case all her three Children, GEORGE
LEE, and the said MARTHA LEE and LETTICE LEE should happen to die without issue, then
she did give and devise her Estate in the County of Suffolk to her Brother, TOBIAS SILK,
and his heirs as by the said Will will more fully appear; And Whereas said MARTHA LEE
the devisee and party to these presents intermarried with GEORGE TURBERVILE, late of
the Parish of Cople in the County of Westmoreland, Gent., deceased, and LETTICE LEE, the
other devisee also intermarried with JOHN CORBIN of County of Essex in the Colony of
Virginia, Gent., and GEORGE TURBERVILE and MARTHA his Wife and JOHN CORBIN and
LETTICE his Wife being in right of their Wives seized of the lands in the County of Suffolk (subject to the charges and incumbrances above recited) and apprehending the
same were entailed did constitute and appoint JAMES BUCHANAN of the City of London,
Merchant, their Attorney as well with intent to receive the rents issues and profits of
the premises and to pay off and discharge the mortgage and incumbrance above mentioned, as to take such proper measures as Council should advise for docking the entail
of the premises, all which has accordingly been done and performed; And whereas
GEORGE TURBERVILE did some years since and the said MARTHA his Widow and Relict
being intermarried with WILLIAM FITZHUGH, said WILLIAM FITZHUGH and MARTHA his

Wife are in right of said MARTHA seized of and in one undivided moiety of all the above mentioned lands in the County of Suffolk; NOW THIS INDENTURE WITNESSETH that in consideration of the sum of Fifteen hundred pounds Sterling money of Great Brittain to WILLIAM FITZHUGH in hand paid by LAURENCE BUTLER, the receipt whereof WILLIAM FITZHUGH doth hereby acknowledge, WILLIAM FITZHUGH and MARTHA his Wife hath and by these presents do bargain and sell unto LAURENCE BUTLER (in his actual possession now being by virtue of a bargain and sale to him thereof made for one whole year and by force of the Statute for transfering uses into possession) and his heirs all that undivided moiety of land situate in County of Suffolk in the Kingdom of Great Brittain; Together with all houses barnes, dovehouses orchards profits and appurtenances to the same belonging; To have and to hold the undivided moiety of lands unto LAURENCE BUTLER his heirs; And WILLIAM FITZHUGH and MARTHA his Wife or either of them except one Lease of part of the premises granted one THOMAS WATSON BACON and a fine and recovery levied and suffered with an Intent to dock an entail of the premises as before mentioned in which MARTHA's name was joined together with the before named GEORGE TURBERVILLE, her former Husband, and JOHN CORBIN, Gentleman and LETTICE his Wife; And WILLIAM FITZHUGH and MARTHA his Wife their heirs unto LAURENCE BUTLER his heirs shall warrant and forever defend by these presents; In Witness whereof the parties to these presents have hereunto interchangeably set their hands and seals the day and year first before written

Sealed and Delivered in the presence of

GEORGE LEE,   WILLIAM FITZHUGH
SAMUEL OLDHAM, CHAS: BEALE   MARTHA FITZHUGH

Westmd. Sct. At a Court held for the said County the 28th day of Augt. 1744 WILLIAM FITZHUGH Esqr., personally acknowledged this Deed of Lease and Release for Lands and Tenements &c. in the County of Suffolk in Great Brittain by him, the said FITZHUGH and MARTHA his Wife, sold and conveyed to LAURENCE BUTLER, Gentleman, to be his proper act and deed and the said MARTHA (she being first privily examined according to Law) relinquished her Right of Inheritance and Dower of in and to the lands and tenements &c., by the said Deed conveyed, all which on motion of the said BUTLER are admitted to Record

Test GEO: LEE, C. W. C.

pp.   (On margin: FITZHUGH & Ux. Power of Atty. to BUCHANAN &c.)
40-   TO ALL TO WHOM these presents shall come, WILLIAM FITZHUGH of Parish of
44   Cople in County of Westmoreland in the Colony and Dominion of Virginia, Es-
        quire, and MARTHA his Wife, send Greeting. Whereass MARTHA LEE (this Power of Attorney repeats the material in the foregoing Release concerning the passing of the land &c.) And whereas WILLIAM FITZHUGH is willing and desirous to sell and dispose of the premises and MARTHA his Wife for that purpose is willing to be barred of all her right and title of Dower in the same testified by her signing and being a party to these presents; NOW KNOW YE that WILLIAM FITZHUGH and MARTHA his Wife for that purpose have and by these presents each of them doth make constitute and appoint JAMES BUCHANAN of the City of London, Merchant, and EDWARD ATHAWES of the same City, Merchant, their true and lawfull Attorneys jointly or either of them separately for them as it may be necesary to enter into the premises and the same to bargain and sell to such person as they or either of them shall think fit to the uttermost profit of WILLIAM FITZHUGH ratifying and confirming whatsoever JAMES BUCHANAN or EDWARD ATHAWES or either of them shall do about the premises; In Witness whereof WILLIAM FITZHUGH and MARTHA his Wife have hereunto set their hands and seals this 28th day of August in the year of our Lord 1744

Sealed and delivered in the presence of
        GEO: LEE,   SAML: OLDHAM,   WILLIAM FITZHUGH
        CHS: BEALE   MARTHA FITZHUGH
    Westmd. Sct. At a Court held for the said County the 28th day of Augut 1744
WILLIAM FITZHUGH, Esqr., and MARTHA his Wife, (she being first privately examined
according to Law) personally acknowledged this Power of Attorney by them made to
JAMES BUCHANAN and EDWARD ATHAWES of the City of London, Merchants, to be their
proper act and deed which is ordered to be recorded
                    Teste   GEO: LEE, C.W.C.

pp.   (On margin: BUTLER's Lease to FITZHUGH
44-   THIS INDENTURE made the 1st day of August in the year of our Lord 1744, Be-
48   tween LAURENCE BUTLER of the Parish of Cople in County of Westmoreland in
        Colony and Dominion of Virginia of one part and WILLIAM FITZHUGH of the
same place, Esquire, of the other part; Witnesseth that LAURENCE BUTLER in consideration of the sum of Five shillings Sterling in hand paid by WILLIAM FITZHUGH, the receipt whereof is hereby acknowledged, hath and by these presents doth bargain and
sell unto WILLIAM FITZHUGH all that undivided moiety or equal half part of all the land
situate in the County of Suffolk in the Kingdom of Great Brittain which were devised by
the Last Will and Testament of MARTHA LEE, late of Mansel Street in Goodmans Fields in
the Parish of St. Matfellow alias White Chappel in County of Middlesex in the Kingdom
of Great Brittain, Widow, deced., to her two Daughter, MARTHA LEE (now Wife of said
WILLIAM FITZHUGH) party to these presents and LETTICE LEE their heirs as tenants in
common and not as joint tenants, together with all houses orchards profits and appurtenances to the same belonging; To have and to hold the moiety of land unto WILLIAM
FITZHUGH his heirs during the term of one whole year paying therefore the rent of
one Ear of Indian Corn on the Feast of St. Michael the Archangel if lawfully demanded,
to the intent that by virtue of these presents and of the Statute for transfering uses into
possession WILLIAM FITZHUGH may be in the actual possession of the premises and be
thereby enabled to take a release of the inheritance thereof to him and his heirs; In
Witness whereof the parties to these presents have interchangeably set their hands
and seals the day and year first above written
Sealed and Delivered in the presence of
        GEORGE LEE, SAMUEL OLDHAM,   LAURENCE BUTLER
        CHARLES BEALE

    (On margin: BUTLER's Release to FITZHUGH
    THIS INDENTURE made the 2nd day of August in the year of our Lord 1744, Between
LAURENCE BUTLER of Parish of Cople in County of Westmoreland, Gent., of one part and
WILLIAM FITZHUGH of the same Parish and County, Esqr., of other part; (the passing of
the land and the material in all the previous entries are repeated in this Release); in trust nevertheless and upon special confidence that the same should be reconveyed to WILLIAM
FITZHUGH and his heirs to the intent and purpose that WILLIAM FITZHUGH and his
heirs should and might stand and be seized of the premises of a perfect inheritance in
fee simple in the lands; NOW THIS INDENTURE WITNESSETH that in consideration of the
said Trust and the sum of fifteen hundred pounds Sterling money of Great Brittain to
LAURENCE BUTLER in hand paid by WILLIAM FITZHUGH, the receipt whereof LAURENCE
BUTLER doth hereby acknowledge, hath and by these presents doth bargain sell and
release unto WILLIAM FITZHUGH (in his actual possession now being by virtue of a
bargain and sale to him thereof made for one whole year and by force of the Statute for

transfering uses into possession) and to his heirs all the undivided moiety above
mentioned; To have and to hold the undivided moiety of land and all the premises with
appurtenances unto WILLIAM FITZHUGH and his heirs free and clear from all
incumbrances; And LAURENCE BUTLER and his heirs the premises unto WILLIAM
FITZHUGH his heirs shall warrant and forever defend by these presents; In Witness
whereof the parties to these presents have interchangeably set their hands and seals
the day and year first above written
Sealed and delivered in the presence of
       GEO: LEE, SAML: OLDHAM,   LAURENCE BUTLER
       CHS: BEALE
   Westmd. Sct. At a Court held for the said County the 28th day of August 1744
This Deed of Lease and Release for lands and tenements &c. in the County of Suffolk in
Great Britain from LAURENCE BUTLER, Gent., to WILLIAM FITZHUGH, Esquire, was
proved in open Court by the Oaths of all the witnesses thereto, which on motion of the
said FITZHUGH is admitted to Record
                  Teste GEO: LEE, C. W. C.

pp.   (On margin: BARNES to McCARTY's Exors.)
48-   THIS INDENTURE made the 28th day of August in the 18th year of the Reign of
50   our Sovereign Lord George the Second by the grace of God of Great Brittain
       France and Ireland, King, Defender of the faith &c., And in the year of our Lord
1744; Between ABRAHAM BARNES of County of ST. MARYS in Province of MARYLAND,
Gentleman, of one part and PRESLEY THORNTON, JOSEPH MORTON, AUGUSTINE
WASHINGTON, LAURENCE BUTLER, Gentleman, Exors. of the Last Will and Testament of
DANIEL McCARTY, late of County of Westmoreland, Gentleman, deceased, of other part;
Whereas THOMAS BARNES, late of County of Westmoreland, Gentleman, deceased, did in
his life time purchase of SNOWDALL HORTON and JOHN ATWOOD two hundred acres of
land more or less situate in the Parish of Washington in County of Westmoreland,
which premises were sold and conveyed by SNOWDALL HORTON and JOHN ATWOOD to
THOMAS BARNES by Indenture of Lease and Release bearing date the 8th & 9th day of
August in the year of our Lord 1725 as by the Indenture recorded in the County of
Westmoreland may more at large appear; And Whereas since the purchase made by
THOMAS BARNES a great part of the two hundred acres of Land has been taken away by
Elder Patents or otherwise so that there remains thereof only Seventy acres or thereabouts of which ABRAHAM BARNES, Eldest Son and heir of THOMAS BARNES, is seized
and possessed in fee, And whereas ABRAHAM BARNES did contract and agree for the
sale of the Seventy acres of land and premises unto DANIEL McCARTY in his life time
but before the same was conveyed DANIEL McCARTY departed this life leaving DANIEL
his only Son and heir having before his death made his Last Will and Testament in
writing and thereof appointed PRESLEY THORNTON, JOSEPH MORTON, AUGUSTINE
WASHINGTON and LAURENCE BUTLER his Exors: NOW THIS INDENTURE WITNESSETH that
in consideration of the sum of Fifty pounds current money to ABRAHAM BARNES in
hand paid by (the Exors.) the receipt whereof he doth hereby acknowledge, hath and by
these presents doth bargain sell and release unto (the Exors.) all that tract of land containing by estimation Seventy acres or thereabouts situate in Parish of Washington in
County of Westmoreland being the remaining part of the Two hundred acres of land
purchased by THOMAS BARNES of SNOWDALL HORTON and JOHN ATWOOD; And all houses
orchards profits and appurtenances to the same belonging; To have and to hold the
tract of land and premises with appurtenances unto (the Exors.) their heirs to the intent
and purposes (that is to the use of DANIEL McCARTY the only Son and heir of DANIEL

McCARTY and of his heirs) And ABRAHAM BARNES for himself his heirs doth covenant with (the Exors.) that he shall warrant and forever defend; In Witness whereof ABRAHAM BARNES to these presents hath set his hand and seal the day and year first above written

Sealed and delivered in the presence of
    GEO: LEE,   B. HARNETT,   A. BARNES, JUNR.
    CHARLES BEALE

    Received the 28th day of August 1744 of PRESLEY THORNTON, JOS: MORTON, AUGUSTINE WASHINGTON and LAURENCE BUTLER, fifty pounds current money it being the consideration mentioned to be by them paid to
Witness GEO: LEE,   B. HARNETT,   A. BARNES, JUNR.
    CHARLES BEALE

    Westmoreland Sct. At a Court held for the said County the 28th day of August 1744 This Deed of Bargain and Sale from ABRAHAM BARNES, JUNIOR, Gentleman, to PRESLEY THORNTON, JOSEPH MORTON, AUGUSTINE WASHINGTON and LAURENCE BUTLER, Gentlemen, Exors. of DANIEL McCARTY, Gent., deceased, together with receipt for consideration, were proved by the Oaths of all the witnesses thereto, which are ordered to be recorded   Teste GEO: LEE, C.W.C.

pp.   (On margin: AYLETT, WILLIAM's Will)
51-   IN THE NAME OF GOD, Amen. I WILLIAM AYLETT of Parish of Cople in County of
54   Westmoreland, Gent., being sick and weak of body but of perfect mind and
       memory (praised be God Almighty) do make this my Last Will and Testament in manner and form following, vizt., It is my will and desire that all those lands and slaves mentioned and expressed in the Deeds of Settlement made between my deced., Father, WILLIAM AYLETT, of the County of KING WILLIAM, and my first Wives Father, Colo. HENRY ASHTON, of the County of Westmoreland, also deceased, on my marriage with my said Wife be equally divided between my two Daughters, ELIZABETH and ANNE, the issue of my first marriage, except five hundred acres thereof sold to JOHN ALLEN of ESSEX County, and if my said two Daughters should die without issue of their body lawfully begotton, I give all the right and title I have may then claim or demand of in or to the same to the Children of my present Wife (to wit) ANNE and MARY, and their heirs and assigns forever.

    Item. It is my will and desire that my beloved Wife have and enjoy all the use and advantage of my land called VAUGHANS NECK which I lately purchased of DANIEL VAUGHAN, as also the land I lately purchased of THOMAS REDMAN, both adjoining to the land I now live on until my said two Daughters of my first marriage shall attain the age of twenty one years and then upon their or their Husbands paying to my Wife and my two Children by her the sum of Two hundred pounds current money, my will is that the said two pieces of land together with the Water Mill thereon lately built be equally divided between my said two Daughters and in case either of them or their proper representative should refuse to pay the moiety of the said two hundred, then my will is that the other shall have the whole on payment of the whole sum of Two hundred pounds as aforesaid; And in case they both shall refuse to accept of the said lands aforesaid on the terms also aforesaid, it is then my will that they shall be sold to the highest bidder at public sale and the money arising therefrom to be equally divided among my Wife and her two Children;

    Item. I give to my dear Wife, ELIZABETH, all my land and appurtenances lately purchased of THOMAS OWSLEY on ACCOTINCK in the County of FAIRFAX adjoining to the land given her by her deceased Father for and during her natural life, and after her decease, I give the same to my two Daughters, ANNE and MARY (her Children) equally between them and to their heirs forever;

Item. It is my will and desire that all my other lands in the Counties of PRINCE WILLIAM and FAIRFAX be equally divided between my said younger Daughters, ANNE and MARY, (reserving always to my Wife her Thirds in the same during her natural life), and all such lands and Negroes as I am heir to from my Brother, JOHN AYLETT, deceased, and his Children, also deceased, to the heirs of my said Daughters lawfully begotton (nevertheless still reserving to my Wife her Thirds during life therein) and if they my said Daughters shall both die without issue lawfully begotton of their bodies, I give the use of the whole unto my Wife during her natural life and after her decease, I give the same and bequeath the said land and premises unto ELIZABETH and ANNE my Daughters by my first Wife and the heirs of their bodies lawfully begotton and for want of such to my Brother, PHILIP AYLETT, and his heirs forever;

Item. My will and desire is that all the slaves given to my present Wife by her Father and all the slaves I claim under my Brother, BENJAMIN AYLETT, deceased, together with all the slaves not mentioned in the Deed of Settlement on my first marriage made between my Father and Colo. HENRY ASHTON be to and for the use of my dear Wife during her widowhood and for the support of her two Children already born, And upon her marriage (should that happen) I then desire my Executors hereafter named may divide the said Negroes into equal parts among my Wife and her two Children and at the decease of my Wife, I desire that all such Negroes as she shall possess may descend to my two younger Daughters, ANNE and MARY and their heirs of their bodies lawfully begotton, But in case my said two younger Daughters should die without such issue, I then give to my Wife the use of all the Negroes I had or may have by her unto her together with the land I bought of THOMAS OWSLEY for her life and to pass to and descend unto the Child or Children of her body lawfully begotton hereafter, and if she should die without any further issue, I give the land and slaves so annexed to my Daughters, ELIZABETH and ANNE by first marriage and the heirs of their bodies lawfully begotton; But in case they die without such issue, then my will is that the same descend unto my Brother, PHILIP, and his heirs forever; And it is my will and desire that if my Daughters ANNE and MARY, by the last (? Qeater) should both die without issue of their bodies lawfully begotton and there should be no further issue between my Wife and I, then and in that case I give all my slaves (not before given to my present Wife) and all my other land in FAIRFAX County (except the land annexed to my Wife slaves aforesaid) to my Daughters, ELIZABETH and ANNE, the first (? Qenter) and their issue lawfully begotton and for want of such I give the land and slaves so annexed to my Brother, PHILIP AYLETT, and his heirs forever, reserving always to my Wife her Thirds in the said Negroes and Land. I give unto my two Daughters, ELIZABETH and ANNE, my first Wifes twenty five head of neat Cattle each to be paid them respectively on the Plantation in ESSEX and reserving in lieu of what Cattle they may claim by settlement and to each of them I give also a Riding Horse.

Item. It is my will and desire that if my Wife should prove with Child hereafter that such Child have an equal dividend of all my Estate real and personal and to descend from heir to heir as the other bequests in this Will;

Item. It is my will that after my just debts are paid, all my Estate of nature or sort soever not before bequeathed shall be equally divided between my two younger Daughters and my dear Wife whom I appoint my sole Executrix of this my Last Will and Testament for and during the term and time of her continuance my Widow, And in case she shall die before my two youngest Children now born or such as hereafter may be born shall arive to the age of twenty one or be married, or in case she my said Wife shall

marry again, then or in either case, it is my desire that my good Friends, Major LAU-
RENCE WASHINGTON, my Son in Law, AUGUSTINE WASHINGTON, my Brother PHILIP
AYLETT and DANIEL McCARTY, Gentlemen take on them the Executorship of this my Last
Will and take my Childrens Estate out of the hands of my said Wife and her Husband if so
it should happen and they think fit so to do, and I do hereby revoke all former Wills by
me made and declare this to be my last; In Witness whereof I have hereunto set my
hand and seal this 29th day of March Anno Dom. 1744
Signed Sealed and published in the presence of
      WILLOUGHBY NEWTON,   WILLIAM AYLETT
      NICHOS: FLOOD, PETER RUST
    Westmd. Sct. At a Court held for the said County the 28th day of August 1744
This Last Will and Testament of WILLIAM AYLETT, Gentleman, deceased, was presented
into Court by ELIZABETH, his Relict and Executrix in the said Will named; who made
Oath thereto and being proved by the Oaths of WILLOUGHBY NEWTON, Gent., and PETER
RUST, two of the witnesses thereto, is admitted to Record; And upon the motion of the
said Exrx. and her performing what is usual in such cases, Certificate is granted her for
obtaining a Probate thereof in due form
            Teste   GEO: LEE, C. W. C.

pp.   (On margin: FOOTMAN, ELIZABETH's Will)
54-   IN THE NAME OF GOD Amen, I ELIZABETH FOOTMAN of Parish of Copley and
55   County of Westmoreland being very sick and weake of body but of perfect mind
       and disposing memory, thanks be given unto God for the same, do constitute
make and ordain this writing to be my Last Will and Testament, revoking all other former Wills by me made either verbal or written and do ordain this to be my Last Will and
no other; And first of all I bequeath my Soul into the hands of God that gave it with a
Christian hope of Salvation thro: the merrits of Christ Jesus my Saviour, and I will that
my body be decently interred at the discretion of my Executors hereafter named; And as
touching such worldly Estate as it hath pleased God to bless and endow me with in this
life, I give devise and dispose of after the following manner. I will that all my just and
lawfull debts be paid.
    Item. I give and bequeath unto my Daughter, FRANCES YOUELL, all my Cloths and
wearing apparel of every kind andnature also my riding horse and saddle, also my
Great Looking Glass, and my Desk that stands in the Hall and it is my will and desire that
neither the Cloaths, Horse, Saddle, Glass nor Desk shall be appraised, but delivered to my
Daughter without.
    Item. I give and bequeath unto my Grandaughter, ELIZABETH YOUELL, my Negro man
named Prince that was given to me by the Last Will and Testament of my Husband, JOHN
FOOTMAN, deceased, and it is my will and desire that my Son in Law, BATTERAW YOUELL,
should have the use of the said Negroe and be accountable unto the aforesaid ELIZA-
BETH YOUELL for the worth of him when she either marries or comes of age;
    Item. I give and bequeath unto my Grandaughter, ELIZABETH YOUELL, one of my Gold
Rings and my Gold boles and Silver tumbler and two Silver spoons and the feather bed
and furniture that I lie in myself;
    Item. I give and bequeath unto WILLIAM RICE, SENIOR, three barrells of Indian Corn.
It is my will and desire that the remainder of my Estate be equally divided amongst my
three Children.
    Lastly, I nominate ordain and appoint my two Sons, WINDOR KENNER, RICHARD KEN-
NER and my Son in Law, BATTRAW YOUELL, whole and sole Exors. of this my Last Will
and Testament; In Witness whereof I have hereunto set my hand and seal this 10th day
of May 1744

Teste   THOMAS REDDALL,   WM. RICE,   ELIZABETH FOOTMAN
        WILLIAM RICE
   Westmd. Sct. At a Court held for the said County the 28th day of August 1744
This Last Will and Testament of ELIZABETH FOOTMAN, deceased, was presented into Court
by her Sons, WINDOR and RICHARD KENNER and her Son in Law, BATTERAW YOUELL,
her Executors, who made Oath thereto and being proved by the Oaths of THOMAS
REDDALL and WILLIAM RICE, two of the witnesses thereto, is admitted to Record; And
upon the motion of the said Executors and their performing what is usual in such cases,
Certificate is granted them for obtaining a Probate thereof in due form
               Teste GEO: LEE, C. W. C.

pp.   (On margin: SMITHs to FEAGINS)
55-   THIS INDENTURE made the 21st day of July in the year of our Lord 1744 Between
57   GEORGE SMITH of County of PRINCE FREDERICK of one part and WILLIAM FEGIN
         of Cople Parish in County of Westmoreland of other part; Witnesseth that
GEORGE SMITH in consideration of the sum of Three thousand pounds of Crop Tobacco and
Five shillings current money to him in hand paid by WILLIAM FEAGINS, the receipt
whereof GEORGE SMITH doth hereby acknowledge, hath and by these presents doth bargain and sell unto WILLIAM FEAGINS his heirs all that parcel of Land containing Fifty
one acres situate in Parish of Cople and County of Westmd., being a parcel of land conveyed to GEORGE SMITH by one JOHN HALL and RUTH his Wife (by Deed bearing date the
19th day of June Anno Dom: 1720), and bounded; Beginning at a marked Spanish Oak
standing by the side of the COACH ROAD near to a Spring commonly known by the name
of HALLS SPRING), on the South side of a Run and extending thence down the Run S.
89d. E. 24 pole, N. 67d. E. 16 poles to a red Oak by a Gully, thence N. 43d. E. 60 poles to another red Oak, then N. 8, W. 99 poles to a red Oak saplin on a Hill, thence S. W. 36 poles to
an Oak, thence continued the said Course farther along the land of ROBERT MIDDLETON
32 poles to a red Oak by said MIDDLETONs Tobacco Ground; corner to his land; thence
along another of said MIDDLETONs lines S. 35d. W. 27 poles to a marked white Oak, thence
along another of his lines N. 24d. W. 31 poles wanting ten links to a white Oak by the
aforesaid Road side corner to said MIDDLETONs Land, thence along the Road S. 2d. W. 15
poles, S. 15d. E. 24 poles, S. 12d. E. 16 poles, the place where it began; Together with all
houses orchards priviledges and appurtenances to the same belonging; To have and to
hold the land and other the premises unto WILLIAM FEAGINS his heirs; said WILLIAM
FEAGINS his heirs forever against GEORGE SMITH his heirs shall warrant and forever
defend by these presents; In Witness whereof GEORGE SMITH hath to this Indenture of
bargain and sale set his hand and fixed his seal the day and year firt above written
Signed Sealed and delivered in the presence of us
         WILLIAM HEADLEY,   JOHN MIDDLETON,   GEORGE SMITH
         WM: HARTLY,   GEO: FEAGINS
   Memo; That on the 31st day of July in the year of our Lord 1744 that peaceable and
quiet possession and seizen of the lands and tenements within mentioned to be granted
was had and received by the delivery of Turff and Twigg in the name of the whole by
the said GEORGE SMITH and by the delivery of the Ring of the Door of the Cheif Mansion
House unto WM: FEAGINS in presence of us
Teste   WILLIAM HEADLEY,   JOHN MIDDLETON,
        GEORGE FEAGINS,   WM. HARTLY

   (On margin: SMITH's Bond to FEAGINS)
   KNOW ALL MEN by these presents that I GEORGE SMITH of PRINCE FREDERICK County

do owe and justly stand indebted unto WILLIAM FEAGINS of Cople Parish in County of Westmoreland his heirs the full and just quantity of Six thousand pounds of Crop Tobacco and Ten shillings current money for payment whereof truly to be made I bind myself my heirs firmly by these presents; Sealed with my Seal and dated the 31st day of July Anno Dom: 1744

THE CONDITION of the above obligation is such that if the above bound GEORGE SMITH his heirs shall perform and keep all the Covenants which on his or their part ought to be performed and kept comprised in one Indenture of bargain and sale made between WILLIAM FEAGINS and GEORGE SMITH according to the true meaning of the same Indenture, That then this obligation to be void and of none effect, otherways to stand and remain in full force power and virtue

Signed Sealed and delivered in presence of

WM: HEADLEY,   JOHN MIDDLETON,   GEORGE SMITH
GEO: FEAGINS,   WM. HARTLY

Westmd. Sct. At a Court held for the said County the 28th day of August 1744 This Deed of Feoffment for lands from GEORGE SMITH to WILLIAM FEAGINS together with Livery of Seizen, together with a Bond for the performance of Covenants, were proved in open Court by the Oaths of the witnesses thereto, (except WILLIAM HARTLY) which on motion of the said FEAGINS are admitted to Record

Teste   GEO: LEE, C. W. C.

pp.   (On margin: DEMOVEL, HANNAH's Will
57-   IN THE NAME OF GOD Amen, this 8th day of September 1744; I HANNAH DEMOVEL
59   of Cople Parish in County of Westmoreland being sick and weak of body but of
        perfect mind and memory, thanks be given to God therefore, calling to mind the mortality of my body and knowing that it is appointed for all persons once to die, doe make this my Last Will and Testament in manner and form following, (that is to say), First and principally I give my Soul to God who gave it me and my body to be buried at the discretion of my Executors hereafter named hopeing through the merits of my blessed Saviour to receive it again at the day of my resurrection by the mighty power of God, And as for what worldly Estate it hath pleased God to bless me with, I give and bequeath as followeth;

Imprimis. I give and bequeath to PETER LAMKIN, Son of GEORGE LAMKIN, deceased, one Shilling Sterling money of England.

Item. I give and bequeath to my Grandaughter, HANNAH DEMOVELL, one feather bed bedstead and furniture and one Crumple'd horn Cow and Calf and one box iron and heaters and one woolen wheel and two boxes and a full third part of what is in them;

Item. I give and bequeath to my Grandaughter, MARY MIDDLETON, one young heifer.

Item. I give and bequeath to my Grandaughter, HANNAH ARMSTEAD, one iron spitt and two pewter and nine pewter plates and one Tankard and one Bason and all my Spoons and one Salt Sellar and one Mustard Pott, and all my Earthen Ware and my Great Chest which hath a whole led and all that is in it and one four gallon iron pott and pot hooks and one Grinding Stone and one feather bed and furniture and two bedsteads and one linnen wheel and one pair of fire tongs, and one fifty gallon cask and runlett

Item. I give and bequeath to SARAH ARMSTEAD, Daughter of JOHN ARMSTEAD and HANNAH his Wife, one pide Cow;

Item. I give and bequeath unto my Grandaughter, JANE MORE, one Chest, one pewter dish and one plate;

Item. I give and bequeath to my Grandaughter, HANNAH HARTLEY, one pewter dish and two pewter plates and one two gallon and a half iron pott.

Item. I give and bequeath to my Grandson, JAMES LAMKIN, one pewter dish & three pewter plates;

Item. I give and bequeath to my Grandson, SAMUEL LAMKIN, one Chest and one Flagon and one plate and one nine gallon iron pott;

Item. I give and bequeath to my Grandaughter, HANNAH BROWN, one Trunk, one pewter plate and one looking glass and one fifteen gallon iron pott;

Item. I give and bequeath to my Grandaughter, MAGDELEN JACKSON, one Negroe man named Tone.

Item. I give and bequeath unto my Daughter, ELIZABETH MIDDLETON, one Negroe woman named Pegg;

Item. I give and bequeath to my Grandaughter, MAGDALEN CLAUGHTON, one gallon a half iron pott;

Item. I give and bequeath to my Son in Law, BENJAMIN MIDDLETON, seven head of Cttle and eight head of hogs and ten pounds current money to be raised out of my Estate after my debts and legacies before bequeathed is paid.

Item. I give and bequeath to JOHN ARMSTEAD, seven head of Cattle and eight head of hogs and ten pounds current money to be raised out of the residue of my Estate after my debts and aforementioned legacies is paid.

Item. I also constitute and appoint BENJAMIN MIDDLETON and JOHN ARMSTEAD whole and sole Executors of this my Last Will and Testament to see the same fulfilled and performed. I hereby revoking and disannulling all former Wills by me made or devised and confirming ratifying and allowing this and no other to be my Last Will and Testament; In Witness whereof I have hereunto set my hand and fixed my seal the day and year above written

Signed Sealed published declared & pronounced by the
said HANNAH DEMOVEL to be her Last Will and Testament
in presence of us   WILLO: HARRISON,   HANNAH her mark 🙢 DEMOVEL
                WM: HARTLEY,
                BENNEDICK his mark β SHORT

Westmd. Sct. At a Court held for the said County the 25th day of Septr. 1744
This Last Will and Testament of HANNAH DEMOVIL, deceased, was presented into Court by BENJAMIN MIDDLETON and JOHN ARMSTEAD, her Exors. in the said Will named, who made Oath thereto, and being proved by the Oaths of the witnesses thereto is admitted to Record; And upon the motion of the said Exors. and their performing what is ususal in such cases, Certificate is granted them for obtaining a Probate thereof in due form
                Teste GEO: LEE, C. W. C.

pp.   (On margin: McCAVE, JOHN's Will)
59-   IN THE NAME OF GOD Amen. I JOHN McCAVE of Westmd. County do make this my
60   Last Will and Testament in manner and form following;
        Imprimis. I give and bequeath to my Loving Wife, DORCAS McCAVE, one half of my Estate during her natural life and after her decease I give and bequeath the half of my Estate before given to my Wife to my Son, SAMUEL McCAVE, and his heirs;

Item. I give and bequeath the other half of my Estate to my Son, SAMUEL McCAVE, and his heirs forever;

Item. Provided my Son, SAMUEL McCAVE should depart this life before he arrive to the age of twenty one years or marry, that then the half of my Estate given to my Son fall to my Loving Wife and her heirs forever;

Item. I nominate my Loving Wife, DORCAS, McCAVE, and my Friend, PETER RUST, my whole and sole Exors., of this my Last Will and Testament; In Witness whereof I have hereunto set my hand and seal the 2nd day of November 1743

Signed Sealed and delivered in the presence of us
  SAMUEL ESKRIDGE,   JOHN McCAVE
  FRANCIS his mark   SELF
  Westmd. Sct. At a Court held for the said County the 30th day of Octr. 1744
This Last Will and Testament of JOHN McCAVE, deceased, was presented into Court by
DORCAS, his Relict, and PETER RUST his Exors, who made Oath thereto, and being proved
by the Oaths of the witnesses thereto is admitted to Record; And upon the motion of the
said Exors. and their performing what is usual in such cases, Certificate is granted them
for obtaining a Probate thereof in due form
    Teste GEO: LEE, C. W. C.

pp. (On margin: JARVIS, JOHN's Will)
60- IN THE NAME OF GOD, Amen. I JOHN JARVIS of County of Westmoreland being
61 very sick and weak in body but of perfect mind memory and understanding,
    thanks be to God for the same; and calling to mind the uncertainty of this life
and knowing that it is appointed for all men once to die, do make and ordain this my
Last Will and Testament; And as touching what worldly Estate it hath pleased Almighty
God of his great goodness to bestow upon me, I will and dispose of in the following
manner and form; But first of all I bequeath my Soul into the hands of Almighty God
which gave it and my body to be buried at the discretion of my Exor. hereafter mentioned.
  I will that my Loving Wife have and enjoy this Plantation whereon I now live during
her life and after her decease to my Son, JOHN JARVIS, and to the heirs of his body lawfully begotton, And in default of such issue, to my Son, FIELD JARVIS, and in default of
such issue, to my three Daughters, ELLENOR, CATHARINE and JANE;
  I will and bequeath unto my Loving Wife the bed she lies on and the pott and spin-
ning wheels. I will that my Daughter, JANE, shall have my best bed which lies upstairs
and a red Cow that hath had a Calf and her increase and a small pot of a gallon and a
half. I will that my Son, JOHN JARVIS, have my Buekanner Gun and a Cow as soon as he
goes to housekeeping. I will that my Son, FIELD JARVIS, shall have the parcel of land I
bought of MURRICE VEALE and to his heirs and in default of such issue to my three
Daughters, ELLENOR, CATHARINE and JANE. I will that the legacy of a bed and pot and
spining wheels I gave to my loving Wife be void and instead of that she shall have and
enjoy all my Estate both within doors and without doors during her life, and then my
Estate to be divided between my two Sons. It is likewise my will and desire and I do
hereby appoint my Loving Wife whole and sole Executrix of this my Last Will and Testa-
ment to see this Will performed. In Witness whereof I have hereunto set my hand and
seal this 7th day of March 1743/4.
Assigned Sealed and published in presence of us
  JOS: BUTLER,   JOHN JARVIS
  NATHL: BUTLER
  Westmd. Sct. At a Court held for the said County the 30th day of October 1744
This Last Will and Testament of JOHN JARVIS, deceased, was presented into Court by his
Relict and Executrix who made Oath thereto and being proved by the Oaths of the wit-
nesses thereto is admitted to Record; And upon the motion of the said Exrx. and her per-
forming what is usual in such cases, Certificate is granted her for obtaining a Probate
thereof in due form   Teste GEO: LEE, C. W. C.

pp. (On margin: MOXLEY, WILLIAM SENR.s Will)
61- IN THE NAME OF GOD Amen. I WILLIAM MOXLEY, SENR. of Westmoreland County
63 in the Parish of Cople being very weak and sickly of body but of perfect sence

and sound memory thanks be to Almighty God for it, and calling to mind the uncertainty of this transitory life and knowing that it is but short and having made several Wills in former times, not being satisfied with the same, doth came me to revoke and lay aside all former Wills and Testament, this only to stand effectual and now this to be my last in manner and form following, vizt., Imprimis. I commit my Soul into the hands of my beloved Saviour and Redeemer Jesus Christ hoping through his merits to obtain everlasting life and salvation and my body to the Ground from whence it was taken to be decently buried according to the direction of the Overseers of this my last Will hereafter named and of what Estate both real and personal God hath blessed me with, I do dispose of as followeth, vizt.

Item. It is my desire that all my lout debts and funeral charges should first be paid of and discharged.

Item. I give and bequeath to my Son, DANIEL MOXLEY, and MARY MOXLEY his Wife, the Plantation whereon I now live and all the profits thereunto belonging during their natural lives and after their decease unto the male heir lawfully begotton of their bodies; But for want of such heirs, my will and desire is that my Grandson, RICHARD MOXLEY, Son of my Son, RICHARD MOXLEY, shall have the above Land and his heirs lawfully begotton forever; And furthermore if it should happen that MARY MOXLEY should live longer than her Husband, DANIEL MOXLEY, and after his decease should marry again, then my desire is that she shall have only one third part of the aforesaid Land and Plantation during her natural life

Item. And all the rest of my lands that is in dispute or that I have any right unto, I do give and bequeath unto my Son, RICHARD MOXLEY, and his heirs forever;

Item. I give and bequeath unto my Grandson, WILLIAM PAYTOR,. my little bay Stallion to him my said Grandson and his heirs forever;

Item. I give and bequeath unto my Son, JOHN MOXLEY, my high bedstead bed and all the furniture that is thereunto belonging to him my said Son, JOHN, and his heirs forever;

Item. I give and bequeath unto my Housekeeper, MARY KILMISTER, my trundle bedstead bed and all the furniture thereunto belonging to her and her heirs forever;

Item. I give and bequeath unto my Son, RICHARD MOXLEY, one Cow yearling and her future increase to him and his heirs forever;

Item. My will and desire is that my Grandson, WILLIAM PAYTOR, may have the Plantation to finish his Crop without any interruption and to reap the benefit of the same after it is finished; as also it is my will and desire that after my decease the said WILLIAM PAYTOR may be his own man clear of all service whatsoever this being a discharge for the same;

Item. It is my will and desire that MARY KILMISTER shall have the benefit of the Plantation two full years after my decease, that is to say, as much ground as she and RICHARD HARRARD can make use of;

Item. I give and bequeath unto my Son, SAMUEL MOXLEY, my pair of Stillards to him my Son SAMUEL and hisheirs forever; they being his full share of my Estate;

Item. I give and bequeath unto my Son, WILLIAM MOXLEY, Ten shillings current money to be paid unto him by my Son, DANIEL MOXLEY, after this my Will proved, also it being his full prt of my Estate;

Item. I give and bequeath unto my Son, THOMAS MOXLEY, Ten shillings current money to be paid unto him by my Son, DANIEL MOXLEY, after my Will proved upon proviso that he the said THOMAS MOXLEY, comes and settles his Account with me before my decease, otherwise he is to have nothing paid him at all;

Item. All the rest of my Estate herein not given or otherways bequeathed, I do give and bequeath it all in general of what kind soever unto my Son, DANIEL MOXLEY, and his heirs forever;

Item. Last of all, I do appoint my youngest Son, DANIEL MOXLEY, whole and sole Exor. and Exrx. of this my Last Will and Testament; In Confirmation whereof I have hereunto set my hand and seal this 8th day of May 1744

Signed Sealed and delivered in the presence of us

    AUGUSTINE SANFORD,   WM: MOXLEY
    OWEN his mark + DOWNEY

Westmd. Sct. At a Court held for the said County the 30th day of Octr. 1744

This Last Will and Testament of WILLIAM MOXLEY, deceased, was presented into Court by DANIEL MOXLEY, his Executor, who made Oath thereto and being proved by the Oaths of the witnesses thereto is admitted to Record; And upon motion of the said Executor and his performing what is usual in such cases, Certificate is granted him for obtaining a Probate thereof in due form

                Teste GEO: LEE, C. W. C.

pp.   (On margin: VIVION & Wife to BAILEY)

63-   THIS INDENTURE made the 21st day of September in the 18th year of the Reign

67   of our Sovereign Lord George the Second by the grace of God of Great Brittain
      France and Ireland, King, Defender of the faith &c., And in the year of our Lord
Christ 1744; Between THOMAS VIVION of the Parish of Hanover in County of KING GEORGE and MARY his Wife of one part and WILLIAM BAILEY of Parish of Lunenburg in County of RICHMOND of other part; Witnesseth that THOMAS VIVION and MARY his Wife in consideration of the sum of Sixty five pounds current money of Virginia to them in hand paid by WILLIAM BAILEY, the receipt whereof THOMAS VIVION and MARY his Wife do acquit WILLIAM BAILEY his heirs, have and by these presents do bargain and sell unto WILLIAM BAILEY his heirs all that parcel of Land containing Two hundred and Seventy eight acres of Land situate in the Branches of NOMONY RIVER in Parish of Cople in County of Westmoreland being pqrt of a Pattent of Eighteen hundred and two acres of Land granted WILLIAM PEIRCE bearing date the 22nd day of March 1665, which Pattent by several conveyances became the right of NICHOLAS SPENCER, Esqr., deceased, and by the Last Will and Testament NICHOLAS SPENCER, Esqr., did give and devise to JOHN SPENCER, his Son, and by JOHN SPENCER sold and conveyed by Deeds bearing dte the 25th day of September 1706 unto JAMES BURN, and by JAMES BURN given and devised to his Sons, JAMES BURN and WILLIAM BURN, and by JAMES BURN and WILLIAMBURN conveyed by Deeds bearing date the 21st day of May 1732 to ISRAEL HILLINGWORTH and by the said HILLINGWORTH conveyed by Deed bearing date the 11th day of May 1733 to THOMAS VIVION, now party to these presents, together with all houses orchards profits and appurtenances to the same belonging; and the rents issues and profits thereof, the Two hundred and Seventy eight acres of land situate on the Branches of NOMONY RIVER and bounded; Beginning at the mouth of a Beaver Dam Swamp by a line of marked trees, S. 5d. W. 450 poles to a marked pohiccory which line divides this land from another part of the aforesaid now in possession of Mr. JOHN SPENCE, formerly belonging to JOHN BUSHROD, Gent., deceased, thence N. 85d. W. 20 poles, thence W. S. W. 95 poles to a marked white Oak standing near the Road that leads to NOMONY FERRY on the North side of said Road, being a corner tree of the Land of Mr. WILLIAM FRYOR, thence N. 5d. E. by a line of marked trees 420 poles to a red Oak, thence down the several meanders of the Branch to the mouth thereof to the aforesaid Great Beaver Dam, thence down the meanders of the Swamp to the first station; And all right

title and demand of THOMAS VIVION and MARY his Wife in the premises; To have and to hold the Two hundred and seventy eight acres of land and premises and appurtenances unto WILLIAM BAILEY his heirs; freely and clearly acquitted saved harmless and ketp indemnified from all incumbrances whatsoever; the quit rents from time to time due to the Lord or Lords of the fee only excepted; And THOMAS VIVION nd MARY his Wife their heirs the premises with the appurtenances to WILLIAM BAILEY his heirs against the claim or demand of every person shall warrant and forever defend by these presents; In Witness whereof THOMAS VIVION and MARY his Wife have to these presents inter-changeably set their hands and seals the day and date within written
Signed Sealed and delivered in the presence of
      THOS: TEMPLEMAN,   WHARTON RANSDELL,   THOMAS VIVION
      RICHD: DOZER,   JOHN TEMPLEMAN
    Memorandum; That on the 21st day of September Anno Dom: 1744 actual and peace-able possession and sizen of the land and appurtenances within mentioned was given and delivered by THOMAS VIVION unto WILLIAM BAILEY by the delivery of Turff and Twigg unto him on the said Land; To have and to hold unto WILLIAM BAILEY his heirs according to the form and effect of the within written; In the presence of
Teste   THOS: TEMPLEMAN,   WHARTON RANSDELL
      RICHD. DOZIER,   JOHN TEMPLEMAN
    Westmd. Sct. At a Court held for the said County the 30th day of Octr. 1744
This Deed of Feoffment for Lands from THOMAS VIVION to WILLIAM BAILEY together with the livery of seizen were proved in open Court by the Oaths of the witnesses there-to, which on motion of the said BAILEY are admitted to Record
                Teste GEO: LEE, C. W. C.

(On margin: VIVION's Bond to BAILEY)
KNOW ALL MEN by these presents that I THOMAS VIVION of Parish of Hanover in County of KING GEORGE, Gent., am held and firmly bound unto WILLIAM BAILEY of Parish of Lunenburg in County of RICHMOND, Planter, in the sum of One hundred and forty four pounds current money of Virginia, to the true and just payment whereof I bind myself my heirs firmly by these presents; Sealed with my Seal and dated this 21st day of September in the 18th year of the Reign of our Sovereign Lord George the Second by the grace of God of Great Brittain France and Ireland, King Defender of the faith &c., Anno Domini 1744
    THE CONDITION of the above obligation is such tht if the above bound THOMAS VIVION his heirs shall perform and keep all Covenants which on his or their part ought to be performed and kept mentioned in a certain Deed of Feoffment made between THOMAS VIVION and WILLIAM BAILEY in all things according to the true meaning of the said Deed; Then the above obligation to be void & of none effect, otherwise to stand & remain in full force power and virtue
Sealed and delivered in the presence of
      RICHARD DOZER,   JOHN TEMPLEMAN,   THOMAS VIVION
      WHARTON RANSDELL,   THOS: TEMPLEMAN
    Westmd. Sct. At a Court held for the said County the 30th day of October 1744
This Bond for performance of Covenants from THOMAS VIVION to WILLIAM BAILEY was proved in open Court by the Oaths of the witnesses thereto, which on motion of the said BAILEY is admitted to Record   Teste GEO: LEE, C. W. C.

pp.   (On margin: ESKRIDGE's Lease to VAULX)
67-   THIS INDENTURE made the 19th day October in the year of our Lord God 1744,
71   Between ELIZABETH ESKRIDGE of Cople Parish in Westmoreland County of one
         part and ROBERT VAULX of Washington Parish in Westmoreland County of other
part; Witnesseth that ELIZABETH ESKRIDGE in cnsideration of the sum of Five shillings
Sterling to her in hand paid by ROBERT VAULX, the receipt whereof is hereby acknowledged, hath and by these presents doth bargain and sell unto ROBERT VAULX all that
parcel of land lying in Parish of Washington in Westmoreland County containing Five
hundred acres be the same more or less which was devised unto ELIZABETH ESKRIDGE
(among other things) by ROBERT VAULX, deceased, Father of the said ELIZABETH ESK-
RIDGE by his Last Will and Testament bearing date the 20th day of March 1684/5; it
being part of a tract of one thousand acres and binding upon the Land of EDWARD MUSE
and the Land of the Honourable THOMAS LEE, Esqr., and the Land now in possession of
said ROBERT VAULX, party to these presents; and all Plantations, houses, orchards profits and appurtenances to the same belonging; To have and to hold unto ROBERT VAULX
his heirs during the term of one whole year paying therefor one Pepper Corn upon the
Feast of Saint Michael the Archangel if demanded to the intent that by virtue of these
presents and of the Statute for transferring uses into possession ROBERT VAULX may be
in the actual possession of the premises and thereby be enabled to take a release of the
inheritance thereof to him and his heirs; In Witness whereof, the said parties to these
presents have hereunto interchangeably set their hands and seals the day and year
above written
Sealed and delivered in the presence of us
         WILLO: NEWTON, GEO: BLAIR,   ELIZABETH her mark ⌇ ESKRIDGE
         ABIGAL+ ESKRIDGE, NATHL: GRAY

         (On margin: ESKRIDGE's Release to VAULX)
     THIS INDENTURE made this 20th day of October in the year of our Lord 1744; Between
ELIZABETH ESKRIDGE of Cople Parish in County of Westmoreland, Widow, of one part and
ROBERT VAULX of Washington parish in aforesaid County, Gent., of other part; Whereas
ROBERT VAULX, deceased, Father of ELIZABETH ESKRIDGE, by his Last Will and Testament
bearing date the 20th day of March 1684/5 (among other things) did give and devise
unto ELIZABETH ESKRIDGE Five hundred acres of his Forrest Land, it being part of a
tract of One thousand acres and binding upon the Land of EDWARD MUSE and the Land
of the Honourable THOMAS LEE, Esqr., and the Land now in the possession of ROBERT
VAULX, party to these presents; NOW THIS INDENTURE WITNESSETH that ELIZABETH
ESKRIDGE in cnsideration of the sum of Ninty pounds current money of Virginia in
hand paid by ROBERT VAULX, the receipt whereof she doth hereby acknowledge, hath
and by these presents doth bargain and sell unto ROBERT VAULX (in his actual possession now being by virtue of a bargain and sale to him thereof made for one whole year
and by force of the Statute for transfering uses into possession), and to his heirs all
that parcel of land containing Five hundred acres (be the same more or less) situate in
Parish of Washington in County of Westmoreland, To have and to hold the premises
with appurtenances unto ROBERT VAULX his heirs And ELIZABETH ESKRIDGE doth pro-
mise ROBERT VAULX his heirs that freed and discharged or otherwise well and suffi-
ciently saved and kept harmless from all incumbrances, the quit rents due and to become due for the premises only excepted; In Witness whereof the parties to these presents have hereunto interchangeably set their hands and seals the day and year above
written

Sealed and deliverred in the presence of us
  WILLO: NEWTON, GEORGE BLAIR,   ELIZABETH her mark   ESKRIDGE
  ABIGAL ESKRIDGE, NATHL: GRAY
  Received of ROBERT VAULX the within mentioned sum of Ninety pounds current
money of Virginia being the consideration mentioned in the within Deed to be paid by
him to me on the perfection thereof; Witness my hand this 26th day of October 1744
Witnesses WILLO: NEWTON, GEO: BLAIR   ELIZABETH her mark ESKRIDGE
  ABIGAL ESKRIDGE, NATHL: GRAY
  Westmd. County Sct. At a Court held for the said County the 30th day of Octr. 1744
This Deed of Lease and Release form ELIZABETH ESKRIDGE, Widow, to ROBERT VAULX,
Gentleman, together with a receipt for the consideration endorsed were proved in open
Court by the Oaths of all the witnesses thereto (except ABIGAL ESKRIDGE) all which are
ordered to be recorded   Teste GEO: LEE, C. W. C.

p. (On margin: CHILTON's Relinqmt. to MONROE)
71 Westmd. Sct. George the Second by the grace of God of Great Brittain France
  and Ireland, King, Defender of the faith &c. to JOHN ELLIOTT, JOHN WATTS, JOHN
MARTIN and JAMES BANKHEAD of County aforesaid, Gentlemen, Greeting; We do hereby
authorise and impower you or any two or more of you at such time and place as you
shall appoint (sometime before the next Court to be held for the County aforesaid) to
take the privy examination of ANNE CHILTON, Wife of JOHN CHILTON of said County apart
from her Husband touching her willingness and unconstrained consent and assent to
the selling and conveying by Deed of Sale her right of Dower to a certain parcel of
Land situate in Parish of Washington and County aforesaid containing One hundred and
fifty acres unto ANDREW MONROE (the Commission for the privy examination of ANNE, the Wife
of JOHN CHILTON); herein you are not to fail; Witness GEORGE LEE Clerk of the said Court
the first day of December in the 18th year of our Reign
         GEO: LEE, C. C. W.
  Westmd. Sct. By virtue of the within Dedimus to us directed we have privately examined ANNE CHILTON, Wife of JOHN CHILTON, apart from her Husband (the return of the
execution of the privy examination of ANNE CHILTON); Given under our hands this 8th day of
November 1744   JOHN WATTS
          JAMES BANKHEAD
  Westmd. Sct. At a Court held for the said County the 27th day of November 1744
This Commission for the privy examination of ANNE, the Wife of JOHN CHILTON, concerning the said ANNEs right of Dower of in and to one hundred and fifty acres of land
by the said JOHN sold and conveyed to ANDREW MONROE, Gent., the said conveyance
being recorded in the Secretarys Office, which Commission being duly exd. as appears
by a Certificate under the hands of JOHN WATTS and JAMES BANKHEAD, two of the Gents.
in the said Commission named, all which on motion of the said MONROE are admitted to
Record   Teste GEO: LEE, C. W. C.

p. (On margin: McCARTYs Relinquishment to her Husband's Will)
72 KNOW ALL MEN by these presents that I ELIZABETH McCARTY, Widow and Relict
  of DANIEL McCARTY, late of the Parish of Washington in County of Westmoreland, Gent., deceased, tho: well satisfied with the generous provision made for me by the
Last Will and Testament of my said Husband, yet on the one hand considering the divers
opinions that have been given on the said Will and the many differences, and Law suits
I should probably be involved in if it should please God to take away my Son in his
infancy, and on the other hand reposing great trust and confidence in the Executors in

Trust appointed by my said Husband's Will, who think it more for my said Sons benefit and advantage to have his part of my said Husband's Estate set apart from him and to be under their care and management and being very sensible that I could not of myself manage the whole Estate according to the true intent and meaning of my said Husband's Will without the assistance of other persons, and thinking none so proper as those my said Husband has thought fit to repose so much trust and confidence in, have for the reasons aforesaid declared and by these presents do declare that I will not accept receive or take any legacy or legacies to me given and bequeathed by my said Husband's Last Will or any part thereof but do hereby renounce and relinquish all benefit and advantage whatsoever which I may or might have claim challenge or demand by or under the said Will; And do hereby delcare that I do and shall demand my Dower of and in the lands and slaves of my said late Husband and such share of his personal Estate as by the Laws of this Colony I am intitled to. In Witness whereof I have hereunto set my hand and seal this 27th day of November in the year of our Lord 1744 Sealed and delivered in the presence of us

      HUMPHRY POPE, WM. BUTLER,   ELIZABETH McCARTY
      HADEN EDWARDS

    Westmd. Sct. At a Court held for the said County the 27th day of November 1744 This Declaration of Renunciation of MRS. ELIZABETH McCARTY, Widow, against the provision for her made in and by the Last Will and Testament of her Husband, DANIEL McCARTY, Gent., deceased, was proved in open Court by the Oaths of WILLIAM BUTLER and HADEN EDWARDS, two of the witnesses thereto, which is ordered to be recorded
               Teste GEO: LEE, C. W. C.

pp.   (On margin: ESKRIDGE, ELIZABETH's Will)
72-   IN THE NAME OF GOD, Amen. this 20th day of October in the year of our Lord
74   Christ one thousand seven hundred and forty four, I ELIZABETH ESKRIDGE of
       Parish of Cople in County of Westmoreland being of sound and perfect mind and memory thanks be to God for the same, do make this my Last Will and Testament in manner and form following, revoking and absolutely annulling all and every Will and Wills hereto made by me either by word or writing, and this only to be my Last Will and Testament and none other; First, I give my Soul to God that gave it and my body to the Earth from whence it came to be buried in such decent and Christian manner as my Executrix hereafter named shall see convenient, trusting through the merits of my blessed Saviour to find pardon for all my sins;
    I give and devise to CRADELL BUTLER, a Negroe boy Tom or Ned, which my Daughter, ELIZABETH ELYLETT pleases to him his heirs, also one bed and furniture with the high bedstead over the parlour, two pair of sheets, three young Cows, three young Steers, half a dozen Sheep, half a dozen flaged Chairs, half a dozen Plates, four dishes and one Iron pot.
    I give bequeath and devise to MRS. BRAY the bed and furniture she lies in and a Quilt that is Callico on both sides, two pair of sheets, two pillow biers and a suit of mourning;
    I bequeath and devise to my God Daughter, JUDITH NEWTON, and her heirs forever one Negroe girl named Peg and two young Cows;
    I bequeath and devise to MARY LUCK nine hundred pounds tobacco, one Callico gound and two shifts.
    I give bequeath and devise to my Daughter, ELIZABETH AYLETT, all the rest of my Estate be it of what nature or kind soever to her and her heirs forever; she paying my just debts and legacies.

And Lastly, I make ordain constitute and appoint my Daughter, ELIZABETH AYLETT, whole and sole Executrix of this my Last Will and Testament. In Witness whereof I have hereunto set my hand and seal the day and year above written
Signed Sealed and delivered in presence of
    WILLO: NEWTON, ROBT. VAULX,   ELIZABETH her mark ⌇ ESKRIDGE
    GEO: BLAIR, NATHL: GRAY

    Westmd. Sct. At a Court held for the said County the 27th day of November 1744 Whereas ELIZABETH AYLETT, Widow, is nominated and appointed sole Executrix of this Last Will and Testament of her Mother, ELIZABETH ESKRIDGE, Widow, deceased, And also whereas the said ELIZABETH AYLETT by reason of a scruple she makes concerning the devise by the said Testatrix in and by the said Will made of two slaves that were left her, the said ELIZABETH AYLETT, by her Father, GEORGE ESKRIDGE, Gent., deceased, hath refused to undertake the proof or burthen of the said Will as Executrix, yet the said ELIZABETH AYLETT is willing and desirous to take administration on the said Decedent, ELIZABETH ESKRIDGEs, Estate with the Will annexed, which is allowed and approved of by the Court; Whereupon the said ELIZABETH AYLETT made Oath thereto and for that the said Will was proved in open Court by the Oaths of WILLOUGHBY NEWTON, ROBERT VAULX and GEORGE BLAIR, Gentlemen, three of the witnesses thereto, the same is admitted to Record; And upon the motion of the said ELIZABETH AYLETT and her giving AUGUSTINE WASHINGTON and JOHN BUSHROD, Gentlemen, for her security and performing what is usual in such cases, Certificate is granted her for obtaining Letters of Administration thereupon with the said Will annexed in due form
           Teste   GEO: LEE, C. W. C.

pp.   (On margin: ASBURY's to EWELL)
74-   THIS INDENTURE made the 26th day of November in the year of our Lord 1744,
76   Between HENRY ASBURY of Parish of Cople and County of Westmoreland of one part and CHARLES EWELL, JOHN TRIPLETT and others, the RAPPAHANNOCK IRON MINE COMPANY, and JOHN PIPER of the other part; Whereas JOHN WRIGHT, late of the County aforesaid did sell and convey unto THOMAS and HENRY ASBURY in cotenancy Four hundred and fifty acres of Land in the Parish of Washington and County aforesaid by Indenture of Release bearing date the 26th day of September 1711, relation being thereunto had may more fully appear; And whereas HENRY ASBURY survived his Brother, THOMAS ASBURY, by which means the whole vested in him and consequently so much thereof as he left undisposed descended to his Son and Heir, HENRY ASBURY, party to these presents; NOW THIS INDENTURE WITNESSETH that HENRY ASBURY in consideration of the sum of Twenty pounds current money of Virginia to him in hand paid by CHARLES EWELL, JOHN TRIPLETT and others of the Company, and JOHN PIPER, the receipt whereof the said HENRY doth hereby acknowledge, hath and by these presents doth bargain and sell unto CHARLES EWELL, JOHN TRIPLETT and others the Company aforesaid, and JOHN PIPER, their heirs all that one moiety of his right and title to the aforesaid tract of land to CHARLES EWELL, JOHN TRIPLETT and other the Company, and the other moiety unto JOHN PIPER and his heirs as Tenants in Common bounded by the Lands of JOHN PIPER, JOHN SMITH, JOHN MARSHALL, THOMAS THOMPSON and ARON HARWICK, together with all houses orchards profits and appurtenances to the same belonging; To have and to hold the tract of land and premises with appurtenances unto CHARLES EWELL, JOHN TRIPLETT and others the Company, and JOHN PIPER their heirs freed and discharged from all incumbrances; In Witness wehreof the said parties have hereunto put their hands and seals the day and year first above written

Signed Sealed delivered in presence of us
         ORIGINAL BROWN,   JOS: SMITH,   HENRY ASBURY
         AUGUSTINE SMITH,   DAVID PIPER
    Livery of Seizen and possession of the within mentioned premises being given by the
delivery of Turff and Twig in the name of the possession for the whole in presence of
us   ORIGINAL BROWN, JOSEPH SMITH
         AUGUSTINE SMITH,   DAVID PIPER
    Westmd. Sct. At a Court held for the said County the 27th day of Novr: 1744
HENRY ASBURY personally acknowledged this Deed of Feoffment for Land by him
passed to CHARLES EWELL, JOHN TRIPLETT and others the RAPPAHANNOCK IRON MINE
COMPANY, and JOHN PIPER, together with Livery of Seizen to be his proper act and deed
which on motion of the said PIPER are admitted to Record
                   Teste   GEO: LEE, C. W. C.

pp.   (On margin: McDANIEL to HABORN)
76-   THIS INDENTURE made the 9th day of January in the 18th year of the Reign of
79   our Sovereign Lord George the Second by the grace of God of Great Brittain
          France and Ireland, King, Defender of the faith &c., And in the year of our Lord
God 1744: Between JAMES McDANIEL of Parish of Cople in County of Westmoreland of
one part and GEORGE HABORN of said Parish and County of other part; Witnesseth that
JAMES McDANIEL in consideration of Forty pounds current money of Virginia to him in
hand paid by GEORGE HABORN, the receipt whereof he doth hereby acknowledge, hath
and by these presents doth bargain and sell unto GEORGE HABORN all that parcel of land
containing Sixty acres situate in The FORREST of NOMONY in Parish and County aforesaid; which Sixty acre one THOMAS MOORE of Parish and County aforesaid, deceased, in
and by his Last Will and Testament among other things therein containing did give and
devise to his Son, WILLIAM MOORE, and his heirs, And said WILLIAM MOORE also in and
by his Last Will and Testament among other things did give and bequeath the Sixty
acres unto WILLIAM MOORE the Younger, who by Deed bearing date 1742 did make a
Deed to JAMES McDANIEL, party to these presents, as also by other writings on the
Records of the County of Westmoreland and all houses orchards and appurtenances to
the sixty acres of land belonging; To have and to hold the sixty acres of land and premises unto GEORGE HABORN; and JAMES McDANIEL and his heirs the premises with appurtenances unto GEORGE HABORN his heirs shall warrant save harmless keep indemnified and forever defend by these presents; In Witness whereof the parties to these
presents have interchangeably set their hands and seals the day and year first above
written;
Sealed and delivered in the presence of
         JA: BAILEY, SAML: his mark + MOORE,   JAMES his mark 𝆑 McDANIEL
         JAS: HABORN, WM. STEVENS
    Memo: That on the 9th day of January in the year of our Lord 1744, peaceable and
quiet possession & seizen of the within bargained and sold premises was sold and given
unto GEORGE HABORN by delivery of Turff and Twigg on the said Land; To have and to
hold the same according to the form and effect of the within written Deed;
In presence of us   JAS: BAILEY,   SAML: his mark + MOORE
                      JAS: HABORN,   WM. STEVENS
    Received the 9th of January 1744 of the within named GEORGE HABORN the sum of
Forty pounds current money of Virginia being the consideration within mentioned to
be by him paid to me.

Witness   JAS: BAILEY,   JAMES his mark ╪ McDANIEL
          SAML: his mark ✝ MOORE,
          JAS: HABORN,   WM. STEVENS

(On margin: McDANIEL's Bond to HABORN)
KNOW ALL MEN by these presents that I JAMES McDANIEL of Parish of Cople in County of Westmoreland, Planter, am held and firmly bound unto GEORGE HABORN of said Parish and County, Planter, in the sum of Eighty pounds current money of Virginia, to the which payment well and truly to be made I bind myself my heirs firmly by these presents; Sealed with my seal and dated the 9th of January in the 18th year of the Reign of our Sovereign Lord George the Second by the grace of God of Great Brittain France and Ireland, King, Defender of the faith &c., Anno Dom: 1744
THE CONDITION of this obligation is lsuch that if the above bound JAMES McDANIEL his heirs shall perform and keep all the Covenants which on his or their part ought to be performed and ketp particularly expressed in one Indenture by wasy of Livery and Seizen made between JAMES McDANIEL and GEORGE HABORN according to the purport of the Indenture, Then this obligation to be void and of none effect or else to remain in full force power and virtue
Sealed and delivered in the presence of
   JAS: BAILEY, SAML: his mark ✝ MOORE,   JAMES his mark ╪ McDANIEL
   JAMES HABORN,   WM. STEVENS
      Westmd. Sct. At a Court held for the said County the 29th day of January 1744 JAMES McDANIEL personally acknowledged this Deed of Feoffment for Lands by him sold and conveyed to GEORGE HABORN, together with Livery of Seizen and Receipt for the consideration endorsed to be his proper act and deed, And JANE Wife of the said JAMES McDANIEL (she being first privily examined according to Law) relinquished her right of Dower in and to the lands by the said Deed conveyed, also a Bond for the performance of Covenants, all which on motion of the said GEORGE are admitted to Record
                  Teste   GEO: LEE, C. W. C.

pp.   (On margin: SORRELLs Deed to BUSHROD)
79-   THIS INDENTURE made the 21st day of January in the year of our Lord God 1745,
82   Between JOHN SORRELL of Parish of Cople in County of Westmoreland of one part
         and JOHN BUSHROD of the Parish and County aforesaid of other part; Witnesseth that JOHN SORRELL in consideration of the sum of Fifty pounds current money to him in hand paid by JOHN BUSHROD, the receipt whereof he doth hereby acknowledge, hath and by these presents doth bargain and sell unto JOHN BUSHROD a certain old Water Grist Mill near the head of NOMONY RIVER in Parish and County aforesaid on a Run lying on West side of said SORRELLs Plantation where JONATHAN RICHARDSON now lives and formerly the Mill of THOMAS SORRELL, Gent., deceased, with two acres of land on South side of the Run and one acre of land on West side at the ends of the Dam the Stream, Mill, Millstones and all the furniture and appurtenances unto the Mill, Mill Stream and land belonging; which said SORRELL hath by virtue of the Last Will and Testament of his Father, THOMAS SORRELL, deceased, or by any other ways, together with all profits and advantages; To have and to hold the land, Mill, Mill house, Stones and other the materials and utensils and premises unto JOHN BUSHROD his heirs; And JOHN SORRELL his heirs &c. the land, mill and other the premises unto JOHN BUSHROD his heirs shall warrant and forever defend so that neither said SORRELL his heirs or any other person shall challenge or lay claim thereto; In Witness whereof JOHN SORRELL hath hereunto set his hand and seal the day & year first above written; the above-

said JOHN BUSHROD agrees with JOHN SORRELL that he his heirs shall be hopper free at the abovesaid Mill.

Signed Sealed and delivered in the presence of

    THOMAS CRABB, WM. DUNBAR,   JOHN SORRELL

    JONATHAN RICHARDSON

    Memo: That on the 21st day of January 1744/5, JOHN SORRELL did put JOHN BUSHROD in the peacible possession of his claim and Estate in the Land and Mill by delivering him Turff and Twigg upon the land and possession of the house in token of Livery of Seizen of the whole land and premises, in the presence of us whose names are hereunto subscribed   THOS: CRABB, WM. DUNBAR

           JONATHAN RICHARDSON

    January 21st 1744/5. Then received of JOHN BUSHROD the sum of Fifty pounds current money, being the consideration above mentioned to be given for the Land and Mill and appurtenances

Teste THOS: CRABB, JONATHAN RICHARDSON   JOHN SORRELL

    Westmd. Sct. At a Court held for the said County the 29th day of January 1744 JOHN SORRELL, Gentleman, personally acknowledged this Deed of Feoffment for three acres of land and an Old Water Grist Mill by him passed to JOHN BUSHROD, Gentleman, together with Livery of Seizen and Receipt for the consideration endorsed to be his proper act and deed, all which on motion of the said BUSHROD is admitted to Record

           Teste GEO: LEE, C. W. C.

    (On margin: SORRELL's Bond to BUSHROD)

    KNOW ALL MEN by these presents that I JOHN SORRELL of Parish of Cople and County of Westmoreland am held and firmly bound unto JOHN BUSHROD of the same Parish and County in the full and just sum of Five hundred pounds of good and lawfull money of Great Brittain to the which payment well and truly to be made I bind myself my heirs firmly by these presents: Sealed with my seal and dated this 12th day of November in the 18th year of the Reign of our Sovereign Lord George the Second by the grace of God of Great Brittain France and Ireland, King, Defender of the faith &c., Anno Dom: 1744

    THE CONDITION of the above obligation is such that Whereas the above bounden JOHN SORRELL hath sold unto JOHN BUSHROD a certain Old Water Grist Mill with two acres of land on the South side and one acre of land on the West side, the said SORRELL to make execute and acknowledge when thereunto required in the County Court of Westmoreland such Deeds of Conveyance as said BUSHROD thinks proper for the safe conveying the Mill; That then the above obligation to be void and of none effect else the same to stand remain and be in full force power and virtue

Signed Sealed and deliveredin presence of

    CHANDLER AWBREY,   JOHN SORRELL

    JOHN his mark ∫ THOMPSON

    Westmd. Sct. At a Court held for the said County the 29th day of January 1744 JOHN SORRELL, Gent., personally acknowledged this Bond for performance of Covenants &c. by him passed to JOHN BUSHROD, Gentleman, to be his proper act and deed, which on motion of the said BUSHROD is admitted to Record

           Teste GEO: LEE, C. W. C.

p.   (On margin: McCARTY's other Exors. qualified)

82   Westmd. SCt. At a Court held for the said County the 29th day of January 1744

    PRESLEY THORNTON and AUGUSTINE WASHINGTON, Gent., the other Exors. of the Last Will and Testament of DANIEL McCARTY, Gent., deced., were this day sworn as such

to the said Will, also to the Codicil thereto which is ordered to be recored; And upon the
motion of the said PRESLEY and AUGUSTINE and their performing what is usual in such
cases, Certificate is granted them for obtaining a joint Probate thereof with the Executors heretofore sworn to the said Will in due form
                    Teste GEO: LEE. C. W. C.

pp.   (On margin: WALKER, GEORGE's Will)
82-   IN THE NAME OF GOD Amen, I GEORGE WALKER of County of Westmd. and Parish
84   of Cople and in Virginia, Planter, being in health of perfect mind and memory
         thanks be to God for it and calling to mind the mortality of my body and
knowing it is appointed for all men once to die, do make and ordain this my Last Will
and Testament (that is to say), principally and first of all I give and recommend my Soul
into the hands of God that gave it me and my body I recommend to the Earth to be
buried in a decent Christian way at the discretion of my Executors, nothing doubting
but at the General Resurrection I shall receive the same again by the mighty power of
God; And as touching such worldly Estate wherewith it hath pleased God to bless me
with in this life, I give devise and dispose of in manner following;
    Imprimis. I give to my beloved Wife, WINIFRED WALKER, all my Land in Westmore-
land County during her life provided she doth not thirds my land in FAIRFAX County,
    Item. I leave to my Wife one Negroe man named Grinock and money out of the Estate
to buy another Negroe man;
    Item. One black horse branded with   on the near buttock named Shaver and the
best feather bed and furniture;
    Item. One white horse branded on the near buttock thus   named Brandy forever.
    Item. I give to my Daughter, BARBARY, my Still and Mare and Colt, one feather bed
and furniture, the second best in the house, and one Negroe girl named Hannah, and
my Daughter WINNIAN is to have the first Colt that the Mare brings forever;
    Item. I give my Daughter, RACHEL, one mulattoe boy named Ned, one black Mare and
third best feather bed and furniture;
    Item. I give to my Daughter, WINNIAN, one Negroe girl named Winney forever;
    Item. I give to my Daughter, FRANKY, one Negroe girl named Gracey forever;
    Item. I give to my four Daughters, BARBARY RACHEL, WINNIAN and FRANKEY fif-
teen hundred and six acres of Land in FAIRFAX County to be equally divided among
them to them and theirs forever, and if any of them die without heirs, the aforesaid
land is to return back to the survivors to be equally divided among them; And as concerning my land in this County after my Wifes death, I desire it may be sold and the
money be equally divided betwixt my two Daughters, WINNIAN and FRANKEY; and if
any of the said two Children die, the survivor to have it and if they should both die before my Wife, to be equally divided betwixt BARBARY and RACHEL. All my remaining
Estate not mentioned after my legacies and debts are paid to be equally divided betwixt
my Wife and four Children and do hereby utterly disallow revoke and make void all and
every other Testaments made before the ratifying and confirming this and no other to
be my Last Will and Testament;
    And Lastly, do conclude this my Last Will and Testament do hereby nominate and
appoint Mr. DANIEL TEBBS and Mr. JOHN MIDDLETON to be my sole Exors. of this my Last
Will and Testament and likeways, my beloved Wife, WINIFRED WALKER; In Witness
whereof I have hereunto set my hand and seal this 13th day of December Anno Domini
1744
Signed Sealed published pronounced and declared by the
said GEO: WALKER as his Last Will and Testament in the

presence of us JAMES CLARKE,   GEORGE WALKER
                CLARKE SHORT,
                HENRY his mark ✝ CALVENER
     Westmd. Sct. At a Court held for the said County the 29th day of Janry. 1744
This Last Will and Testament of GEORGE WALKER, deceased, was presented into Court by
WINIFRED, his Relict, and JOHN MIDDLETON of the Executors in the said Will named, who
made Oath thereto and being proved by the Oaths of the witnesses thereto, is admitted to
Record; And upon the motion of the said WINIFRED and JOHN and their performing
what is usual in such cases, Certificate is granted them for obtaining a Probate thereof
in due form   Teste GEO: LEE, C. W. C.

pp.   (On margin: CARR to TEBBS)
84-   THIS INDENTURE made this 22nd day of December in the 18th year of the Reign
86   of our Sovereign Lord George the Second by the grace of God of Great Brittain
         France and Ireland, King, Defender of the faith &c., And in the year of our Lord
God 1744; Between JOSEPH CARR of Cople Parish and Westmoreland County of one part
and DANIEL TEBBS of same Parish and County of other part; Witnesseth that JOSEPH
CARR in consideration of the sum of Fifteen pounds current money of Virginia to him
in hand paid by DANIEL TEBBS, the receipt whereof JOSEPH CARR doth hereby acknowledge, hath and by these presents doth bargain and sell DANIEL TEBBS his heirs all that
parcel of land containing One hundred and fifty acres be the same more or less situate
in Parish of Cople in County of Westmoreland, it being all the land which JOSEPH CARR
hath or claims a right to the same by the death of his Brother, JAMES CARR, deceased, it
being all the land which JOSEPH CARR hath any right to in the County of Westmoreland with all its rights members and appurtenances; Together with all houses orchards
profits and appurtenances; To have and to hold the One hundred and fifty acres of Land
and other the premises unto DANIEL TEBBS his heirs; And JOSEPH CARR his heirs
against every person shall warrant and forever defend by these presents; In Witness
whereof the parties to these presents have interchangeably set their hands and seals
the day and year first above written
Signed and delivered in the presence of
          WILLO: NEWTON, JOS: SMITH,   JOS: CARR
          STEPHEN BAILEY, JUNR.
     Received of DANIEL TEBBS the sum of Fifteen pounds current money of Virginia in
full payment for the consideration within mentioned; Witness my hand this 22nd day of
December 1744
Teste WILLO: NEWTON, JOS: SMITH   JOSEPH CARR
       STEPHEN BAILEY, JUNR.
     Westmd. Sct. At a Court held for the said County the 29th day of January 1744
This Deed of Feoffment for Lands from JOSEPH CARR to DANIEL TEBBS together with the
Receipt for the consideration endorsed were this day proved in open Court by the Oaths
of WILLOUGHBY NEWTON, Gent., and STEPHEN BAILEY, JUNR., two of the witnesses there-
to, which on motion of the said TEBBS are admitted to Record
               Teste   GEO: LEE, C. W. C.

pp.   (On margin: MOTT & Wife to LEE, Esqr.)
86-   THIS INDENTURE made the 29th day of January in the 18th year of the Reign of
89   our Sovereign Lord George the Second by the grace of God of Great Brittain
         France and Ireland, King, Defender of the faith &c, And in the year of our Lord
1744; Between JOSEPH MOTT of County of NORTHUMBERLAND, Schoolmaster, and JANE

his Wife of one part and THOMAS LEE of County of Westmoreland, Esquire, of other part;
Witnesseth that JOSEPH MOTT and JANE his Wife in consideration of Twenty pounds current
money of Virginia in hand paid and One hundred and fifty acres of Land of said
LEE's at the DIVIDING CREEKE in County of NORTHUMBERLAND, the receipt whereof
JOSEPH MOTT and JANE his Wife doth hereby acknowledge, have and by these presents
do bargain and sell unto THOMAS LEE his heirs all that Plantation parcel of land situate
in Parish of Washington in County of Westmoreland containing by estimation four
hundred and fifty acres be the same more or less which land descended to JAMES, heir
at Law of his Father, JOHN SPENCE, or by any other way and is now in the occupation of
said JOSEPH and JANE; And all houses gardens profits and heriditaments to the same
belonging; To have and to hold the premises with appurtenances freely and clearly
discharged of Dower unto THOMAS LEE his heirs; And said JOSEPH and JANE for them
and their heirs against every person to THOMAS LEE his heirs shall warrant and forever defend by these presents; In Witness whereof the parties to these presents have
hereunto interchangeably set their hands and seals the day and year first above
written
Signed Sealed and delivered in the presence of
            ALEXANDER WHITE, DAVID DOAK,   JOSEPH MOTT
            EDMUND PARTINGTON   JANE her mark ⅄ MOTT
    Signed Sealed and delivered by JANE MOTT above named in the presence of
            BALDWIN MATHEWS SMITH,
            GEORGE BALL, JUNR., JOSEPH McADAMS, ALEXR. WHITE
    Received the day within mentioned of THOMAS LEE, Esqr., the sum of Twenty pounds
current money of Virignia and a sufficient assurance in Law for the lands within
mentd., being the full consideration mentd. in the Deed
Teste ALEXANDER WHITE, DAVID DOAK,   JOSEPH MOTT
            EDMUND PARTINGTON   JANE her mark ✝ MOTT
    Memorandum; That on the 29th day of January in the year of our Lord 1744; full
possession and sezen of the lands and premises within granted was given by JOSEPH
MOTT and in the name and behalf of his Wife, JANE, unto THOMAS LEE Esquire, to hold to
him and his heirs according to the true meaning of the Indenture;
In presence of ALEXR: WHITE,   DAVID DOAK,
            EDMUND PARTINGTON
    Westmd. Sct. At a Court held for the said County the 29th day of January 1744
JOSEPH MOTT of NORTHUMBERLAND County, Schoolmaster, personally acknowledged this
Deed of Feoffment or Exchange of Lands by him passed to THOMAS LEE, Esqr., together
with livery of seizen and Receipt for the consideration endorsed to be his proper act
and deed and to give a great sanction thereto the same were proved in open Court by
the Oaths of all the witnesses thereto, which on motion of said LEE dare ordered to be
Certified   Teste GEO: LEE, C. W. C.

    Westmd. Sct. At a Court held for the said County the 26th day of February 1744
At January Court last, this Deed of Feoffment or Exchange for Lands from JOSEPH MOTT
and JANE his Wife to THOMAS LEE Esqr., together with livery of seizen and Receipt
endorsed were acknowledged by the said JOSEPH MOTT and proved in the preceeding
Certificate as set forth and now at this Court the said Deed and Receipt were proved by
the Oaths of ALEXANDER WHITE to have been signed sealed and delivered by the said
JANE, which said ALEXANDER also swore that in his sight BALDWIN MATHEWS SMITH,
GEORGE BALL JUNR. and JOSEPH McADAM subscribed their names as witnesses to the
said JANEs acknowledgment aforesaid, And also the said JANE by virtue of a Commission

for privy examination relinquished her right of inheritance of in and to the lands by the said Deed exchanged and conveyed as appears by a Certificate under the hands of two of the Commissioners for that purpose appointed, all which on motion of the said LEE are admitted to Record   Teste GEO: LEE, C. W. C.

(On margin: MOTTs Relinqt. to LEE, Esqr.)
Westmd. Sct. George the Second by the grace of God of Great Brittain France and Ireland, King, Defender of the faith &c. to ROBERT JONES, GEORGE BALL, BALDWIN MATHEWS SMITH and ARGAIL TAYLOR of County of NORTHUMBERLAND, Gentlemen, Greeting; We do hereby authorise and impower you or any two at such time and place as you shall appoint (some time before the next Court to be held for the County of Westmoreland) to take the privy examination of JANE, the Wife of JOSEPH MOTT, of the County of NORTHUMBERLAND, Schoolmaster, apart from her said Husband (the Commission for the privy examination of JANE, the Wife of JOSEPH MOTT); herein you are not to fail; Witness GEORGE LEE, Clerk of the said County Court of Westmoreland the first day of February in the 18th year of our Reign   GEORGE LEE, C. W. C.
NORTHUMBERLAND Sct. By virtue of the within Commission to us directed we have privately examined JANE, the Wife of JOSEPH MOTT (the return of the execution of the privy examination of JANE MOTT); Certified under our hands this 18th day of February 1744
GEORGE BALL, JUNR.
BALDWIN MATHEWS SMITH
Westmd. Sct. At a Court held for the said County the 26th day of February 1744 This Commission for the privy examination of JANE the Wife of JOHN MOTT concerning her the said JANE's Right of Inheritance to the within mentioned land by them sold exchanged and conveyed to THOMAS LEE, Esquire, being returned executed as appears by a Certificate under the hands of GEORGE BALL, JUNR., and BALDWIN MATHEWS SMITH two of the Gentlemen in the said Commission named, all which on motion of the said LEE are admitted to Record   Teste GEORGE LEE, C. W. C.

pp.   (On margin: WILSON & ROGERS to RUST)
89-   THIS INDENTURE made this 26th day of November in the year of our Lord Christ
91   1744, Between ALLEN WILSON and MARY ROGERS of Parish of Cople and County
         of Westmoreland of one part and MATHEW RUST of Parish and County aforesaid
of other part; Witnesseth that ALLEN WILSON and MARY ROGERS in consideration of the sum of Two thousand pounds of lawfull tobacco to them in hand paid, the receipt whereof they doth hereby acknowledge, hath and by these presents doth bargain and sell unto MATHEW RUST his heirs a certain parcel of land containing Ninety acres in County aforesaid be the same more or less lying on North side of YEOCOMOCO RIVER binding S. E. on BAILEY's back Creeke, N. E. on the land called KINGS SAILE, N. W. on PETER RUST's MILL and S. W. on the land of WILLIAM BAILEY and may it more fully appear was sold by WILLIAM WALKER to WILLIAM GARLAND and then sold by WILLIAM GARLAND to JOHN WILLSON by whom the aforesaid ALLEN WILSON claims a Right by him being Heir at Law to the parcel of land now being in the tenure of ALLEN WILSON and MARY ROGERS; To have and to hold the land and premises with appurtenances unto MATHEW RUST his heirs &c. and ALLEN WILSON and MARY ROGERS for themselves their heirs &c. the land and premises unto MATHEW RUST his heirs against all persons shall warrant and forever defend by these presents; In Witness wherof the parties to these presents have interchangeably set their hands and seals the day and year first above written

Signed Sealed and delivered in the presence of
    ARTER⨯ KING,   MARY her mark B ROGERS
    MICHAEL his mark T TOBEN   ALLEN his mark LU WILLSON
    RICHARD his mark R PARTRIDGE

Memorandum; That on the 4th day of December in the year of our Lord Christ 1744, peacible and quiet possession and seizen of the lands and premises within mentioned was made and delivered by ALLEN WILSON unto MATHEW RUST by delivering Turff and Twigg according to the true meaning of the within Deed, in the presence of us
    DANL: TEBBS,   MICHAEL his mark T TOBEN,
    ARTHUR his mark V KING, RICHD: 2f PARTRIDGE

Received of Mr. MATHEW RUST the within consideration of two thousand pounds of lawfull tobacco, this 4th day of December 1744
Teste DANIEL TEBBS, VINCENT RUST.   ALLEN his mark LU WILSON

    Westmd. Sct. At a Court held for the said County the 26th day of February 1744 ALLEN WILSON personally acknowledged this Deed of Feoffment for lands by him and MARY ROGERS sold and conveyed to MATHEW RUST together with livery of seizen and receipt for the consideration thereon endorsed to be his proper act and deed, all which on motion of the said RUST are admitted to Record
                    Teste   GEO: LEE, C. W. C.

pp.   (On margin: MOORE's to BAILEY)
92-   THIS INDENTURE made the 25th day of February in the 18th year of the Reign
94   of our Sovereign Lord George the Second by the grace of God of Great Brittain
        France and Ireland, King, Defender of the faith &c., And in the year of our Lord God 1744; Betwen WILLIAM MOORE of Parish of Cople in County of Westmoreland, Planter, and REBECCA his Wife of one part and JAMES BAILEY of the same Parish and County, Planter, of other part; Witnesseth that in consideration of the sum of Two thousand five hundred pounds of tobacco to WILLIAM MOORE in hand paid by JAMES BAILEY, the receipt whereof WILLIAM MOORE doth hereby acknowledge, hath and by these presents WILLIAM MOORE and REBECCA his Wife doth bargain and sell unto JAMES BAILEY his heirs all that parcel of land situate in Parish of Cople and County aforesaid containing by estimation Sixty six acres be the same more or less being the Plantation now in the occupation of said WILLIAM MOORE, formerly purchased by one PATTY HAILE of one STEPHEN SELF and JANE his Wife, and by them conveyed to PATTY HAILE by Indenture of Lease and Release bearing date the 18th & 19th days of September in the year of our Lord 1714, and afterwards sold and conveyed by PATTY HAILE to JOHN FROUD (Father of WINIFRED MARMADUKE, Wife of JOHN MARMADUKE) by Indenture of Feoffment bearing date the 24th day of September 1717; which JOHN FROUD in and by his Last Will and Testment in Writing bearing date the 4th day of March in the year 1717, gave and devised the same to the aforesaid WINIFRED in fee simple, which land one JOHN MARMADUKE and his Wife, the aforesaid WINIFRED, sold and conveyed to JAMES McDANIEL by Deed of bargain and sale bearing date the last day of July in the year of our Lord 1741, and JAMES McDANIEL by Deed of Feoffment bearing date the 21st day of February 1742 sold and conveyed the same to WILLIAM MOORE, which Sixty six acres of land was first devised and given to JANE JOICE in and by the Last Will and Testament of her Father, JOHN GARNER, as by the several Conveyances and Wills proved and recorded in the Court of County of Westmoreland may more fully appear; And all houses orchards profits and appurtenances belonging; To have and to hold the parcel of land and premises with appurtenances unto JAMES BAILEY his heirs; And WILLIAM MOORE and his heirs the premises unto JAMES BAILEY his heirs shall warrant and forever defend

by these presents; In Witness whereof the parties to these presents have interchangeably set their hands and seals the day and year first above written
Signed Sealed and delivered in presence of

GEO: LEE. B. HARNETT,   WILLIAM MOORE
GARLAND MOORE, GEO: HABORN,   REBEC: her mark R MOORE
JNO: SELF

Memorandum; That on the 25th day of February 1744, peacible and quiet possession
and seizen of the within premises was delivered by WILLIAM MOORE to JAMES BAILEY
by delivery of Turff and Twigg on the land; To have and to hold according to the form
and effect of the within written Deed, in presence of

GARLAND MOORE, GEORGE HABORN,
JOHN SELF

Received this 25th day of February 1744 of JAMES BAILEY Twenty five hundred
pounds of tobacco, being the consideration mentioned to be paid by him to me
Witness GEO: LEE, B. HARNETT   WILLIAM MOORE
JOHN COLVIN

Westmd. Sct. At a Court held for the said County the 26th day of February 1744
WILLIAM MOORE and REBECCA his Wife (she being first privately examined according
to Law relinquished her right of Dower to the land herein conveyed) personally acknowledged this Deed of Feoffment for land by them sold and conveyed to JAMES BAILEY
to be their act and deed, And the said WILLIAM MOORE also personally acknowledged
the Livery of Seizen and Receipt endorsed to be his proper act and deed, which on
motion of the said BAILEY are admitted to Record
                        Teste   GEO: LEE, C. W. C.

(On margin: MOORE's Bond to BAILEY)
KNOW ALL MEN by these presents that I WILLIAM MOORE of Cople Parish in County of
Westmoreland, Planter, am held and firmly bound unto JAMES BAILEY of the same
Parish and County, Planter, in the sum of Five thousand pounds of tobacco to which
payment well and truly to be made I bind myself my heirs firmly by these presents;
Sealed with my Seal and dated the 25th day of February 1744 and in the 18th year of the
Reign of our Sovereign Lord George the Second &c.
THE CONDITION of this obligation is such that if WILLIAM MOORE his heirs shall per-
form and keep all Covenants which on his or their part ought to be performed and kept
particularly expressed in one Deed of Bargain and Sale made between WILLIAM MOORE
and JAMES BAILEY according to the purport of the said Deed; Then this obligation to be
void and of none effect, otherwise to be and remain in full force power and virtue
Sealed and delivered in presence of

GEO: LEE, B. HARNETT,   WILLIAM MOORE
JOHN COLVIN, GARLAND MOORE,
GEO: HABORN, JOHN SELF

Westmd. Sct. At a Court held for the said County the 26th day of February 1744
WILLIAM MOORE personally acknowledged this Bond for performance of Covenants by
him passed to JAMES BAILEY to be his proper act and deed, which on motion of the said
BAILEY is admitted to Record   Teste   GEO: LEE, C. W. C.

p.   (On margin: FLEMING, JOHN's Will)
95   IN THE NAME OF GOD, Amen. I JOHN FLEMING of County of Westmoreland and
        Parish of Cople in Virginia, Planter, being in health and of perfect mind and
memory (thanks be to God for it) and calling to mind the mortality of my body and

knowing that it is appointed for all men once to die, do make and ordain this my Last Will and Testament (that is to say), principally and first of all I give and recommend my Soul into the hands of God that gave it me and my body I recommend to the Earth to be buried in a decent Christian way according to the discretion of my Executor, nothing doubting but at the General Ressurection I shall receive the same again by the mighty power of God, And as touching such worldly Estate wherewith it hath pleased God to bless me with in this life, I give devise and dispose of in manner following;

Imprimis. I nominate and appoint JAMES BAILEY of the said County my sole Executor of this my Last Will and Testament and do hereby leave my Son, PETER, to the sd. BAILEY till he arrive to the age of Eighteen.

Item. To my Daughter, SARAH, one feather bed and all that belongs to it;

Item. I leave to my Daughter, ANNE, one feather bed and furniture;

Item. I leave to my Son, PETER, my own bed and furniture;

Item. I leave to my Son, THOMAS, two pounds, ten shillings currency to be raised out of my movable Estate and my little Trunk and Gun;

Item. I leave to my Son, WILLIAM, two pounds, ten shillings currency to be raised out of my movable Estate, my Sword and Belt;

Item. I leave to my Exor. one case of bottles and after all the Legacies are paid, if there be anything remaining, I desire it may be equally divided among my Children and do hereby utterly disallow revoke and make void all and every other Testaments made before this ratifying and confirming this and no other to be my Last Will and Testament; In Witness whereof I have hereunto set my hand and seal this 15th day of November Annoque Domini 1744

Signed Sealed published pronounced and declared by the
said JOHN FLEMING as his Last Will and Testament in
presence of us   JAMES CLARKE   JOHN FLEMING
          WM: BAILEY

Westmd. Sct. At a Court held for the said County the 26th day of February 1744 This Last Will and Testament of JOHN FLEMING, deceased, was presented into Court by JAMES BAILEY, his Executor, who made Oath thereto and being proved by the Oaths of the witnesses thereto is admitted to Record; And upon the motion of the said Exor. and his performing what is usual in such cases, Certificate is granted him for obtaining a Probate thereof in due form   Teste GEO: LEE, C.W.C.

p.   (On margin: REYNOLDS, ROBERT's Will)
96   IN THE NAME OF GOD, Amen, I ROBERT REYNOLDS of Parish of Washington being weak of body but of a sound mind and judgment (blessed be God) do make this my Last Will and Testament in manner and form following; In the first place, I recommend my Spirit to Almighty God and commit my body to the Earth in hopes of a joyfull resurrection and as for the worldly goods the Almighty has blessed me with, I bestow and dispose of in the manner following;

First, I leave my Loving and dear Wife and do hereby appoint her the sole Executrix of all my Estate whatsoever as long as she continues unmarried, and in case of marriage she is to have what the Law allows and pay of my dear Children with the residue and I desire that my Son may be put to some honest and commendable Trade as soon as he is capable thereof and my will and pleasure is that my Son shall have a Horse saddle and bridle to the value of Ten pounds currency over and above his equal share with my two Daughters, who I desire may live along with their Mother as long as she and they shall think convenient and my desire is that my loving Wife shall pay off my Children (as above directed) either in money goods or chttles as is most convenient for her and I

desire she may school and educate my Children till once they can read & write, and my
Son is to have so much arithmetick as shall be sufficient for learning his Trade. In
Witness whereof I have hereunto set my hand and seal this 14th day of February in the
year of our Lord 1744/5
Signed Sealed and delivered in the presence of
       CHARLES CUPPLES,   ROBERT REYNOLDS
       CHARLES PALLARON
    Westmoreland Sct. At a Court held for the said County the 26th day of February 1744
This Last Will and Testment of ROBERT REYNOLDS, deceased, was presented into Court by
NANCY, his Relict and Executrix, who made Oath thereto, and being proved as well by
the Oath of CHARLES CUPPLE, one of the witnesses thereto, as by the Oath of ALEXANDER
WHITE, who wrote the same (altho not subscribed a witness thereto) is admitted to
Record; And upon the motion of the said Executirx and her performing what is ususal
in such cases, Certificate is granted her for obtaining a Probate thereof in due form
               Teste GEO: LEE, C. W. C.

pp.   (On margin: DODD, JOHN's Will)
96-   IN THE NAME OF GOD, Amen. September the 16th day in the year of our Lord
98   1740; I JOHN DODD of Parish of Washington in Westmoreland County being in
        health of body and of good and perfect sence and memory, thanks be to God, do
make this my Last Will and Testament in manner and form as followeth;
    Imprimis. First, I bequeath my Soul and Spirit into the hands of Almighty God by
whom of his mercy through the death and merrits of my Lord and Saviour Jesus Christ,
I sett the only hope of my salvation, my body I commit to the Earth to be buried in a
Chritian manner;
    Item. I do give and bequeath unto my Son, JOSEPH DODD, all that Plantation in KING
GEORGE County which the said JOSEPH now liveth upon to him the said JOSEPH DODD and
his heirs forever; with all the land thereto belonging;
    Item. I do give and bequeath unto my Son, NATHANIEL DODD, all that Plantation and
parcel of land I now live on lying in Westmoreland County with the appurtenances and
every part and parcel thereof to him the said NATHANIEL DODD, and his heirs forever;
    Item. I do give and bequeath unto my Son, BENJAMIN DODD, one feather bed, rugg,
blankett and one pair of fine sheets, one boulster and one pillow and curtains and
vallens, to the said Bed, I do also give to my said Son, BENJAMIN, three pewter dishes and
three pewter plates and one pewter bason and one small iron pott;
    Item. I do give and bequeath unto my Daughter, MARY McKENNEY, all my whole
right title and interest of a Servant Maid which now liveth with me and was bought by
me and JOHN McKENNEY, Husband to my said Daughter, at equal charge which said
Servant womans name if ELIZABETH WASHINGTON.
    Item. I do give and bequeath unto my Son in Law Six shillings current money, WIL-
LIAM GEARING by name;
    Item. My will and desire is that all and every part of my personal Estate goods
chattles and appurtenances whatsoever thereto belonging after the aforesaid legacies
are delivered be equally divided amongst my Five Children hereafter named, (that is to
say) my Eldest Son, JOHN DODD, my aforesaid Son, JOSEPH DODD, and my said Son, BENJA-
MIN DODD, and my said Daughter, MARY McKENNEY and my youngest Daughter, ELIZA-
BETH (? UREDNE) each and every one of the said five to have and equal part as aforesaid of my said personal Estate and every part and parcel thereof, And I do make constitute and appoint my Eldest Son, JOHN DODD, my Exor. of this my said Will revoking and
disannulling all former Wills by me heretofore made ratifying and declaring this and

no other to be my Last Will and Testament. And in confirmation thereof have hereunto
set my hand and seal the day month and year above written
Sealed and delivered in presence of
      EDWARD ELMS,   JOHN his mark ╪D DODD
      ROBERT FORGIE, DANIEL WHITE, JUNR.
    Westmoreland Sct. At a Court held for the said County the 26th day of March 1745
This Last Will and Testament of JOHN DODD, deceased, was presented into Court by JOHN
DODD his Executor who made Oath thereto and being proved by the Oaths of EDWARD
ELMS and ROBERT FORGIE, two of the witnesses thereto, is admitted to Record; And upon
the motion of the said Executor and his performing what is usual in such cases, Certi-
ficate is granted him for obtaining a Probate thereof in due form
                Teste   GEORGE LEE, C. W. C.

p.   (On margin: SCULL, JAMES Nuncupative Will)
98   JAMES SCULL late of Parish of Cople & County of Westmoreland, deceased, on the
        Second day of January 1744/5, being on his death bed and his pefect sence and
memory said that he did not design to make any Will but entirely gave all his Estate
both real and personal to his Wife for her to act and do with it as she pleased. Witness
JOHN MINOR and ELIZABETH YATES this 3rd day of January 1744/5; Given under my
hand and seal the day and year above written
Teste   JOHN MINOR,   HENRY LEE
       ELIZABETH YATES
    Westmd. Sct. At a Court held for the said County the 26th day of March 1745
This Last Will nuncupative of JAMES SCULL, deceased, was presented into Court by
MARY his Relict and Executrix who made Oath thereto and being proved by the Oaths of
JOHN MINOR and ELIZABETH YATES, witnesses thereto, is admitted to Record; And upon
the motion of the said Executrix and her performing what is usual in such cases, Certi-
ficate is granted her for obtaining a Probate thereof in due form
                Teste GEO: LEE, C. W. C.

pp.   (On margin: RILEY, EDWARD's Nuncupative Will)
98-   Westmd. County Sct. ELIZABETH BOYTON and JANE OLIVE came before me, one of
99   his Majestys Justices of the Peace for the said County, and made Oath on the Holy
        Evangelists that on the 22nd day of February 1744/5 and in the 18th year of the
Reign of our Sovereign Lord George the Second of Great Brittain &c., King, that they
were present and in company with EDWARD RILEY of the said County who there lay
upon his death bed and in his perfect sence and memory and declared that he gave all
his Estate to his Wife, ELIZABETH RILEY, except one of his heaviest hogsheads of tobacco
of his share of the Crop which he gave to MRS. MARY LEE; Given under my hand and
seal this 28th day of February 1744/5
Teste ELIZABETH BOYTON,   WHARTON RANSDELL
       JANE OLIVE
    Westmoreland Sct. At a Court held for the said County the 26th day of March 1745
This Last Will and Testament nuncupative of EDWARD RILEY, deceased, was presented
into Court by ELIZABETH his Relict and Executrix who made Oath thereto, and being
proved by the Oaths of ELIZABETH BOYTON and JANE OLIVE, witnesses thereto, is admitted to Record; And upon the motion of the said Executrix and her performing what
is usual in such cases, Certificate is granted her for obtaining a Probate thereof in due
form   Teste   GEO: LEE, C. W. C.

pp.   (On margin: FRESHWATER to LINTON)
99-   THIS INDENTURE made the 26th day of March in the year of our Lord 1745, Be-
101   tween JOHN FRESHWATER of Lunenburg Parish in RICHMOND County of one part
           and JOHN LINTON of County of RICHMOND and Parish aforesaid, Planter, of other
part; Witnesseth that JOHN FRESHWATER in consideration of the sum of Twenty five
pounds current money to him in hand paid by JOHN LINTON, the receipt whereof JOHN
FRESHWATER doth hereby acknowledge, hath and by these presents doth bargain and
sell unto JOHN LINTON his heirs one parcel of land situate in County of Westmoreland
and Parish of Cople, Beginning at a Sassafras corner tree to JOHN DUNKIN and WILLIAM
LAIN, thence along a line of mrked trees that divides this land and the said LAINs to a
large Hiccory, another corner to LAIN, thence N. 44d. 30m. E. 145 poles to a red Oak
corner the aforesaid LAIN, thence So. 59d. W. 84 poles to a corner Oak standing in Colo.
PATONs line, thence S. 33d. W. 120 poles to a Hiccory in said PATONs line, thence S. 40d. E.
28 poles to a small red Oak, thence along a line of marked trees that divides this land and
WILLIAM PORTER to a marked Hiccory corner in the aforesaid DUNKINs land crossing
the Main Road, thence along a line of marked trees between this land and the said DUN-
KIN to the beginning Sassafras; which land was formerly WILLIAM LINTONs, deceased,
Father to said JOHN LINTON, and Sixteen acres which is taken in the above courses adjoining to the aforesaid WILLIAM LINTONs, deceased, land which was taken lup by said
JOHN FRESHWATER as Surplass Land which the whole quantity is One hundred and sixty
acres be the same more or less; and now by JOHN FRESHWATER and ELIZABETH his Wife
unto JOHN LINTON with all its rights members and appurtenances; To have and to hold
the premises unto JOHN LINTON his heirs and JOHN FRESHWATER and ELIZABETH his
Wife shall warrant and forever defend by these presents; In Witness whereof the parties have hereunto set their hands and fixed their seals the day and year first above
written
Signed Sealed and delivered in presence of
       WM. GARLAND, JUNR.   JOHN FRESHWATER
       MARTIN HUGHES, JUNR.   ELIZA: FRESHWATER
    Westmd. Sct. At a Court held for the said County the 26th day of March 1745
JOHN FRESHWATER and ELIZABETH his Wife (she being first privately examined according to Law relinquished her right of Dower &c.) personally acknowledged this Deed of
Bargain and Sale or Feoffment for Land by them passed to JOHN LINTON to be their proper act and deed, which on motion of the said LINTON are admitted to Record
              Teste   GEO: LEE, C. W. C.

pp.   (On margin: SMITH and Wife to SMITH)
101-   THIS INDENTURE made the 9th day of February in the 19th year of the Reign of
105   our Sovereign Lord George the Second by the grace of God of Great Brittain
           France and Ireland, King, Defender of the faith &c., And in the year of our Lord
God 1744; Between JOHN SMITH JUNR. of Parish of Dettengan in PRINCE WILLIAM County, Planter, of one part and JOHN SMITH SENR. of the Parish of Washington in County of
Westmoreland within the Dominion of Virginia, Planter, of other part; Witnesseth that
JOHN SMITH, JUNR. in consideration of the sum of Thirty five pounds current money to
him in lhand paid by JOHN SMITH, SENR. the receipt whereof is hereby acknowledged,
hath and by these presents doth bargain and sell unto JOHN SMITH, SENR. his heirs all
that parcel of land containing One hundred and sixty acres of land more or less situate
in County of Westmoreland and Parish of Washington and bounded; Beginning at a
marked white Oak saplin standing in North side of COVENTRY RUN, thence N. West to a
small Spanish Oak tree, thence N. to the head of a small Branch, thence down the

Branch to a Run, thence to a marked red Oak a corner tree to the land of JOHN MAR-
SHALL, thence to a marked Poplar standing in a Branch, thence up the water courses of
the Branch to a tract of land belonging to JOHN PIPER, thence E. to BLAGG's line,
thence along BLAGG's line to COVENTRY RUN, thence down the Run to the first mentioned beginning; Together with all houses orchards profits and appurtenances to the
same belonging; To have and to hold unto JOHN SMITH SENR. his heirs during the term
of one whole year paying therefore the rent of one Ear of Indian Corn at the expiration
of the term to the intent that by virtue of these presents and of the Statute for transfering uses into possession, JOHN SMITH SENR. may be in the actual possession of the
premises and be better enabled to take a release of the inheritance thereof, said JOHN
SMITH JUNR. hath to this present Indenture set his hand and affixed his seal the day
and year first above written
Sealed and delivered in the presence of us
    JOHN FARGUSSON, JUNR.   JOHN SMITH
    AUGUSTINE SMITH,   PATIENCE SMITH
    MARY FARGUSSON,   SAMUEL STONE
  Westmd. Sct. At a Court held for the said County the 26th day of March 1745
This Deed of Lease for Land from JOHN SMITH, JUNR. and PATIENCE his Wife to JOHN
SMITH SENR., was proved by the Oaths of the witnesses thereto, And on motion of the
said SMITH, SENR., is admitted to Record
          Teste GEO: LEE, C. W. C.

    (The Release after the foregoing Lease is the same insofar as participants, the amount of
money paid, the description of the Land). In Witness whereof JOHN SMITH hath to this pre-
sent Indenture set his hand and affixed his seal the day and year first above written
Sealed and delivered in the presence of us
    JOHN FARGUSSON, JUNR. AUGT. SMITH   JOHN SMITH
    MARY FARGUSSON, SAML: STONE   PATIENCE SMITH
  Received February 9th 1744/5 of Mr. JOHN SMITH, SENR. the sum of Thirty five
pounds current money of Virginia for value received in full
Teste   JOHN FARGUSSON,   p me   JOHN SMITH, JUNR.
    AUGUSTINE SMITH,
    MARY FARGUSSON,   SAMUEL STONE
  Westmd. Sct. At a Court held for the said County the 26th day of March 1745
This Deed of Release for Land from JOHN SMITH JUNR. and PATIENCE his Wife to JOHN
SMITH SENR. was proved by the Oaths of the witnesses thereto as also the receipt
endorsed, which on motion of the said SMITH, SENR. are admitted to Record
         Teste GEORGE LEE, C. W. C.

  (Westmoreland County Deed and Will Book, 1744-1748, will be continued in another book beginning on page 105 with the Deed of BENJAMIN RUST to THOMAS BOGGESS, dated the 25th day of
March, 1745).

KIRK. Ann (Widow of Jos: Hardwick) 48, 49.
KIRKHAM. William 73.

LAIN. William 109.
LAMKIN. George (deced. -61), 87;
  James (G-Son of Hannah Demovil) 88;
  Peter (Son of Geo., deced) 87; Samuel
  G-Son of Hannah Demovil, deced) 88.
LANDMAN. Daniel 29.
LEE. George (County Clerk-1), (Capt.-32), 65,
  74, 79-83, 105; George (Son of Richard, Gent.,
  deced) 60; Henry 1, (Gent.-30), 31, 51, 52,
  108; John (deced.-60); Lettice (Dau. of Martha
  Lee of England, Wife of John Corbin of Essex
  Co.) 79, 81; Martha (Dau. of Martha Lee of Eng-
  land, Widow of Geo. Turbervile, now Wife of
  Wm. Fitzhugh) 79, 81; Martha (deced. of Eng-
  land) 79, 81; Richard 74; Richard Esqr.,
  (deced. -31); Richard (Gent., deced., Son of
  Richard, Gent., deced) 60; Richard (deced.
  Gent., Bro. of John, deced.) 60). Thomas Esqr.
  39, 30, 44, 45, 60, 61, 93, 102.
LEGG. Robert 77.
LELAND. John 32.
LINTON. John (of Richmond Co.) 109;
  William (deced. -109).
LORD. William 11, 27.
LOVEL. Mr. (Ferry-53); Robert 53.
LUCK. Mary 95.

McADAM. Joseph 29, 55, 102.
McAULEY. Andrew 45.
McCARTY. Billington (Bro. of Daniel, deced) 75;
  Daniel (Gent.-13), 14, 15, 24-28, 38, (Capt.-58)
  85; Daniel (deced., Will of -74, 75), 82, 94, 95,
  99; Daniel (Son of Daniel, deced) 74, 75, 82;
  Dennis (Bro. of Daniel, deced) 75; Elizabeth
  (Widow & Relict of Daniel) 94, 95.
McCAVE. Dorcas (Wife of John) 88, 89;
  John 5; John (deced., Will of -88, 89);
  Samuel (Son of John deced) 88).
McCULLY. John 32, 33.
McDANIEL. James 17-19, 97, 98, 104;
  Jane (Wife of James) 17-19).
McKENNEY. John 107; Mary (Wife of John,
  Dau. of John Dodd, deced) 107.

MACCULLOCK. Roderick (Reverend) 16), 78.
MARMADUKE. John 17, 104; Winifred (Wife of
  John, Dau. of John Froud, deced) 17, 104.

MARSHALL. James 37; John 96.
MARTIN. John 7, (Gent.-43), 63, 77, 94.
MARYLAND. St. Marys Co. 82.
MATTHEWS. Hopkins 51.
MIDDLETON. Benjamin (Son in Law & an Exr. of
  Hannah Demovil) 88; Elizabeth (Dau. of Hannah
  Demovil) 88; John 86, 87; John (an Exr. of Geo.
  Walker) 100, 101; Mary (G-Dau. of Hannah
  Demovil) 87; Richard 71; Robert 86.
MINOR. Elizabeth (Dau. of Nicholas deced) 72;
  Jemima (Wife & Exrx. of Nicholas) 72, 73;
  John 64, (Gent. of Fairfax Co.) 65, 108;; John (an
  Exr of Nicholas) 73; John (Son of Nicholas deced)
  72, 73; Nicholas (deced., Will of -72, 73);
  Nicholas Junr. 8, 9, 55, 56; Nicholas (Son & an
  Exr. of Nicholas) 72, 73; Stewart (Son of Nicho:
  deced) 72, 73; William Stewart (Son & an Exr.
  of Nicholas, deced) 72, 73.
MONROE. Andrew (Gent.-45), 94; William 45.
MOON. William 49.
MOORE. Garland 105; Jane (G-Dau. of Hannah
  Demovil, deced) 87; Rebecca (Wife of Wm.) 104,
  105; Samuel 97, 98; Thomas 79; Thomas
  (deced.-97); William 17-19, 104, 105,
  William (Son of Tho., deced) 97.
MORTON. Joseph 13-15; Joseph (an Exr. of Danl:
  McCarty) 75, 82, 83.
MOTHERSHEAD. Christopher 38.
MOTT. Jane (Wife of Joseph) 101-103; Joseph
  (of Northumberland Co., Schoolmaster) 101-103.
MOXLEY. -8; Daniel (Son & Exr. of Wm.) 90, 91;
  John 42, 43; John (Son of Wm., deced) 90;
  Joseph (deced.-43); Mary (Wife of Daniel) 90,
  91; Richard 16, 17; Richard (Son of Wm., deced)
  90; Richard (G-Son of Wm., deced., Son of Richd.)
  90; Samuel (Son of Wm., deced) 90; Thomas (Son
  of Wm. deced) 90; William 9; William (Son of
  Wm., deced) 90; William Junr. 9; William Senr.
  (deced., Will of 89-91).
MURDOCK. Jane (Wife of Jeremiah) 3;
  Jeremiah Gent. of King George Co.) 3, 4.
MURPHY. Elizabeth (Dau. of John deced) 8;
  John 38; John (deced. Will of -8); John (Son of
  John (deced) 8; Mary (Wife of John, deced) 8;
  Samuel (Son of John, deced) 8.
MUSE. Edward 93; John 23; Thomas 3.

NEALE. P. 9, 12, 13; Presley 33, 34, 71, 72.
NEWMARCH. Ann (Wife of Jonathan) 9; Jonathan
  9, 10; Thomas (Son of Ann & Jonathan) 9.

NEWTON. Judith (God Dau. of Eliza: Eekridge, deced) 95; Thoams (Gent. -6); Willoughby 6, 32, 33, 45, 57, 58, 66, 71, 72, 85, 93, 94, 96, 101.

NOWLES/KNOWLES. Edward 41, 42, 67.

NUTT. Elizabeth (Wife of Richard) 5; Richard 5; Richard (Cozen of Lazarus Smith, deced., Son of Elizabeth & Richard) 5.

OLDHAM. Samuel 30, 31, 79-82.

OLIVE. Jane 108.

OMOHUNDRO. Ann (Wife of Richard) 10; John 21, 22; Richard 9-11, 21.

OSBORN(E). Penelope 7; Richard (Gent. of Fairfax Co.) 65.

OVERETT. William 47.

OWSLEY. Thomas (of Fairfax Co.) 83, 84.

PAGAN. John 64, 65.

PALLARON. Charles 107.

PARRY. John (deced.-16).

PARTINGTON. Edmund 102.

PARTRIDGE. Richard 104.

PAYTON. Anthony (of King George Co.) 46, 47; John 46, 47; William 46, 47.

PAYTOR. William (G-Son of Wm. Moxley, deced) 90.

PEIRCE. William 4, 91.

PIPER. David 97; John 67, 70, 96, 97, 110.

PLACES. Lower Machotick Neck 1, 2, 22; Washington's Path 9; Quarter Swamp 9; The Black Swamp 19; Rogers' Dam 19; Wolf Pit Swamp 21; Mattox Neck 24, 25; Black Forrest 28; Yeocomoco Forrest 31; Iron Mine Stone 31; Washington's Mill 35, 36; White's Mill 35; Irish Neck 36; Forrest Old Field 41; Stoney Nole 43; College of Surveys 44; Yeocomoco Church 56, 57; Horse Bridge 70; The White Marsh 72; Little Dicks 76; Vaughans Neck 83; Nominy Ferry 91; Nominy Forrest 97; Kings Saile 103.

PLUNKETT. John (of King George Co.) 4.

POPE. Humphrey 12, 13, 27, 35, 38, 95; Nathaniel 11.

PORTER. William 109.

POWNALL. Elizabeth (Relict of John Butler, now Wife of John Pownall) 38; John 38.

PRATT. Thomas (of King George Co.) 19-21.

PRICE. John 40-42; John Junr. 42; Thomas (Cousin of Cath: Butler, deced) 37.

QUESENBURY. Humphry (Gent.-43).

RALLINS. Samuel 68-70.

RANSDELL. Wharton 92, 108.

RAPPAHANNOCK IRON MINE CO. 96, 97.

READ/REID. Coleman 47, 48, 51; Joseph 49, 50.

REDDALL. Thomas (Joyner) 1-3, 86; Thomas (an Exr. of John Murphy) 8.

REDMAN. Thomas 83.

REMY. Asbury 28; Daniel 28; James 28; William (deced., Father of James) 28.

REYNOLDS. Nancy (Relict & Exrx. of Robert) 107; Robert (deced., Will of -106, 107).

RHODS. John 6.

RICE. John 51; Sarah (Wife of Zorobabble) 56; Thomas (Son of Zorobabble) 56; William 56, 86; William (an Exr. of John Murphy) 8; William Senr. 85; Zorobabble 55, 56.

RICHARDSON. John 29; Jonathan 98, 99.

RIDLEY. Margaret 11, 12.

RILEY. Edward (deced., Will of -108); Elizabeth (Relict & Exrx. of Edward) 108.

RIVERS: Nominy 91, 98; Yeocomoco 103.

ROADS. Coach 86; Mattox 56.

ROBINS. Thomas 3, 4.

ROBINSON. Michael 13; William 70, 71.

ROE. Bunch 45; Bunch (deced., Will of -45); Henry (Nephew of Bunch, deced) 45.

ROGERS. Mary 103, 104.

RUNS. Accotink in Fairfax Co. 83; Coventry 40, 109, 110; Cradenhill 40; Sugarland in Prince William Co. 44; Tuckers 58; Turks 30; Wolf Trap 69.

RUST. John 44; Mathew 103, 104; Peter 10, 11, 26, 51, 52, 65-67, 85, (Mill-103); Peter (an Exr. of John McCave) 88, 89; Vincent 104.

SANDERS. Philip 21; William 21.

SANFORD. Augustine 28, 91; John 9, 16, 17, 43; John (deced., Son of Robert, deced) 16; Joseph (deced.-16); Richard 13, Richard (Son of Robert deced) 16, 17; Richard Junr. 16, 17; Robert 16; Robert (deced. -16), 42, 43; Thomas 8, 13; Thomas (Son of Robert deced) 16.

SCOTT. Joseph 73.

SCULL. James (deced., Will of -108); Mary (Relict & Exrx. of James) 108.

SELF. Francis 89; Jane (Wife of Stephen) 104; John 18, 19, 105; Robert (old) 32; Stephen 104.

SETTLES. John 76.

SHAW. Thomas 11-13, (Gent.-43), 44, 51.

SHORT. Benedict 88; Clarke 101.

SHOTWELL Anne (Wife of John) 63;
 John (Taylor 53-55); 63.

SIMS. Alexander 23; Samuel 54, 55.

SHROPSHIRE. John 78; St. John 4, 5, 78;
 Saint John (deced., first Husband of Eliza-
 beth Stonehouse) 15; St. John (Son & Exr. of
 Elizabeth Stonehouse) 15, 16; Winkfield 4, 5;
 Winkfield (Son of Elizabeth Stonehouse) 15.

SKINNER. Peter 54.

SMITH. Augustine 97, 110; Baldwin Matthews
 102, (Gent. of Northumberland Co.-103);
 Elizabeth (Wife of Tho.) 39, 70; George (of
 Prince Frederick Co.) 86, 87; James (Bro. of
 Lazarus) 6; John 38-40, 96; John (Bro. & Exr.
 of Lazarus) 6; John Junr. 109, 110; John Senr.
 109, 110; Joseph 39, 40, 68-70, 97, 101, Judith
 Judith (God. Dau. of Lazarus, Dau. of Wm.) 6.
 Lazarus (deced, Will of -5, 6); Mary (Mother of
 Tho.) 39, 40; Patience, Wife of John Junr.) 109,
 110. Peter 18, 19; Robert (Weaver -30), 61;
 Spencer (God Son of Lazarus, Son of Tho: deced)
 5; Thomas (of Orange Co). 38-40, 69, 70;
 Thomas (deced.-5); William 6, 37.

SORRELL. John 30, 31; John (Son of Tho. deced)
 98, 99; Thomas 1, 2, 56; Thomas (Gent., dece
 -98).

SPENCE. James (Son of John deced) 102;
 John 36; John (deced.-102); Patrick (Gent.
 -43); Thomas 42, 43.

SPENCER. John (Son of Nicholas) 91;
 Nicholas Esqr. (deced. -91).

STEEL. John 42-44; John (deced.-42);
 John (deced., Will of -50, 51); Margaret 50;
 Margaret (Relict & Exrx. of John) 42; Mary
 alias Weeks (Dau. of young Margaret) 50;
 Richard 43, 44; Thomas 50; Thomas (Son of
 Margaret) 42.

STEPTOE. James 30, 31, (Gent.-51, 52).

STEVENS. William 97, 98.

STONE. Samuel 110; Thomas 13.

STONEHOUSE. Elizabeth (deced., Will of -15,
 16).

STORK. John 26.

STROTHER. Sarah (Dau. of Nathl. Gray) 36;
 William 78; William (Exr. of Nathl: Gray) 36,
 37.

STURMAN. Thomas (deced.-6); William 13.

SUTTON. Jacob 43.

SYDENHAM. Jona: 28.

SYMS. Job 36.

TANCIL. Edward 20, 21.

TAYLOR. Argail (Gent. of Northumberland Co.)
 109; Elizabeth (Wife of Wm.) 21, 22;
 William 21, 22, 45.

TEBBS. Daniel 56-59, 62, 64-67, 101, 104;
 Daniel (Exr. of Charnock Cox, Junr.) 74;
 Daniel (an Exr. of Geo. Walker) 100, 101.

TEMPLEMAN. John 92; Thomas 22, 43, 73, 92.

THOMAS. Elizabeth (Dau. of James deced) 44;
 George (Son of James deced) 44, 55; Hannah
 (Dau. of James deced) 44; Hugh 28, 29, 65-67;
 James 29, 58; James (deced., Will of -44, 45),
 55, 56; James (deced. -64); James (Son of James
 deced) 56; John 55-58; John (Son & Exr. of
 James) 45. Katherine 29; Katherine (Dau. of
 James (deced) 44; Mary (Wife of Hugh, Sister of
 Joseph Carr) 29, 66, 67; Sarah (Wife of James
 deced) 45; Sarah (Dau. of James deced) 44;
 William (G-Son of James deced, Son of Katherine
 -44); Winifred (Dau. of James deced) 44.

THOMPSON. James 42; John 99; Thomas 96.

THORNTON. Anthony 75; Francis 75;
 Presly (Colo., an Exr. of Danl. McCarty) 75, 82,
 83, 99, 100.

TOBEN. Michael 104.

TRIPLETT. Catharine (Wife of John) 68-70;
 Francis (Old) 41; John (of King George Co.)
 67-70, 96, 97.

TURBERVILLE. George (deced.-79); Martha
 (Widow of Geo. now Wife of Wm. Fitzhugh) 79.

TURNER. William 65, 66.

TYLER. Benjamin 20, 21; William (Gent.-20),
 21, 36, 63, 76, 77.

UNDERWOOD. Major 41.

VAUGHAN. Daniel 83; John 39.

VAULX. R. or Robert (Gent.-6), 7, 13-15, 28, 44,
 77, 93, 94, 96; Robert (deced.-93).

VEALE. Maurice/Morris 15, 89.

VIVION. Mary (Wife of Tho.) 91, 92;
 Thomas (Gent. of King George Co.) 91, 92.

WADDEY. Benjamin (deced. -29); Jeane/Jane (of
 Northumberland Co., Widow of Benja.) 29, 45.

WALKER. Barbary (Dau. of Geo.) 100; Franky
(Dau. of Geo.) 100; George (deced., Will of -100,
101); Har: 49, 50; John 47; Rachel (Dau. of
Geo.) 100; Samuel 49, 50; William 103;
William (Son of Geo.) 100.

WASHINGTON. Augustine (Gent. of King George
Co. -13), 14, 15, 23-26, 96; Augustine (an Exr.
of Danl. McCarty) 75, 82, 83, 99, 100; Augustine (Son in Law & an Exr. of Wm. Aylett) 85;
Elizabeth 107; Henry 46; Henry Junr. 13-15;
John 4, 23-26; Lawrence 9; Lawrence (Major,
an Exr. of Wm. Aylett) 85.

WATTS. Daniel 79; John (Gent.-43), 63, 77, 94.

WEBB. William 54.

WEEKS. B. or Benjamin 7, 10, 11, 23, 38, 42;
Benjamin (Exr. of John Steel) 51.

WELCH. John 54, 55, 75-77; Mary (Wife of John
a Dau. of John Hudson and Mary his wife, deced)
75-77; William 6, 31, 32, 43.

WHEELER. Samuel 37, 54, 55, 76, 77.

WHERRELL. Elizabeth (Dau. of Nicho: Minor,
deced) 72.

WHITE. -36; Alexander 55, 102, 107;
Daniel 19, 20, (Mill Dam-54); Daniel Junr.
108; Daniel Senr. (deced. -19); James 63;
John 53.

WHITFIELD. James 22, 63.

WHITING. Thomas 415; William 54.

WILLIAMS. Jane (Wife of Tho.) 73, 74;
John 31, 32, 43; John (deced., Father of John)
32; Thomas 49, 73, 74.

WILSON. Allen 103, 104; John 103.

WRIGHT. Charles 3, 4; John (deced. -96).

WROE. Original 41, 42.

YATES/YEATTS. Eleanor 6; Elizabeth 108.

YOUELL/YEWEL. -1; Batteraw (Son in Law & an
Exr. of Elizabeth Footman) 85, 86; Elizabeth
(G.-dau. of Elizabeth Footman) 85; Frances (Dau.
of Elizabeth Footman) 85.

Heritage Books by Ruth and Sam Sparacio:

Abstracts of Account Books of Edward Dixon, Merchant of Port Royal, Virginia, Volume I: 1743–1747

Abstracts of Account Books of Edward Dixon, Merchant of Port Royal, Virginia, Volume II

Albemarle County, Virginia Deed and Will Book Abstracts, 1748–1752

Albemarle County, Virginia Deed Book Abstracts, 1758–1761

Albemarle County, Virginia Deed Book Abstracts, 1761–1764

Albemarle County, Virginia Deed Book Abstracts, 1764–1768

Albemarle County, Virginia Deed Book Abstracts, 1768–1770

Albemarle County, Virginia Deed Book Abstracts, 1776–1778

Albemarle County, Virginia Deed Book Abstracts, 1778–1780

Albemarle County, Virginia Deed Book Abstracts, 1780–1783

Albemarle County, Virginia Deed Book Abstracts, 1787–1790

Albemarle County, Virginia Deed Book Abstracts, 1790–1791

Albemarle County, Virginia Deed Book Abstracts, 1791–1793

Augusta County, Virginia Land Tax Books, 1782–1788

Augusta County, Virginia Land Tax Books, 1788–1790

Amherst County, Virginia Land Tax Books, 1789–1791

Caroline County, Virginia Order Book Abstracts, 1765

Caroline County, Virginia Order Book Abstracts, 1767–1768

Caroline County, Virginia Order Book Abstracts, 1768–1770

Caroline County, Virginia Order Book Abstracts, 1770–1771

Caroline County, Virginia Order Book, 1765–1767

Caroline County, Virginia Order Book, 1771–1772

Caroline County, Virginia Order Book, 1786–1787

Caroline County, Virginia Order Book, 1787, Part 1

Caroline County, Virginia Order Book, 1788

Culpeper County, Virginia Deed Book Abstracts, 1795–1796

Culpeper County, Virginia Land Tax Book, 1782–1786

Culpeper County, Virginia Land Tax Book, 1787–1789

Culpeper County, Virginia Minute Book, 1763–1764

Digest of Family Relationships, 1650–1692, from Virginia County Court Records

Digest of Family Relationships, 1720–1750, from Virginia County Court Records

Digest of Family Relationships, 1750–1763, from Virginia County Court Records

Digest of Family Relationships, 1764–1775, from Virginia County Court Records

Essex County, Virginia Deed and Will Abstracts, 1695–1697

Essex County, Virginia Deed and Will Abstracts, 1697–1699

Essex County, Virginia Deed and Will Abstracts, 1699–1701

Essex County, Virginia Deed and Will Abstracts, 1701–1703

Essex County, Virginia Deed and Will Book, 1692–1693

Essex County, Virginia Deed and Will Book, 1693–1694

Essex County, Virginia Deed and Will Book, 1694–1695

Essex County, Virginia Deed and Will Book, 1753–1754 and 1750

Essex County, Virginia Deed Book, 1742–1745

Essex County, Virginia Deed Book, 1749–1751

Essex County, Virginia Land Trials Abstracts, 1711–1716 and 1715–1741

Essex County, Virginia Order Book Abstracts, 1699–1702

Essex County, Virginia Order Book Abstracts, 1716–1723, Part 1

Essex County, Virginia Order Book Abstracts, 1716–1723, Part 2

Essex County, Virginia Order Book Abstracts, 1716–1723, Part 3

Essex County, Virginia Order Book Abstracts, 1716–1723, Part 4

Essex County, Virginia Order Book Abstracts, 1723–1725, Part 1

Essex County, Virginia Order Book Abstracts, 1723–1725, Part 2

Middlesex County, Virginia Deed Book, 1679–1688

Middlesex County, Virginia Deed Book, 1688–1694

Middlesex County, Virginia Deed Book, 1694–1703

Middlesex County, Virginia Deed Book, 1703–1709

Middlesex County, Virginia Deed Book, 1709–1720

Middlesex County, Virginia Order Book, 1686–1690

Middlesex County, Virginia Record Book, 1721–1813

Northumberland County, Virginia Deed and Will Book, 1650–1655

Northumberland County, Virginia Deed and Will Book, 1655–1658

Northumberland County, Virginia Deed and Will Book, 1662–1666

Northumberland County, Virginia Deed and Will Book, 1666–1670

Northumberland County, Virginia Deed and Will Book, 1670–1672 and 1706–1711

Northumberland County, Virginia Deed and Will Book, 1711–1712

Northumberland County, Virginia Order Book, 1652–1657

Northumberland County, Virginia Order Book, 1657–1661

Northumberland County, Virginia Order Book, 1665–1669

Northumberland County, Virginia Order Book, 1669–1673

Northumberland County, Virginia Order Book, 1680–1683

Northumberland County, Virginia Order Book, 1683–1686

Northumberland County, Virginia Order Book, 1699–1700

Northumberland County, Virginia Order Book, 1700–1702

Northumberland County, Virginia Order Book, 1702–1704

Orange County, Virginia Deeds, 1743–1759

Orange County, Virginia Order Book Abstracts 1747–1748

Orange County, Virginia Order Book Abstracts 1752–1753

Prince William County, Virginia Deed Book, 1749–1752

Prince William County, Virginia Order Book Abstracts, 1752–1753

Prince William County, Virginia Order Book Abstracts, 1753–1757

(Old) Rappahannock County, Virginia Deed and Will Book Abstracts, 1656–1662

(Old) Rappahannock County, Virginia Deed and Will Book Abstracts, 1662–1665

(Old) Rappahannock County, Virginia Deed and Will Book Abstracts, 1663–1668

(Old) Rappahannock County, Virginia Deed and Will Book Abstracts, 1665–1677

(Old) Rappahannock County, Virginia Deed and Will Book Abstracts, 1668–1670

(Old) Rappahannock County, Virginia Deed and Will Book Abstracts, 1670–1672

(Old) Rappahannock County, Virginia Deed and Will Book Abstracts, 1672–1673/4

(Old) Rappahannock County, Virginia Deed and Will Book Abstracts, 1673/4–1676

(Old) Rappahannock County, Virginia Deed and Will Book Abstracts, 1677–1678/9

(Old) Rappahannock County, Virginia Deed and Will Book Abstracts, 1678/9–1682

(Old) Rappahannock County, Virginia Deed and Will Book Abstracts, 1682–1686

(Old) Rappahannock County, Virginia Deed and Will Book Abstracts, 1686–1688

(Old) Rappahannock County, Virginia Deed and Will Book Abstracts, 1688–1692

(Old) Rappahannock County, Virginia Order Book Abstracts, 1683–1685

Richmond County, Virginia Deed Book Abstracts, 1692–1695

Richmond County, Virginia Deed Book Abstracts, 1695–1701

Richmond County, Virginia Deed Book Abstracts, 1701–1704

Richmond County, Virginia Deed Book Abstracts, 1705–1708

Richmond County, Virginia Deed Book Abstracts, 1708–1711

Richmond County, Virginia Deed Book Abstracts, 1711–1714

Richmond County, Virginia Deed Book Abstracts, 1715–1718

Richmond County, Virginia Deed Book Abstracts, 1718–1719

Richmond County, Virginia Deed Book Abstracts, 1719–1721

Richmond County, Virginia Deed Book Abstracts, 1721–1725

Richmond County, Virginia Order Book Abstracts, 1694–1697

Richmond County, Virginia Order Book Abstracts, 1697–1699

Richmond County, Virginia Order Book abstracts, 1699–1701

Richmond County, Virginia Order Book Abstracts, 1714–1715

Richmond County, Virginia Order Book Abstracts, 1719–1721

Richmond County, Virginia Order Book, 1692–1694

Richmond County, Virginia Order Book, 1702–1704

Richmond County, Virginia Order Book, 1717–1718

Richmond County, Virginia Order Book, 1718–1719

Spotsylvania County, Virginia Deed Book, 1722–1725

Spotsylvania County, Virginia Deed Book, 1725–1728

Spotsylvania County, Virginia Deed Book: 1730–1731

Spotsylvania County, Virginia Order Book Abstracts, 1742–1744

Spotsylvania County, Virginia Order Book Abstracts, 1744–1746

Stafford County, Virginia Deed and Will Book, 1686–1689

Stafford County, Virginia Deed and Will Book, 1689–1693

Stafford County, Virginia Deed and Will Book, 1699–1709

Stafford County, Virginia Deed and Will Book, 1780–1786, and Scheme Book Orders, 1790–1793

Stafford County, Virginia Deed Book, 1722–1728 and 1755–1765

Stafford County, Virginia Order Book, 1664–1668 and 1689–1690

Stafford County, Virginia Order Book, 1691–1692

Stafford County, Virginia Order Book, 1692–1693

Stafford County, Virginia Will Book, 1729–1748

Stafford County, Virginia Will Book, 1748–1767

Westmoreland County, Virginia Deed and Will Abstracts, 1723–1726

Westmoreland County, Virginia Deed and Will Abstracts, 1726–1729

Westmoreland County, Virginia Deed and Will Abstracts, 1729–1732

Westmoreland County, Virginia Deed and Will Abstracts, 1732–1734

Westmoreland County, Virginia Deed and Will Abstracts, 1734–1736

Westmoreland County, Virginia Deed and Will Abstracts, 1736–1740

Westmoreland County, Virginia Deed and Will Abstracts, 1740–1742

Westmoreland County, Virginia Deed and Will Abstracts, 1742–1745

Westmoreland County, Virginia Deed and Will Abstracts, 1745–1747

Westmoreland County, Virginia Deed and Will Abstracts, 1747–1748

Westmoreland County, Virginia Deed and Will Abstracts, 1749–1751

Westmoreland County, Virginia Deed and Will Abstracts, 1751–1754

Westmoreland County, Virginia Deed and Will Abstracts, 1754–1756

Westmoreland County, Virginia Order Book, 1705–1707

Westmoreland County, Virginia Order Book, 1707–1709

Westmoreland County, Virginia Order Book, 1709–1712